Guide Library

Hillwood Museum
Washington, D.C.

◆§ MARIE AVINOV
Pilgrimage Through Hell

MARIE AVINOV

Pilgrimage Through Hell

❧

An Autobiography told by
PAUL CHAVCHAVADZE

Prentice-Hall, Inc., Englewood Cliffs, N.J.

ACKNOWLEDGMENTS

My heartfelt gratitude goes to my friend Jane Soames Nickerson, who spent so much of her time and energy preparing the material for this book, listening to my stories, reading and translating my French notes, checking dates and sequences, and, finally, writing the first draft of my memoirs. It was a tedious and complicated task, done out of love and friendship. I can't thank her enough.

Without this groundwork I might never have brought these memoirs to the attention of Paul Chavchavadze, and this book might never have been written. His writing of this Memoir was a godsend to me, for the close understanding and affinity that exists between us has enabled him to render here a true portrait of me—of my mind and heart, of the full gamut of my life experience.

—MARIE AVINOV

I should like to thank Charles R. Walker, Jr. for permission to reprint the passage from his translation of Sophocles' *Oedipus at Colonus*, to be found at the conclusion of this volume.

PAUL CHAVCHAVADZE

CONTENTS

PROLOGUE

❧

Advice from the Kremlin

"Hold on a minute: the Kremlin wishes to speak to you."

That's what I heard one morning when the telephone rang in my room and I lifted the receiver. I confess, shivers ran down my spine. In Stalin's Russia of 1935, attentions from the Kremlin usually proved fatal to a "former person" like myself; and I might add that anyone who blew his nose in a handkerchief was apt to find himself included in this category. But on this occasion my fears proved groundless. A man's soft-spoken, "cultured" voice at the other end of the wire was saying to me: "You don't know me personally, Citizeness Avinov, but perhaps you have heard of me? I am Bontch-Bruyevitch." Bontch-Bruyevitch—Lenin's friend and collaborator, who had recently established a commission for the preservation of Russia's literary and artistic treasures.

"Of course I've heard of you," I exclaimed. "And I've often wished you well—ever since I heard of your Commission."

Thus began an unexpectedly pleasant conversation with an invisible inhabitant of the Kremlin. And little did I suspect that it would end up with this staunch supporter of Lenin, this important Communist "boss," urging me, a so-called "enemy of the people," to write my memoirs.

First, Bontch made himself explicit: it was in connection with his Special Commission that he was calling me; he had heard that my family owned some precious archives—letters of prominent writers; interesting sketches, some drawn by the famous poet Lermontov, and so on. Then, he topped his long preamble with an offer: "Would you care to sell them to us for a good price?"

I was taken aback. I would gladly have given him the archives had they still been in existence. I told him so. I told him more. I said the peasants—or rather the "liberated masses," as one was supposed to call them now—had burned our hereditary estate. Everything that was in the house had perished with it.

His reaction was brief but poignant: "How dreadful!" I went on to explain that the few things I had managed to save had already been donated to various institutions: letters from the poet Fet to Tolstoy, for instance, transcribed by the poet himself for his friend, my Grandfather Novosiltsev's sister, were now in the Museum of Literature; and a long letter from Pushkin was in the "Pushkin House." But, I added, I still possessed a diary of my father's Grandfather Novosiltsev, one of the defenders of Sebastopol during the Crimean War. There were also the diaries of my mother's grandmother, Princess Scherbatov née Apraxin, wife of a hero of the War of 1812 against Napoleon, who had been sung by Joukovsky in his poem "A Bard in the Camp of Russian Warriors." I told Bontch that my great-grandmother's diaries offered a wealth of material for the study of life and conditions in early nineteenth-century Russia. "Thirty volumes in all," I said. "And all of them stacked under my bed, now that we're allowed only one room to live in. Of course their place is in a museum!"

Bontch thanked me nicely. Then, after a brief pause. "In your parents house and later in your own you must have met many outstanding people. I think it's your civic duty to write your memoirs. They'd be so valuable. . ."

"Oh no!" The cry escaped me of its own volition; "and for two reasons. First, if I, a 'former person,' started writing by reminiscences, I know I'd end up in prison. Later still, in a concentration camp!"

There was a shocked silence from the Kremlin. Then Bontch's voice again: "Oh, but why so pessimistic?"

Pent-up outrage and my own intemperate tongue got the better of me: "Don't you realize in what fear of the G.P.U. we are all living? Hasn't it occurred to you that never was the French saying —'if you wish to live happily, hide yourself'—more appropriate than it is right here, today, in Moscow?"

I stopped, appalled at what I had done. Somehow the silence from the Kremlin did not seem too ominous. And presently Bontch's voice was with me once more, sounding, if anything, slightly amused: "And your second reason, Citizeness?"

Instantly my tongue was loosened.

"My second reason? I adore memoirs! But I have come to the conclusion that when a woman gets to writing hers she invariably undermines their authenticity by heaping roses around her own pedestal."

The voice in the Kremlin was actually chuckling now: "Very witty. But since you know the snares, you can avoid them." He then urged me again at length and in no uncertain terms to start writing my memoirs, ending up with: "If I can be of help, let me know."

A click. The Kremlin fell silent. This time for good.

More than thirty years have passed since that curious telephone conversation. Yet it is only now, far away from the Kremlin, from Moscow, from Russia, in the security of Ellie's comfortable home on Long Island, gazing with admiration at the many potted flowers around me, that I have at last decided to follow the Kremlin's advice and write my memoirs. The flowers did it, not the Kremlin. Flowers have always been the delight of my life, ever since the age of two, when finding myself one day in an orchard with my mother and seeing the grass under the fruit trees covered with violets, I tore myself from Mamma's hand and rolled among those fragrant little flowers.

That was over eighty years ago. Today I gaze at Ellie's flowers —especially at the beautiful cyclamen across the room from me. Flowers carry me back to my beloved Kotchemirovo, with its avenue of lindens and maples, its white-columned porch framed by century-old lilacs: so remote now in space and time that it seems like a dream, separated from today's reality by a long dark night.

In my old age I am again surrounded by the comforts which, during many gruelling years, I had been unable even to imagine as still existing anywhere on earth. Ellie gave them back to me, together with the flowers. Ellie is my sister-in-law, Nika's only sister. We are both getting on. Although only five years behind me, she still carries her age like a light English saddle, whereas I have reached the stage of spacious robes and snow-white hair. Ellie is away, painting someone's portrait. And so today I am alone, but never lonely. How could I be with such an abundance of memories to fall back on? And since I am about to relate them, I may as well start from the very beginning, from my earliest childhood days in the great Scherbatov house in Moscow, the home of my maternal Grandfather, Prince Alexander Scherbatov, in the mid-eighties of the last century.

PART ONE

❧❀❧

The Closing of a Dream

CHAPTER ONE

❧

The French writer Barbey d'Aurevilly once gave this advice to a young friend: "You who stand at the crossroads of history, take careful note of those of a former generation who are disappearing into the mists, for there will be no more like them."

In my life the first figure to step out of those "mists" is my great-grandmother, Princess Scherbatov. Indeed, there will never again be anyone quite like her. I was a small child when I was taken to see her for the first time, but her image still remains indelibly stamped upon my memory: a regal old lady in a big, curly white wig and lace cap, enthroned in a huge armchair, a basket of freshly plucked violets at her feet.

Great-grandmamma had been only eighteen when Prince Alexis Scherbatov (already closing on fifty) asked for her hand. "My dear Sophie," her father said, "the Prince is noble and generous. He is of the most distinguished ancestry, and a hero of 1812. He enjoys the confidence of our lord the Emperor, who has appointed him Governor-General of Moscow. His offer is a great honor, but because of the disparity in your ages, you are free to decide for yourself. When you come downstairs in the morning wear a ribbon in your cap. If it's pink, your mother and I will know the answer is yes. If blue—well, no questions will be asked. We will consider the matter closed. Now go up to your room, my child, and pray for guidance."

"And so I did," Sophie recorded in her diary. "Next morning I came downstairs with a pink ribbon in my cap."

On their honeymoon Prince Scherbatov brought her to St. Petersburg where they were given an apartment in the Palace of Tsarskoye Selo. The young Princess would rise early every morning and go for a stroll in the park. It was soon noticed that the Emperor,

9

Alexander I, frequently accompanied her. He is said to have become violently attracted to her. One morning, seated with Sophie on a bench in the park, he cut short an impassioned speech to protest: "But Princess, you are not listening to me!" "Sire," she replied, "I am listening, but I don't hear a word." The Emperor, they say, took this witty rebuff in good part and remained devoted to her to the end of his life.

As the wife of the Governor-General of Moscow, Sophie Scherbatov was nonetheless aware of the needs and miseries of the poor. Plunging into what would now be called social work, she mobilized Moscow ladies and their money to help run schools, homes for the aged, creches, and soup kitchens, which she had founded and managed with immense energy.

She showed her practical good sense in many other ways. To the astonishment of her family, she sold the jewels that had been part of her dowry and bought large properties in the south of Russia at very advantageous prices. These investments founded the family fortune. "My children are my jewels," she declared, "and I'm determined to assure them incomes sufficiently large to enable them to lead useful lives in the service of their countrymen."

After Prince Scherbatov's death Sophie moved into a stately house in the center of Moscow, and continued to live there in much the same style as she had with the Prince in the Governor-General's Palace. She entertained largely, presided over her many charities, and wrote a copious daily diary into those thirty big leather-bound volumes that ended up stacked under my bed.

Leafing through them, I was able to recreate a clear picture of the old Princess and her manner of life. Like the kings of France, she had a daily ceremonial *levée*, with five maids in attendance; the first held a silver basin, the second a silver ewer, the third a sponge, the fourth soap and toilet water, the fifth a lace-edged towel. After her ablutions, she would withdraw into another room and seat herself before a huge gilt mirror. Her women then helped her into an embroided dressing gown, and covered her totally bald head with that profuse white wig and lace cap I remember so well. Thus attired, she took her morning coffee served on the finest *Sèvres*.

This was the hour when she liked to receive her intimates. One morning, shortly before my mother's marriage, Great-grandmamma sent for her and said, "My child, I fear your dowry is smaller than those of your cousins. You haven't much jewelry. Tell Glasha [her personal maid] to bring my work-basket." After rummaging among embroidery silks, she produced a large miniature of the late Empress, mounted in fine diamonds. "There my dear! Have the stones reset and you'll have a nice brooch to go with your ball gowns."

I was only four when my mother took me on that first visit. When I saw the basket of violets at the foot of the big armchair, I buried my face in them before kissing my Great-grandmamma's hand. This so pleased the old lady, who ordinarily was not overly fond of small children, that she told my mother to ring the bell. "Tell Glasha to bring the box of lace." And out came yards and yards of *Alençon, Point de Venise*, priceless Brussels. "For little Masha," she said. "When she grows up and is presented at Court, it will come in handy, and she'll have a beautiful veil for her wedding."

Such were my earliest impressions of Great-grandmamma. I was duly awed by her striking appearance at the time. Later however, at sixteen, the age when young people turn a critical eye upon their elders, and when rebellion was already beginning to seethe in me, I asked my mother: "Why, if Great-grandmamma is so intelligent, does she persist in such archaic customs—five women to dress her!"

My grandfather, Prince Alexander Scherbatov, had been Great-grandmamma's youngest child and also her favorite. In his youth he served as *aide-de-camp* to the Governor-General of eastern Poland, where he met and fell in love with my Grandmother, Marya Pavlovna Moukhanov, daughter of the Minister of Education and then belle of Warsaw. Before proposing to her, Alexander traveled all the way back to Moscow by sleigh to get Great-grandmamma's approval. With Sophie's blessing, he brought his bride to Moscow, where she was much admired for her charm and beauty.

Alexander had freed his serfs on his own initiative, long before Alexander II's Decree of Emancipation (1861); and when local self-governing bodies (such as the *zemstvos* and municipal councils) were created, he was elected Mayor of Moscow.

After Sophie's death, Alexander and his two older brothers

presented her splendid mansion to the city of Moscow. It was converted into a hospital dedicated to St. Sophia, her patron saint. Two life-size portraits of my great-grandparents by Vigée le Brun were left hanging in the entrance hall.*

Our home in Moscow was our Grandfather Scherbatov's house, a mansion that might be compared to a palace in size. Many times on sleepless nights I have wandered in thought through that house, remembering every detail of it with the vivid first impressions of childhood: first was the main entrance, protected by a small glassed-in porch from the bitter Moscow cold; and old Vassili, the butler, stooping over the guest book to write down the names and addresses of callers. I can still see him, the Scherbatov coat-of-arms on the silver buttons of his spotless livery, obsequiously announcing the names of some important visitors.

A marble staircase led from the hall to a second floor occupied entirely by reception rooms: The Red and Blue rooms, and finally a ballroom with a great chandelier. Benches upholstered in pale blue silk lined the walls. Above each of the four doors was a plaster medallion with our grandmother's initials under a princely crown. When Mother sold the house after the Revolution, she made my brothers knock down those handsome decorations with hammers. "I won't leave my mother's name here," she said. "I can just imagine what will go on in this room after we are gone!"

The great marble staircase in the hall rose to a landing set with a large wall mirror. I have always thought that Tolstoy might have had that staircase in mind when in *Anna Karenina* he described Kitty going to her first ball and stopping to adjust the black ribbon round her neck. It may well have been so, for our marble staircase and the hall below evoke a memory of Tolstoy himself. It was on a New Year's Eve; I must have been fifteen at the time. We were

---

* After Lenin seized power, the Bolsheviks erased the name "Scherbatov" from the facade of the St. Sophia Hospital, and replaced it by that of some doctor whose name escapes me. When I learned that they had torn down the two Vigée le Brun portraits and thrown them away, I went that same night, accompanied by a faithful servant, into the park that surrounded the hospital. We crept about until we found the portraits lying face down in the snow. But they were too large for us to carry away. We cut the heads out of the canvases and smuggled them out of the park under our coats.

all gathered around Grandpapa in the pink drawing room, waiting
to go, as we always did, to the church in the Kremlin Palace for a
midnight *Te Deum*. Vassili hurried into the room, looking
thoroughly baffled.

"Count Leo Tolstoy," he announced, "to see the Prince."

The upward flight of my grandfather's eyebrows seemed to reflect Vassili's perplexity.

"Are you sure it is Count Tolstoy?"

"No mistake about it, Your Excellency. He is dressed like a
peasant."

Grandpapa's feelings for Tolstoy were ambivalent, equally
split between admiration for his works and repugnance at his
particular philosophy and his criticism of the Orthodox Church.
Rising heavily to his feet, Grandpapa went down the stairs into the
hall where Tolstoy was standing in his habitual pose. His hands
were thrust deep into the pockets of his sheepskin coat, and his
beard was long and untidy. Grandfather asked him the reason for
a visit at such a late hour. Tolstoy's answer was characteristic:
"Prince, you and I are both old. I suggest that we spend this New
Year's Eve together, reading the Gospel and meditating upon it."

Grandfather drew himself up to his full and very corpulent
height: "My dear Count, I read the Gospel every evening before
going to bed. On New Years's Eve, it is my custom to go to the
midnight service in the Kremlin with my family. We are leaving
shortly. Pray accept my best wishes."

My father was a man of great erudition but also a very busy
one, who left our education largely in our mother's hands. Mother,
for all her sensitivity and perception, was not intellectual in the
strict sense, but nonetheless she insisted on giving us the soundest
possible education.

We were educated at home because Mother had a poor opinion
of the educational system in our *gymnazias* (public schools). Consequently, the best professors in Moscow came to lecture to us in a
rigorous course of studies. We were taught history, geography,
mathematics, literature, philosophy, the history of art and music,
and the history of the Church, as well as French, German, and
English. Our German professor, Dr. Krueger, had a particularly
strong influence over me. Very tall, in a long frock coat and with
a great shock of white hair, I thought he looked exactly like a

German poet of the eighteenth century. I admired him immensely, became deeply immersed in German literature, and learned quantities of German poetry by heart.

Our heavy program of studies did not prevent us from having a good time, especially at Christmas. A huge Christmas tree would be set up in the ballroom, the room itself being kept carefully under lock and key, so that we children should not catch a glimpse of the preparations. On the great day the doors would be thrown open, and we would rush in to admire the glittering tree and the tables loaded with packages. The servants' children would be there too, with clean clothes and freshly scrubbed faces standing in a shy little group by the door. There were presents for them too, of course, but they were never as elaborate or expensive as ours. Even as a child, this inequality troubled me. I saw their envious glances and felt distressed, a bit guilty. Since then I have often thought that those Christmas parties, in their way, may have played their part in bringing about Bolshevism: even though Grandfather gave our servants' children a good education at his own expense and provided their daughters with dowries on their marriage, most of them eventually became Communists.

During those winters of our early youth, we led a life of untroubled ease. We went to the theater and opera, saw all the classics, and heard Chaliapin sing. There was one theatrical performance in particular I shall never forget. Grandpapa, who hardly ever went out in the evening, was persuaded to go with us on this occasion. We had chosen *Die Einsame Menschen* by Gerhart Hauptmann, one of the most successful plays in the Moscow Art Theater's repertory.

With the appearance of Anna Marr, the heroine, the first scene takes place in the home of a young, married German pastor, it becomes immediately evident that the young husband is violently attracted to this lovely but enigmatic stranger. Tensions kept mounting. All of a sudden Grandpapa, completely identifying himself with the action on the stage, began thumping his cane on the floor. "Get out, you snake in the grass," he exclaimed in loud indignation, "Get out!" Mother blushed scarlet, but the audience seemed only sympathetically amused to see the old Prince, with his white mustache and long, white side-whiskers, raking the play as seriously as a child. As my mother said later, it was at once an embarrassing and a most moving experience.

We did not know Grandmamma enough to love her. She died when I, the eldest, was still too young to appreciate her intelligence and wit, yet old enough to stand in fear of the tongue-lashings she gave us for misbehavior. But we were brought up on amusing stories about her. Father, for instance, always remembered with a chuckle her caustic remark to Grandpapa after a visit to our nursery:

"Sasha, please go to the best toy shop tomorrow and buy the biggest drum you can find. I just heard little Sasha asking God to send him one for Christmas, and I should like to see at least one prayer granted before I die." Anyone else would have been rebuked for such impious sarcasm, but Grandmamma could do no wrong in Grandfather's eyes.

Dead, she played a recurring role in our lives: every 12th of December, the anniversary of her death, we accompanied Grandpapa to a Requiem Mass for her soul at the Donskoy Monastery where she was buried. Donskoy is about eight miles outside Moscow, and necessitated quite an expedition at that time of year, when the cold is intense and snow is often falling. But what we children dreaded more than the weather was the stuffy air in the closed carriage.

One such journey stands out in my mind as particularly tedious.

At the front door stood Grandpapa's large black carriage with its two huge black horses. We called them "The Elephants" because of their size. These two, at once funereal and spectacular, were kept exclusively for trips to the cemetery. But by far the most impressive figure on the carriage was the old coachman, Guryan, perched high on his box. On less solemn occasions—in the country, for instance, where informality reigned—he was a jovial man who let us drive the pony-cart. But now, getting ready to drive the old Prince, he was "officiating." He became another being, formidably dignified and remote.

Respectfully assisted by the butler Vassili and the footman Alexey, Grandpapa came slowly down the front steps. He seemed bigger than ever in his fur coat and *valenki* (knee-high felt overshoes). The rest of us were equally well insulated: Mother wore her black-fox furs, and we children—my sister Katya, my brother

Sasha, and I—were wrapped in thick padded coats and astrakhan caps. I heard the springs of the carriage creak and groan as we settled down. Alexey shut the door, climbed onto the box beside Guryan, and slowly the carriage began to move.

The atmosphere in the carriage became gloomy and unbearably close. The "Elephants" moved at a slow, measured trot. Grandpapa kept sighing. And nothing could be seen of the sparkling day outside, for the tightly shut windows were coated with frost. To cheer Grandpapa, I began telling a story of how one of my dolls had turned into a chimney sweep. Grandpapa was about to laugh when he noticed Sasha writhing in his seat and pulling at his *bashlyk* (hooded camel-hair scarf). Mother quickly opened a window, and the influx of sunshine, fresh air, and voices from the street saved Sasha from being sick.

At long last we reached our destination. The Donskoy Monastery was a huge building, outside whose high walls lay the extensive cemetery. The last resting place of generations of Muscovites, it was crowded with urns, crosses, blocks of granite, and statues of angels. One such kneeling angel, with chubby cheeks and a chipped nose, was our favorite. With shouts and laughter Katya, Sasha, and I rushed forward to greet it, and climbed the pedestal to brush the snow off it wings. Mother tried to remind us of where we were, but Grandpapa was on our side as usual. "Let them be, Masha. They have such a very long service ahead of them."

We walked on down a path swept and sanded especially for us. It led through the cemetery to our family mausoleum—a small chapel built on classical lines, with an iron railing round the plot where Grandmamma and other members of the family lay buried. At the entrance to the chapel, we were met by the Treasurer of the Monastery, Father Anastasy, with black soutane and silver crucifix. Grandpapa received his benediction, and they exchanged a ritual kiss on the shoulder. We children then kissed his hand. During this little ceremony, Sasha's voice resounded in an all-too-audible whisper:

"Mamma, why are his nails so black?"

I, the eldest, already knew that Father Anastasy's black nails came from passionate gardening; but Sasha did not, though he was easily the most observant of us all, and certaintly the most in-

quisitive. In the carriage on the way home his thin, piping voice
rang out again.

"Mamma, tell me about that icon—the one where the Archangel
Gabriel offers a lily to the Virgin Mary. He is wearing shoes just
like the ones Papa wears to go riding. Did the Archangel bring her
that lily on horseback?"

Grandpapa shook with laughter and patted Sasha on the cheek:
"My dear boy, with your analytical mind you'll go far."

"Where will I go, Grandpapa?"

"That I cannot tell you. I shan't be there to see."

"Where will you be?"

"Why, in my coffin—in the cemetery at Donskoy."

The thought of Grandpapa dead and buried was too much. Loud
sobs filled the carriage. And nothing would stop our grief until he
promised to live as long as possible and see us all grow up.

The high point in our year came when at last the long Moscow
winter broke up and we got ready to go to our country place for
the summer. My parents' property, Kotchemirovo (about 25,000
acres), was in central Russia in the province of Tambov, and it
bordered on vast forests that extended all the way to the Volga.
When I was a small child there was no railway anywhere near
Kotchemirovo. We had to travel by horse and carriage.

The journey meant three days of excitement and fun for us
children. But they were a trial for Mother, who had to plan the
transportation of five small children, as well as nurses, governesses,
cooks, maids, and footmen. On our way back to Moscow in the
autumn, the snow and bitter cold made traveling with children
even more difficult. The five of us with our nurses would be packed
into two carriages, each drawn by three horses. Wheels had been
removed and sleigh runners attached, so that the vehicles glided
easily over the snow. However, sleigh-borne carriages overturned
at the slightest bump or furrow in the road, and there were many
of them when traveling through the forest. I can still clearly recall
the scene when our carriage overturned: huge pines towering over
us, their branches weighed down with snow; a line of sleighs; jolly
Russian faces reddened by the frost. Our nurses making frantic
efforts to prevent us from rolling out; shouting coachmen pulling

on the horses' reins. Other men straining and struggling to right
the vehicle, while joyful screams and squeals issued from inside.

The relay station where our horses were changed was always a
welcome break. We would enter the *izba* (a sizeable wooden
peasant's house) to find a samovar steaming on the table, on which
our chef had already laid out a picnic luncheon: *pirojki* (small
individual pies stuffed with meat or cabbage), cold chicken, and
hard-boiled eggs. But Mother, harried and nervous (she was
mortally afraid of horses) only drank a glass of tea. Father, meanwhile, his short well-trimmed beard coated with rime, would
linger outside to oversee the harnessing of fresh horses and to drink
a glass of vodka with the master of the posting station—a burly,
bearded peasant who crossed himself devoutly before downing his
glass at one gulp.

But it was our springtime returns to the country that always
filled us with special joy. We alighted at the little Kotchemirovo
station in the morning to find the troika for our mother at the head
of a line of carriages. All the coachmen were dressed in the traditional costume of red shirt, black velvet vest, and round hat with
a peacock feather. How intoxicating it was to drive through the
reborn forest! Fresh young leaves rustled overhead, and anemonies
and lilies-of-the-valley grew on both sides of the road. When we
emerged into the open we could see pools of melted snow reflecting the blue sky. Here and there along the way, groves of wild
cherry trees would be shedding their white petals down on the
brown, crumpled leaves of the last autumn.

Very soon our village church's onion-shaped cupola would come
into view. And at last, as we turned into an avenue of lindens and
maples, our house itself would appear, surrounded by lilacs in
bloom, with windows wide open and white curtains fluttering in
the breeze. Dogs would be barking, and all the servants would be
gathered on the steps to grin a "welcome home." Traditionally we
first inspected the greenhouse where the gardner Artamon waited
to show us blooming masses of cyclamen and polyanthus.

Quite a character, this Artamon was: a habitual drunkard, he was
nonetheless a marvelous gardener. When Mother, who could not
endure intemperance, complained about him, Father would say,
"My dear, what's the use? Plenty of people we know have the

same weakness. If he neglected his work, I'd feel differently, but just look at those cyclamens!"

Father was full of understanding for human weaknesses. There was an old former pensioner of Mother's, whom she had abandoned upon discovering that he spent every kopek on vodka and had become the village drunkard. One day when Father and I were sitting in our Kotchemirovo drawing room, this pitiful man wandered into the garden and peered in through the window. Father handed me a ruble. "Give it to him, but don't tell Mamma. She is right, but after all—it's all the poor chap has."

In Kotchemirovo, Mamma continued some of the good works that occupied her in Moscow. Her thoughts were constantly with the sick of the village. Every Tuesday when a doctor visited our village, she risked contagion by accompanying him to the small hospital she had had built. While the doctor prescribed medicines, she supplied the patients with other things they needed. Father saw, among the things brought from Moscow, a large case of Tokay wine. He looked at Mother in surprise.

"Two dozen bottles? Five rubles a bottle? Why, Masha dear, what extravagance! But," he added slyly, "it's my favorite wine," and his hand reached out for a bottle.

"No, no, no, no! That's for the peasant children! Tokay is so good for stomach upsets."

Father looked at her, pleadingly: "Not even a bottle?" He got one in the end.

One should not conclude from this incident that Papa was a henpecked husband. On the contrary, in our house his word was law, for he was greatly respected, and also a bit feared. Mother, on the other hand, never "gave orders," yet no one in the household ever dreamt of going against her wishes. Catching sight of her on her way to confession, our old chef was once heard to say, "There goes our saintly dove to repent for her sparrow-like sins."

When we reached our later teens, our summer house was always full of young people: my brothers brought their friends, cousins arrived, and tutors for the younger boys, as well as our own painting and music teachers.

With so many thrown together, romances were bound to flourish: thus Katya fell madly in love with Igor. After a year of the romantic courting one thinks of finding only in English novels, she married into a lifetime of marital bliss. As for me, I came very close to making a fool of myself and wrecking a man's life.

Our French music teacher was twenty years my senior and married, though not living with his wife. My passion for music drew us together, but I let my vivid imagination get the better of me. For awhile I fancied myself acting George Sand to his Chopin. He in turn began dedicating his piano compositions to me, playing them over and over again while I listened in blissful rapture. I gave no thought to consequences, until the thunderclap fell one evening. My horrified parents summoned me to announce that Chopin intended to get a divorce in the hopes of obtaining my hand.

At my mother's dictation, I had to write a letter telling him that this state of affairs was all a mistake, that he had misunderstood my feelings. I didn't sleep a wink that night, and early next morning I heard carriage bells at the door. Peering out the window, I saw the poor man being driven away to the station.

My parents took me to Italy that year—to forget. I don't know which emotion was uppermost in me, infatuation or humiliation— but it took me a whole year to get over them both.

CHAPTER TWO

☙⚜❧

From an early age, I had tended to support any reform that proposed to let vivifying air into the stale old chambers of the Russian Monarchy. Thanks to the influence and examples of my family, I had grown up to be a rebel, or at least a young woman of advanced liberal ideas.

Admirable as my grandparents' civic-mindedness had been, it was still of the nature of paternalism, belonging to the past. More liberal men like my father, loyal to the monarchy yet recognizing the inevitable, got nothing but frowns from the Throne they were trying so hard to serve. Father kept as far away as he could from the dangerously reactionary elements surrounding the Throne, spending his energies on the improvement of social rather than political conditions. He collaborated with many of those who later took part in the Provisional Government that followed the Emperor's abdication in 1917. As loyal monarchists, they originally had tried to strengthen the monarchical order with the support of an elected assembly, or *Duma*. They felt that the people's aspirations would then be legitimately expressed, abuses corrected, and the Throne's prestige enhanced. But the government of Nicholas II regarded such initiatives as "revolutionary."

Monarchist though my father was, at the same time he was gravely aware of the growing social unrest. I remember that one day, upon our return to Kotchemirovo, the peasants of our village greeted my parents with the traditional bread and salt to express their loyalty. Mother was touched. "Oh, they do love us," she exchaimed. But Father only shook his head, smiling sadly. "I'm afraid some day we'll pay dearly for these expressions of devotion." In the face of current conditions, such lavish displays of gratitude did seem somewhat exaggerated.

21

The advocacy of any education among the peasantry beyond bare literacy was frowned upon as premature and dangerous, for it was feared that education would arouse a desire for changes in the methods of agriculture and landholdings. Yet God knows how sorely such changes were needed!

When the serfs had been freed in 1861, a certain area of land was assigned to every village. Individual farms, distributed among separate families, rotated every seven years. In this way, farmers held no permanent titles to their properties and had no incentive to improve the land, which naturally deteriorated. The great Russian Premier Stolypin, whose agrarian reforms tried to end this hangover from the past, was opposed by the extreme political Right. He also faced opposition from the subversive parties on the Left, who feared that if Stolypin's reforms became effective, peasants would lend less amenable ears to revoluntionary propaganda. In 1911 Stolypin was assassinated by an *agent provocateur*, whose plans had been previously known to the Okhrana (the tsarist Secret Police). Like Stolypin, we moderates found ourselves between the ultraconservatives, headed by the Empress, on one side; and the left-wing extremists on the other.

In my youth there was a general fermentation of thought all over Russia. My family became deeply involved in the political and economic discussions that were taking place everywhere. Katya and I used to type reports of the meetings of our "Kadet" Party. We shared the hopes of those who beseeched the Emperor to promulgate the badly needed reforms and thereby to preserve the dynasty and the imperial regime. We typed more than one such "Address to the Throne," which only fell on deaf ears.

From childhood on, my training had been preparing me to supervise welfare projects. At sixteen I was entrusted with the care of a foundation for old women, originally built by Sophie Scherbatov. The rest home had its own chapel and garden. Grandpapa Scherbatov had endowed it with a large sum of money, and during Grandpapa's lifetime I often accompanied him on his tours of inspection from ward to ward. He would beam at the old women, who smiled in turn at his kindly jokes. Later there would be a *Te Deum* in the ugly gold-and-pink chapel, and prayers of thanksgiving for Grandpapa and his bounty. But somehow I was never happy during those visits. I intuitively felt a false and strained atmosphere about the place.

Every time I visited the rest home now, I walked from ward to ward just as Grandpapa had done, but could not get rid of the tightly corseted, ax-faced matron who dogged me with a sugary smile. I had wanted to establish direct contact with the old ladies; to chat and ask if they were happy, whether they needed anything; but with the watchful matron at my side, I was tongue-tied. I could sense the old women were afraid of her.

Outwardly, everything about the place was in perfect order: the floors shone, the beds were neatly covered, and small cupboards were provided for every inmate. When I first peeked inside these, my heart ached to see the pathetic little belongings: bundles of yellowed letters, old faded photographs, dried flowers, prayer books. The matron's voice buzzed in my ear.

"I've told them time and again not to keep rubbish there because of the mice. They refuse to obey!"

I tried to explain that the poor souls had no other place to store their keepsakes. She only scoffed: "Keepsakes? You are too kind! Trash like that ought to be burned, I say!"

I saw hate glimmering in the eighty pairs of old eyes, and felt sick at heart. No warmth or love was here; only clean floors and oppressively tidy beds, on which the poor women ought to have been allowed to rest during the daytime. But no! Against the rules! They had to sit in the reception room on stiff hard benches.

"And what about the food?" I asked, entering the kitchen.

"Oh, excellent, excellent! See? Macaroni and a little ground meat for them today, and gruel and a little ground meat tomorrow. Everything has to be soft, you know, for those toothless mouths."

"Lies! All lies, vile lies!"

The indignant voice came from behind me. Turning, I saw a stout woman in gray. Her face was transformed by fury, and a gold medal for valor was pinned to her heaving bosom. She was Glafira Petrovna, a Red Cross nurse who'd served in the Turkish War. Having faced the Turk in her day, she now faced the matron with blazing eyes:

"Yes, yes, I'll tell her everything! You can have your revenge later, you crocodile!"

The matron gasped. I tried to pacify Glafira Petrovna, begging her not to use such language. "It's bad for your heart, too," I reminded her as a last resort. But she only screamed louder:

"Heart? Why my dear young lady, my heart is bursting with hate, and that's bad enough. Excellent food indeed! Why can't we have some salted cucumbers, some mushrooms, or a bit of herring now and them? The old Prince, God rest him, left enough money for such small pleasures. But not anymore! It goes elsewhere, into somebody's pocket, that's where it goes! The old Prince, God rest him, would've thrown this matron out the window, but you're too young of course, much too young!"

I decided to do the same, young or not. Rushing home, I burst into Mother's boudoir. It all came pouring out: the poor frightened old women, their meager belongings, the dreadful food, the horrible matron, and Glafira Petrovna. I was sobbing with rage. Mother heard me out quietly, but dismissed me without saying a word. A few days later, she summoned me to her room.

"I have thought it over, Masha, and I believe this particular activity is not in your line. I will take care of the rest home. I'll find another matron, and you must look for something else to do that will suit you better."

"I'm simply bursting—to work, to help, and be useful! But how, and where?"

"It'll come, dear—the right work—in its proper time and place. You'll find it soon enough."

And I did, a couple of years later. Many men in Kotchemirovo had gone away to the cities to look for work, leaving behind their wives and families. Since there was no local employment for women, I conceived the idea of employing their skills in embroidery and lace-making. I studied traditional Russian designs and sent to Italy and France for others to be executed by the peasant women. This modest enterprise grew so fast that before long, over five hundred women were employed in it. Orders came pouring in, not only from fashionable women, but also from the best shops in St. Petersburg and Moscow. What had started as a scheme for providing employment became a flourishing financial success. I had had to borrow the initial capital, but that was soon repaid. It was a great joy watching the wives grow rich enough to repair their homes and buy new heads of cattle, while the single girls added to their dowries.

In 1913 there was an all-Russian exhibition in St. Petersburg, where I took a booth to display the beautiful workmanship of the Kotchemirovo women. The designs were greatly admired, and I was given the gold medal of the exhibition. The Empress, Alexandra Feodorovna herself, visited my booth and gave a substantial order, which was the best possible advertisement for our enterprise.

Nevertheless, my feelings for the Empress remained unchanged. True to my principles, I avoided meeting her on this occasion. Having heard of her proposed visit, I arranged to stay away that day and left another woman in charge of the exhibit.

From the very beginning, I had taken a firm stand against the Imperial Court. At eighteen, the age when a girl "came out" into society, I might have been presented at Court together with many other girls of my social standing. But I balked at the idea. My parents did not insist. "Petersburg society," my father used to say, "is like a growth of sunflowers, always turning their faces to the sun." (In general, Moscow did not attach as much importance to such things as St. Petersburg did.) But a few months later, in 1903, my determination to remain "unpresented" was brought to a test.

A momentous event was to take place in our district: the Empress, who had already given birth to four daughters, was coming with the Emperor to pray for a son and heir at the nearby shrine of St. Seraphim of Sarov. As Marshal of Nobility of the district, Father would have to entertain Their Majesties. Mother was ill, unable to be of help, and I was in Moscow at the time. A very important person at Court intimated that, should I act as his hostess, I would be appointed honorary maid-of-honor and given a *chiffre*—an imperial crown over the combined initials of the two empresses, dowager and reigning, all in diamonds, hung with a pale blue bow of the ribbon of St. Andrew (the highest Order of the Russian Empire). Such a *chiffre* gave a woman entrée to Court during her whole lifetime. Knowing how I felt about such things, Father said he would have to consult me before giving an answer. He had fully anticipated my reaction: "No! Honorary or not, no Court functions for me!" I remained in Moscow, and a female relative took my place.

St. Seraphim, to whose shrine the Empress made this pilgrimage, was one of the most revered saints in Russia. Born into a merchant family toward the end of the eighteenth century, Grace moved him early in life to retreat into the depths of the forest, near the Monastery of Sarov, where he led a life of prayer, contemplation, and abstinence. Before long, the rumor of his saintly life spread. It was said that a huge bear kept him company in his solitude, but that he forbade the animal to appear when anyone came to see him least the friendly beast frighten the visitor. People from all walks of life and from all parts of Russia came to him for guidance.

On great Church feasts, St. Seraphim would attend Mass at the Cathedral of Sarov, but otherwise he was on distant terms with the monks because of their too wordly attitude and too easy life. After his death, they buried him in their Cathedral nonetheless. His miracle-making shrine there and his hermitage in the forest nearby both became places of pilgrimage.*

There is a story of St. Seraphim which illustrates why the people, especially the simple peasant folk, loved him so. On one occasion a group of local dignitaries had come to his retreat to consult him on some important matter. A peasant woman inter-rupted their discourse with wails and lamentations, and begged the Saint's help. A landowner, she told him, had employed her to take care of his turkeys, but now the turkey chicks were all dying. Soon the outraged landowner would return and turn her out, and her children would starve. What was she to do?

The Saint listened to her patiently, and told her not to fear, but rather to pray. "And I will also pray that your turkey chicks should live and prosper."

When the woman had left, comforted and happy, the visiting dignitaries reproached the Saint for allowing people to waste his time with such trivial matters. But he smiled. "That poor woman's not unique, you know. We all have our turkey chicks."

The Sarovka, as the monastery was commonly called, lay thirty miles from the nearest railway station; but every year on St. Seraphim's Feast Day in July, there was a pilgrimage to his shrines. A most impressive procession took place at night as thousands of pilgrims chanted and carried lighted tapers through the forest.

---

* The Bolsheviks later removed the remains of St. Seraphim from Sarov to Moscow, where his bones were displayed in an antireligious musuem beside the relics of many other Russian saints.

One day in 1903, the Emperor and Empress drove the thirty miles from the railway station in the first of a row of open landaux, followed by their suite. It was a glorious morning full of spring sunshine, with not a cloud in the blue sky above, and blue flax blooming on the sides of the road.

Peasants dressed in native costume lined the streets of every village to cheer the passing sovereigns. But their joy and jubilation were marred by a single, sinister figure: in one of the open carriages rode a shabby eccentric with long hair and beard—one of those forerunners of Rasputin who held periodic sway over the Empress' mind. The peasants, with eyes only for their "little father, the Tsar," may not have paid much attention to that bizarre figure, but to people like my Father, the presence of such a disreputable creature on such an important occasion came as a shock.

The Empress prayed at the Saint's tomb, then went to his hermitage and plunged herself fully dressed into a nearby spring which was said to have curative properties. Next year her wish was granted. The Tsarevich was born and named Alexey, after the baptismal name of St. Seraphim.

Even though the Russo-Japanese War was then raging, the whole land rejoiced: a new heir was born to Russia, and with him, new hope. Yet somewhere deep in our hearts a formless fear kept stirring—a foreshadowing of disasters as yet unperceived but already dimly sensed.

Shortly after returning to Russia from Italy, I met Nicholas Avinov—Nika. It happened in Moscow. Katya, already married for a year to Igor Demidov, was giving a reception. When I entered her crowded drawing room, I became keenly aware of a young man standing against a white wall. He looked my way. He was young—twenty-five or so—handsome, and slender. He made me think of a tall young tree, of a white sail in the wind.

Someone introduced us: "Nikolay Nikolayevich Avinov—Marya Yuryevna Novosiltsev." Those were formal days. For months our first names and patronimics would have to suffice. We talked a lot together that first time, but I remember little. My heart was beating too furiously. I knew from the eyes that looked into mine— innocent and gentle, trusting but indomitable—that here was an exceptional man.

The next day he paid a formal visit on my parents. Two days later he called again, and that same evening I told Katya I intended to marry Avinov. She looked horrified: "But you don't even know the man!"

I guessed what was on her mind—my affair with the Frenchman. Half closing my eyes, I began to recite: "Oh, but I do know him. He is young and handsome! An intelligent, benevolent panther with the kindest eyes on earth! His political views as liberal as yours or mine, and what's more, he has an adorable smile!" I saw Katya's lips move, but I forestalled her: "Is he serious? Oh yes, very! Does he lack our lighter touch, our gift of fun? Perhaps. But he has the ability to give of himself, and his love of his country borders on the sublime. No sensible woman would let such a man slip by, and I won't either, mark my words!"

Katya was left speechless and a bit disgusted with me, but my determination to marry Avinov never flagged. From our first meeting to our wedding, I knew. But it took me a long time to become convinced that he cared for me. For weeks I lived tormented by recurring doubts: does an unusual, such a remarkable, such an extraordinary man ever love such an ordinary girl? One evening, I entered our pink drawing room where Mother welcomed me with open arms: "Go into the Blue Room, darling. Hurry. Avinov is waiting for you."

I remember little of the next half hour. All I can recall are my own silly, faltering words: "Is . . . is it possible that you love me. . . ?" Without a word, he put his arms around me. I do believe that in that instant we were spiritually joined for life; but we had to wait another year before acting formally on our intentions.

There were several reasons for a prolonged engagement. First, Nika's parents had left him in charge of Shideyevo, their estate in Little Russia. When they returned in the fall, Nika was faced with months of heavy studying to prepare himself for a final examination in economics. All day Nika's studies and my work at the university mess hall kept us apart, but every evening we spent together at my home.

At last—just as it was beginning to seem as if it would never come—our wedding day arrived, May 14, 1906. From top to bottom, the old Scherbatov house was exquisitely decorated with flowers. In my own room, where the entire floor was covered with clean white sheets, I was getting dressed for the altar in a·long gown and veil made from the Brussells lace my great-grandmother had given me when I was a child. Mother's soft, luminous eyes sobered me, while the words she said sank deeply into my memory.

"I honestly think that your Nika is a saint; in the most profound and beautiful sense of the word. He is so thoughtful, and yet so detached that one would think he's living on some higher plane. But at the same time, he's head over heels in love with you." She appeared puzzled.

"But what's wrong with that, Mamma? I love him too."

"Simply this, Masha: you are passionate, high-strung, impulsive, and outspoken—in short, you're entirely of *this* world. You may easily hurt Nika if you're not careful. You may find yourself standing in his way some day." She took a deep breath. "Remember, my child: you are marrying an extraordinary person who would give up his ideals for you. It won't be easy, but see that you never become his Achilles' heel!"

CHAPTER THREE

❧

During our long engagement, I had a chance to learn much about Nika's family background. The Avinov family had originally come from the north, from the Ancient Free City of Novgorod, whose two governors were traditionally chosen from among the Avinov clan.

The whole clan perished in the fighting which ended with Ivan the Terrible's conquest of the city after a long seige. Through the care of his nurse, only one male infant survived, and through him General Avinov, Nika's father, traced the family lineage back to those freedom-loving men of Novgorod. Perhaps it was that independence, reflected in his eyes and in the folds of his smile, that drew me to General Avinov from the very start.

I had met Nika's parents, his younger brother Andrey, and his sister Ellie at the time of my wedding in Moscow, but my brief memory of them was dimmed by the intense emotions of the wedding day. Not until the early fall of 1906, after our return from our honeymoon abroad, did I get to know my in-laws in their own home.

Nika and I arrived at Shideyevo after dark on a clear, star-lit evening. Getting off the train, the first thing I noticed was the strange, pungent smell of burning straw and dung. Nika inhaled rapturously. (Later I too grew fond of that characteristic odor: hanging on the air, it was so much an essential part of that lovely place.) We were met by the Station Master and a welcoming committee from the village, all of them shouting. "Long live Nikolay Nikolayevich Avinov and his bride!" We shook hands all around. The three grays hitched to the riding carriage had pink ribbons in their manes. After a fairly long drive, at last I saw a row of lighted windows shining through the warm darkness. Nika took my hand

and drew me close to him, "Welcome to Shideyevo, Sweetheart."

His family was waiting assembled on the twelve-pillared porch: my father-in-law, in general's uniform, held a silver icon. My mother-in-law, tall and stout, carried the traditional Russian plate of bread and salt used in welcoming a bridal couple. Nearby were my young brother-in-law Andrey, whose pale face showed great sensitivity and intelligence; and my sixteen-year-old sister-in-law Ellie, with large dark eyes like Nika's. The group of servants behind them seemed to consist solely of giggling maids in red Ukrainian skirts and black velvet bodices.

After the first embraces, we moved into a spacious dining room that extended the whole breadth of the house. The long table bore a fabulous display of food: roast suckling pig, turkey, ham, and pastry of every kind. My mother-in-law sat down at a brass samovar to pour tea. I suddenly realized how beautiful she must have been in her youth. Even now, though her body had grown heavy, her matured features were of that chiselled perfection so often found among Georgian woman, whose blood, through a great-grandmother, coursed in her veins. All of us settled around the table, but Nika remained standing, looking for something. His mother glanced at him fondly, then smiled at me.

"Look at that Nika of yours!" she said, "Round and round he goes, in search of rice and kasha. That's all he really likes. Before the General and I went abroad last year, I sat down with Olga, our cook, and we spent hours together thinking up wonderful menus for Nika. I left a dozen fat geese and turkeys in the coop, and had asparagus planted in the garden. Well! What do you think? When we got back, there were the birds strutting around fatter than ever, the asparagus tall and gone to seed, and Olga ringing her hands. When Nika hadn't been eating borsch and kasha, he'd just shared whatever food the workers had brought to the fields. Such a Spartan diet! One would think he was preparing for a convict's life." Little did we dream how prophetic her joke was to be.

Not much more was said that evening. My mother-in-law, rightly guessing that Nika and I wanted most to be left alone, stood up and swept ahead of us to the charming room she had prepared for us, bright with chintzes and flowers. On a table lay a wonderful antique tea set—her wedding present. A full moon had risen high and was shining through our window. The only other light came from a *lampada* (image lamp) before a holy icon in a distant corner. She bade us good night and closed the door. Nika's strong arms enfolded me.

Next morning I was shown through the house. By daylight, I saw it to be a splendid mansion, standing on a ridge overlooking a wide plain. The huge green cupola resting on twelve massive white pillars was a local landmark, and from the porch beneath, one enjoyed a truly panoramic view of the plain. I could see many individual villages, lying among orchards of fruit trees turned to rectangles of red and gold by the autumn sun. In the spring, so I was told, the lilacs, jasmines, and acacia trees in the garden gave out a perfume so strong that one had to shut the windows at times.

I soon discovered how devout the family was. A whole wing was given up to a house-chapel and living quarters for the priest, who was always in residence during the summer months. Divine services were held every Saturday evening and Sunday morning.

The south wing contained reception rooms. The red drawing room was old-fashioned and formal, with walls of scarlet and gold brocade. Two rows of massive armchairs, in which guests sat according to rank on formal occasions, were placed opposite each other. Next came the much cosier blue drawing room, with quaint old mahogany furniture, white muslin curtains, and a portrait of Catherine the Great (who had originally donated the Shideyevo estate). Each of these large rooms had its own special atmosphere and its own peculiar smell.

What appealed to me most about Nika's home was the ingenious lack of any attempt at period decorating. The house had simply grown, amplifying itself with each succeeding generation. Every inch of it had been lived in. Objects totally unrelated to their surroundings were to be found in unexpected places. On the window sills of the drawing rooms sat huge bottles filled with fruit fermenting into delicious homemade wines. There was a riotous abundance of furniture, china, and valuable bibelots, as well as fine works of art collected by my mother-in-law's father, an art expert who had held a prominent position at Court. When commissioned to purchase paintings for the Hermitage Museum in St. Petersburg, he had always bought one or two for himself.

While conducting me on a tour of the house, my mother-in-law came to a stop before a closed door. "Masha," she said to me, "prepare yourself for a shock!" With that she flung the door open and pointed into Andrey's sanctuary: "Have you ever seen such a chaos?"

I shook my head in dismay. Books, paint-boxes, and unfinished sketches were thrown together pell-mell, with prints, pamphlets, and rows of case-mounted butterflies. Still more butterflies were pinned to the walls and window curtains.

"Now tell me," my mother-in-law exclaimed in mock despair, "how can any work be done in such disorder?" Everyone laughed. Andrey smiled his whimsical smile.

"Well, Mama, I've actually done quite a lot. Yesterday I finished this miniature on ivory, and today I've written a paper for the Entomological Society."

Then we moved on to General Avinov's study, next to which Andrey's room seemed like Neatness itself. Not without a certain affectionate malice, Andrey whispered to me, "Behind Father's back, we call it the Dump Room."

No name could have been more appropriate: dusty piles of yellowing newspapers were stacked almost ceiling-high in a corner. Littering the sofa were sample bags of oats, barley, peas, sunflower seeds, wheat, and corn. The dates scribbled on some of those bags amazed me: "Why have you kept them for ten years?"

The General looked pleased. "Because," he said, "I like to check the progress of the farm."

Nika smiled and winked at me surreptitiously. *He* was the one who had done all the planning and who was responsible for the estate's abundance; but his father had long cherished the notion that their success was the reward of his personal supervision. The rest of the family was never to disillusion him.

Despite this one vanity, the General was an intelligent man of excellent taste. As my eyes grew accustomed to the extraordinary disarray of his study, I began to glimpse a few real treasures amidst the litter: old silver, cameos, snuff boxes, and a splendid collection of old coins. Already, the Avinov home with its comforts and incongruities, its loftiness and rusticity, was becoming dear to me. Yet what I enjoyed most that first day was walking with Nika through the fields and village of Shideyevo.

"This is the richest, most fertile black soil in the world," Nika expounded as we strolled together, arm in arm. "It's not surprising that this land is a coveted granary! It supplies western Europe with millions of tons of the best white flour every year, in addition to feeding the whole of Russia!"

The local peasants had a gaiety and self-assurance about them never displayed in central Russia. Nika told me that in the Ukraine, serfdom had not been established until the reign of Catherine the Great. Those pernicious seven-year rotations of individual farms had never existed here. "The peasants in Shideyevo own their own land. They know it's theirs to pass on to their sons. They cherish it and do all they can to improve it, and see the difference that makes!"

Nika was right; prosperity was evident from the moment we entered the village. Everyone, of course, knew Nika and greeted us both like old friends. I then learned that Nika had taught the peasants to use the new agricultural machinery and to improve their breed of cattle. This was Nika in still a new light! He seemed to have studied agronomy and farming for years. The peasants listened to him as to an oracle.

Now and then, as we moved through the village, a peasant would invite us into his clean cottage that smelled of dried herbs and was whitewashed every Saturday. A long table covered with gaily embroidered cloth would be set out with dishes of cottage cheese, freshly baked bread, fruit, eggs, and pitchers of cream. The host and his merrily bustling, pink-cheeked wife would welcome us as equals.

On our way home Nika said, "Don't think all their hospitality was simply a special display for our benefit. They're always like that. Every morning when our peasants go to work, they leave the door to the cottage open and the table set, so that unexpected guests and passing travelers can come in and help themselves to food."

Life in Shideyevo was delightful. One golden day followed another, like amber beads on a string. After breakfast the family dispersed, each to his chosen occupation. I sewed useless embroidery onto blouses and napkins, or else wrote poetry. Andrey wrote entomological articles, painted miniatures, and from time to time dashed into the garden with a butterfly net after an insect he had seen through his window. At sixteen, his sister Ellie already showed a marked skill at portrait painting. She could copy old masters so admirably that the art critic, Grabar, once exclaimed, "This young lady is a genius! For the life of me I couldn't tell her copy from the original."

Nika spent his mornings more simply, in the fields or else working over the estate's account. His mother—a real chatelaine if there ever was one, with a large bunch of keys at her waist—busied herself with the household, and dispensed remedies to anyone sick in the village. I am not sure what the General did in the mornings, but in the evenings he was a brilliant raconteur who entertained us with stories that always rang true.

During the Red Terror, Shideyevo was burned to the ground together with all its contents.

CHAPTER FOUR

❦

The outbreak of World War I in the summer of 1914 found Nika
and me in Moscow. Nika was then heading the financial department of the town *Duma* (City Council). With the declaration of
war, an enthusiastic wave of patriotism swept the country, and
with it came a strong, chauvinistic intolerance of everything German—Teutonic names, the German language, and even German
music. By popular demand, the German name of "Petersburg" was
replaced with its Russian equivalent, "Petrograd." * But the war
enthusiasm was genuine and overwhelmingly sincere. Everyone
wanted to work for the armed forces, or to sacrifice—time, energy,
or money for the cause. I did too, of course. Yet when I was
offered the management of the Evacuation Center of Moscow's
largest hospital, I would never have accepted if it hadn't been for
Nika's faith in my ability.

It was a stupendous task. The immense garage of the Municipal
Tramway System had been requisitioned and furnished with two
thousand beds. The wounded were brought here direct from the
railway station, given first-aid treatment, and sent on to various
special hospitals. Trains bearing casualties kept arriving day and
night. Thus the turnover had to be a rapid one, with beds ready
and food freshly cooked for every new trainload. An immense staff
was required to run the place. In addition, a disinfection center
had been set up with expert personnel, since the wounded were

*I might point out that this renaming of a large city was previously
unheard of in Russia's thousand-year-old history. Later the Bolsheviks,
drunk with desire to immortalize themselves and their heroes, transformed "Petrograd" into "Leningrad," and then frantically began
changing geographical names throughout the country.

traveling straight from the front, and often arrived with their clothes filthy and vermin-ridden. I was appalled simply by the responsibilities of managing such a place.

Nika told me not to worry. "It's only a case of supervising and coordinating. You can do that. Besides, you have a gift of express-ing your appreciation. That's important: the ward-maids will keep the wards clean and the beds tidy in order to win your approval. The kitchen staff will strive to prepare good food and serve it hot. Even the doctors will realize that any delay will be instantly re-ported to you. No detail should escape you, but I know none will."

"But that's a man's job," I cried, more awed than ever by the prospect.

"So what?" said Nika.

He reminded me of Weininger's theory that every human being possessed both masculine and feminine genes in varying degrees. A faint, self-deprecatory smile appeared in Nika's eyes, as it always did when he was afraid of sounding too serious: "You are a striking example of this theory. Your masculine genes provided you with brains, energy, and the ability to exercise authority. Your feminine ones, on the other hand, have brought tact, a kind heart, and the faculty of seeing the best in people. Accordingly—" Nika's eyes were laughing outright—"your iron fist will be wrapped in soft velvet, and you'll get on famously with everyone. Why should you worry?"

I was still hesitant. My fear brought out a last protest: "You see nothing but good in me because you love me!"

"Not at all, not at all," said Nika, shaking his head. "I know all your weaknesses. You are oversensitive, emotional, excitable—what is commonly known as 'high-strung.' But all you have to do is take hold of yourself." He reminded me of the maimed bodies, the blood and sufferings I would have to witness, and again he insisted that I would have the strength to remain calm: "Does a surgeon break down and weep over a patient while operating? Of course not! Neither will you." His voice took on a soothing tone. "I'll draw up a plan of work for you. If anything does go wrong, you'll always have me to help you out."

Whenever Nika expressed a firm wish, there was always an inflexible will behind his "soft velvet." With the promptings he had given me, I had no choice but to accept the appointment.

The wounded and the dying had to be unloaded from the long trains immediately upon arrival, and one of my first problems was to find enough stretcher-bearers. I organized a volunteer corps made up of students from the University and the Technological Institute. Within a month we had three hundred volunteers in three shifts working night and day. Some came from rich families, but most of them were poor boys whose shabby coats were inadequate in winter. It was pitiful to watch them carrying heavy stretchers in the bitter cold, sometimes for hours at a time. But their cooperation was invaluable. Before long, our personnel became a large, friendly unit held together by pride in our work and devotion to the wounded. Yet having become the model hospital of Moscow had its drawbacks. The High Command brought visiting foreign dignitaries to inspect us, which of course seriously disrupted our routine.

The Grand Duchess Elizabeth Feodorovna, the Empress' sister, had taken the veil in 1905 after the assassination of her husband, the Grand Duke Serge, Governor-General of Moscow, and had dedicated herself to good works. She became one of our most admiring patrons and insisted that the wounded going to her convalescent home in the south of Russia should come from our hospital. Every time a trainload left for the south, she went to the station herself to bless the departing men. She was always extremely kind to me and asked me to accompany her and carry the basket of little crucifixes and religious books which she distributed among the soldiers. She was a lovely sight as she made her rounds in her trailing pearl-gray robes and white veil. But this charming, saintly woman never realized how much her presence hindered our work: while she made the rounds of railway carriages packed with convalescents, the freshly arrived patients had to wait on a siding.

During the first two years of the war, the men seemed flattered by the attentions of a member of the Imperial Family. But as the conflict dragged on, bringing disaster and disillusionment, their attitude subtly began to change. The Grand Duchess was often received with surly, sullen looks. One day a wounded soldier refused to accept the cross she offered, muttering, "She thinks she's doing us a favor—a glass of vodka would be more welcome!" I glanced at her anxiously, but she only smiled sadly: "Don't worry, my dear. He's just tired and grumpy. The Russians are a kind people."

The Grand Duchess had spent part of her childhood and youth in England, where one of her married sisters lived. (Like the Empress, she was by birth a Princess of Hesse-Darmstadt, and a granddaughter of Queen Victoria.) After the outbreak of the Revolution she had an opportunity of returning there. My mother pleaded with her to go, insisting that she was in mortal danger as long as she stayed in Russia. But the Grand Duchess replied that along with her marriage vows, she had embraced her husband's country; that she loved Russia and was determined to share its fate. Shortly afterward, in 1918, the Bolsheviks threw her and an attendant nun into a disused Siberian coal pit, and hurled hand grenades and rocks down upon the two women.

Every day at the hospital brought new problems. My student stretcher-bearers and the younger nurses presented a particular headache. I was no prude. I have always loved young people and understood their mutual attraction. But besides three hundred students, the hospital employed a hundred nurses, some of whom were young and very pretty.

During the day nothing much went wrong. But I soon discovered that strict supervision was necessary at night. I took to staying at the hospital late to patrol the wards myself. One particularly handsome stretcher-bearer had been working extremely well before he grew infatuated with a pretty red-headed nurse. I found them one night sitting together at her ward desk, too enraptured with one another to hear a severely wounded soldier moaning and crying for water. When I appeared, the couple sprang to their feet guiltily. I told the girl to attend to the sick man at once. "And you, Makeyev, come with me!"

Leading him into my small office, I gave him a tongue-lashing; red-faced and penitent, he begged forgiveness and promised never again to neglect his duties. I should have known he was too much in love for such promises to be worth much, but I tried to be patient. Again I reminded him of our responsibilities to the wounded and of the high reputation of our hospital.

But the little red-head's charms proved too strong. A week later I caught them together again, and this time I was absolutely firm.

Makeyev left, but apparently bore me no grudge. At Christmas, when the students and nurses presented me with a very touching handwritten tribute, he turned up at the hospital and asked me to let him embellish it with a drawing.

In the end I found a solution to romantic distractions, or at least a way of giving these young cavaliers a chance to let off steam. There were large halls in one of the hospital annexes. I arranged monthly parties there for the students and nurses, and for any doctors who cared to come. I hired dance orchestras to play and also provided the suppers. I was fortunate to be able to afford such things.

Every morning I brought to the hospital a supply of coffee, cookies, and cigarettes. Everyone—student, nurse, or doctor—was welcome to drop into my office for a cup of coffee, a smoke, and a few minutes of relaxation. This way, I not only promoted a friendly ambience, but also got to know my staff. We began working closely together, and for a time all went well.

The first signs of trouble came not from the staff, but from the wounded. Their patriotism had been decimated along with the ranks of the army. Those first splendid units (such as the Siberian regiments) had suffered terrible losses during the first two years. Their troops had been replaced two and even three times. The peasant lads who had predominated before were now replaced with factory-hand recruits. Socialist propaganda had been rife for years among industrial laborers, and now their dissatisfaction had found worse grievances: the terrible incompetence, graft, and corruption among those trusted to supply the armies with food, ammunition, and clothing. Even soldiers in the front lines lacked arms, and for a rifle to be shared by ten men was not an uncommon occurrence. Our soldiers were attacking German barbed wire fences with their bare hands; often the artillery could not give covering fire for lack of shells. The wounded began to arrive from the front in a rebellious state of mind, complaining bitterly of the hardships they had suffered and blaming them on the government, the generals, and even the Empress.

The hospital itself underwent a change. Most of our stretcher-bearers had been gradually drafted, and their replacements came from military convalescent hospitals. We had no choice but to employ soldiers who were still slow and feeble, loudly resentful, and inflamed by revolutionary propaganda. Where students had once carried a stretcher cautiously and smoothly, these weakened and disgruntled men dragged it with bumps and jerks that were a torture to the wounded. The unloading of trains proceeded at a slow pace and held up our entire schedule.

Immediately after the outbreak of the Revolution in March of 1917, committees of soldiers sprang up at the front. Officers were insulted, even killed. Kerensky, then Minister of Justice and later Head of the Provisional Government, toured the front lines urging men to fight, promising land and liberty to all once victory had been won. "Of what use is land and liberty to me if I'm killed?" one of the soldiers shouted back. The cry was picked up by others: "We've had enough!" "Let the general fight!" "We'll grab what we can and head for home!" Thus began a total collapse of morale, and a tragic exodus from the front which no amount of Kerensky's oratory could check.

Alexander Kerensky, that loquacious figure at once pathetic and burlesque, who strutted so very briefly across the stage of Russian history! I once asked a mutual acquaintance how he could explain that incompetent statesman's amazing popularity.

"Simple enough," my friend replied, "He's a soap bubble. Soap bubbles reflect all the colors of the spectrum, and so does Kerensky. Everyone who talks to him gets the impression that Kerensky shares his views. People like that sort of illusion, but then of course, a soap bubble soon bursts."

Recently Kerensky has written his memoirs, in which he fully acknowledges his mistakes, and I regret that Nika's diary of those times has been lost. It would have been interesting to compare the two accounts. Nika had known Kerensky all his life. Although his opinion of Kerensky was none too high, Nika wrote down everything that happened from day to day over the six months or so while Kerensky was in power. As Undersecretary of the Interior under Prince Lvov's Provisional Government and later under Kerensky, Nika heard and saw a great deal personally. He knew even more. For years I managed to preserve his diary, but when one night the G.P.U. found it in the samovar where I had hidden it, and that was the end of that.

In Moscow as everywhere else in Russia, committees of soldiers and workmen were formed in every hospital. In ours, the wounded, the ward-maids, the orderlies, and the stretcher-bearers formed an organization; nothing could be done without their consent. They even decided what diets to give the patients, when operations should begin, and which doctors should perform them. Needless to say, our efficiency began to fall apart. The medical staff was already growing panicky when our chief surgeon resigned. He had tears in his eyes when he came to say goodbye, and I threw up my hands in despair: "But Professor, what will happen here if you leave?"

He shook his head despondently: "The same as everywhere else in Russia—mob rule! Prince Lvov is a fool and a coward. Kerensky a hopeless demagogue and blunderer—Oh, I suppose it's easy to criticize, but those imbeciles don't seem to realize they've made it impossible to *do* anything!" There was a moment's silence, during which he looked at me with something akin to pity: "Dear lady, take my advice. Leave the hospital. You heard what happened at the Morozov Hospital yesterday? Dr. Alexeyev, that beloved, respected, hard-working man, was reviled by the committee. They threw him into a wheelbarrow, and dumped him outside in the snow. Something of the sort may happen to you any day!"

I didn't know what to do. I needed advice, but Nika was in Petrograd. It was then late April. Early in March, in his newly appointed capacity of Undersecretary of the Interior, Nika headed a Commission to draw up procedures for electing the Constituent Assembly which was to decide Russia's future form of government. All our hopes were pinned to that Constituent Assembly. We felt that upon the establishment of a regularly constituted national authority, the country might awaken from its nightmare. But there was still much to be done before the novelty of a universal secret free ballot could be achieved in Russia. Nika worked on the project night and day. Nonetheless, he tore himself from his work long enough to spend a couple of days with me in Moscow, where he made my decision for me. "Masha," he said, "Leave the hospital! At once! There is nothing more you can do there, and I can't work in Petrograd knowing that you are in danger here."

His eyes were tender, as always, but his voice was very firm. The next day, I went to the hospital for the last time. The place had become unrecognizable: the wards were dirty and unswept; ward-maids sat on the beds of wounded men, giggling and carrying on;

doctors ran in circles not knowing what to do. Yet when I told the Committee that I was leaving, tears and lamentations broke out. "Why?" "We have nothing against you!" "You are well-liked." "What'll we do without you?"

Their appeal found no response in me. I felt nothing but bitter disgust and, true to my nature, I could not hide it: "Do as you like. In a few short weeks you have turned our hospital into a pigsty. I'll have no part of it!"

A hard lump rose in my throat as I left the hospital for the last time, the place where for two years I had worked and given my utmost energy and goodwill.

CHAPTER FIVE

I will not recount the story of how Lenin seized power early in November of 1917 (late October, by the old-style calendar—hence the so-called "October" Revolution), nor how he dispersed the Constituent Assembly at the point of Lettish bayonets upon finding that Russia's mandates had turned against him. Long before that, it had become clear to us that our former mode of life would not be possible. Consequently, my parents sold the Scherbatov house early in 1917. It fetched them a million rubles in gold (about a half million dollars), which was an incredible sum to receive in those unsettled times. Friends all advised them to transfer at least part of this capital abroad, so as to have a nest egg outside of Russia, just in case. But my parents' sense of patriotism made that inconceivable. Instead, they decided (as my father put it) "to help Russia in her hour of need." Every kopek was invested in bonds launched by the Provisional Government. Before the year had expired, all of the money was lost, melted into nothingness, a valueless heap of printed paper.

I, too, put my house up for sale. I even found a buyer, but was never able to collect. By the time I was ready to move out, the newly formed Government of People's Commissars had requisitioned the house, and my prospective buyer was unable to take possession.

Disappointed but not disheartened, Nika and I moved into the house of friends who had left for France. It had twenty rooms besides a ballroom, and a vast basement which contained a large storage room in which the absentee-landlord had locked his possessions. The main floor became crowded with our belongings and with furniture from the Scherbatov house: eighteenth-century tables and chairs, Aubusson carpets, priceless Persian and Bokhara rugs, Gobelains, family portraits, and a magnificent silver dinner service engraved with the Scherbatov coat-of-arms. Quite obviously, it was dangerous to live surrounded by such treasures; perhaps even slightly insane. We could never take them with us if the Bolsheviks chose to pack us off to garret, prison, or grave. But then what else was there to be done but live with our familiar belongings and wait for the future to decide what to do with us?

We still had six servants. In many cases family servants represented yet another source of danger, liable to be bribed into spying upon their masters. Our staff included my grandfather's butler, Joseph, who had succeeded old Vassili and who had continued in my mother's service after Grandpapa's death. Joseph was a kind of family relic left in my care when my parents sold their town house and moved to our country house in Kotchemirovo. I must say I found Joseph a fearful nuisance.

For years his eccentricities—the white tie and tails he insisted on wearing, his absurdly solemn pomposity, the psalms he chanted as he went about his business—had made us all laugh. But there he was; I had to make the best of him.

At the outbreak of the Revolution, four or five of Nika's friends had taken refuge in Moscow and moved in with us as our guests. This meant that I had to feed them as well as ourselves and our staff. With increasing prices and dwindling supplies, planning meals for seventeen people became more of a problem with every passing day. Before long, we were reduced to boiled potatoes and gruel (without butter, of course); and roast horseflesh as a rare treat. It seemed ludicrous to go on serving pauper's food on silver platters, but when I broached my feelings to Joseph, the aged butler struck a pose of wounded dignity:

"Madame, when old Joseph is dead you'll make whatever changes you see fit, but as long as he is alive and at the head of your household, dinner will be served as it always was under the late Prince and under my lady, your mother!" He kissed my shoulder to show that he held me in respect too—by virtue of inheritance no doubt. Roast horseflesh, with its concomitant gruel or boiled potatoes, continued to be served on silver platters to the vast amusement of our guests.

The first time the G.P.U. (then known as the Cheka) came to the house, Joseph received them in the front hall with all the stateliness of an eighteenth-century majordomo: "My friends, what can I do for you?"

The Chekists, with their leather coats and drawn revolvers, stood gaping in consternation at this strange apparition. When they were gone, I asked Joseph why he had called them "friends." He drew himself to his full measure of pomp. "Madame, I couldn't call such rabble 'gentlemen.' The word 'comrade' shall never cross my lips. And since our Lord Jesus Christ commanded us to love one another, I deemed 'friends' to be the most appropriate form of address."

Much to my relief, I finally got rid of Joseph by persuading him to go live with his daughter. He agreed in his characteristic manner: "Yes, the time has come. I'm getting old. I'm tired. And my daughter, thank God, is very well off. She has an excellent husband who manages a large store. No day goes by without his bringing home a piece of cloth, a length of silk, or a dozen shirts or blouses. And thus my daughter wants for nothing. Ah, indeed, God's mercy is infinite!"

After much hand-kissing and a few crocodile tears, Joseph left. But no sooner had he gone, than my maid Natasha came rushing into the room: "For Heaven's sake, Madame, look out the window at that saintly Joseph of ours! The old fraud! Too weak to lift a samovar, was he?"

I ran to the window. There was Joseph, slowly making his way down the street, bowed under the weight of my French marquetry writing desk. Bolshevik propaganda was certainly beginning to take effect!

I've already mentioned how the relationship between masters and servants was becoming precarious. Bolsheviks urged servants to spy on their masters, promising rewards for any talk inimical to the new order and for the location of hidden valuables. I knew many families who had lost everything they owned through servants' tips, and still others who were sent to prison on the strength of some imprudent remark. We were very fortunate in this respect. After Joseph's departure, the loyalty of our remaining staff was unshakable. Basil, Father's former valet, was a priceless friend during this difficult period. We also had serene confidence in Filipich, the chef, although his hot temper was a source of constant danger. He swore he would knife the first Bolshevik who struck his nose into his kitchen. "If you do," I retorted, "we'll all find ourselves hung up to dry." In the end I persuaded him it was better to curb his fiery temper, and he did manage to control it, even though our house was searched over and over again. Many a Bolshevik went trampling through his kitchen, but he never uttered a word. Instead, he and Basil quietly saved many of our most valuable possessions by hiding them, at the risk of their lives.

Both men were devoted to Nika and were as upset as I was on the night of Nika's first arrest. A band of Chekists had ransacked the house from top to bottom, ostensibly searching for incriminating papers, but at the same time smashing up any object they felt like. When they got through with this routine, they declared Nika under arrest. Filipich and Basil embraced him, calling blessings upon him as he was led away. The eyes of the Chekist in charge registered amazement: "Since when do servants grieve when their master is taken to prison? Yours is a strange family!"

As usual, I couldn't restrain myself. "Yes," I cried, "you think class hatred governs everything, but has it ever entered your head that there can be affection and loyalty in its place?" He stared at me and shrugged with mild disgust.

But Nika was soon released. "It was all a mistake."

Early in May 1917, Kerensky was still in power and I was still alone in Moscow, filled with anxiety for Nika in Petrograd, where things were going from bad to worse. I received a telegram from my sister Sonya, who had worked as a Red Cross nurse at the front until the front itself had begun to disintegrate. She was now with our parents in Kotchemirovo. "COME AT ONCE VERY URGENT" read the message. Knowing Sonya's courage and self-control, I realized that something very serious was afoot. I had no way of communicating with Nika at such short notice, but I knew he would want me to go. The question was *how*. All the passenger trains were overloaded, packed with deserters from the front. Soldiers were hurrying back to make sure they got their share of the land Lenin had promised them, to pillage the great estates which the Communists had assured would be broken up and handed over to them. They were an ugly, angry horde, armed to the teeth (every man had bolted with his rifle and as much ammunition as he could lay hands on). Not even overflowing carriages could slow their wild rush; if unable to get inside, they perched on the roof, rode the buffers, or hung from the steps like grapes. There was absolutely no chance of my obtaining a seat in the regular way. After some deliberation, I decided to apply to an old friend for help.

There was a porter at the Kazan station who had once been my grandmother's footman. Before the Revolution, we had always given him a ten ruble gold piece for putting our luggage on the train on our way to Kotchemirovo. What with class hatred spreading and the relationship between different social levels becoming more strained every day, I knew I might be taking a chance. But I decided to risk it. I got in touch with the porter. When I told him what I wanted, he blanched. I could almost see him mentally ringing his hands. He couldn't promise anything. "But," he whispered after a brief inner struggle, "come to the station at six. I'll meet you on the steps."

I donned my Red Cross uniform and, at the appointed hour, made my way to the great square outside the station. I had to struggle through teeming crowds of Red soldiers, drunken, swearing, pushing. I finally managed to win my way to the steps, where I found my friend making discreet signs for me to follow him.

Carrying my suitcase and pretending to be on my own, I trailed him through the tremendous station—through several waiting rooms, a restaurant, along a seemingly endless platform, and finally to open tracks, where an empty train stood in readiness. With his pass key, the porter opened a carriage door, helped me climb the high steps, and literally shoved me into the first compartment.

"Ugh! That's done with! Thank God!" He wiped the sweat off his forehead. "Now keep very quiet, like a mouse. Say nothing when the soldiers come. Let's hope they'll respect your uniform."

I thanked him with all my heart, offering him the usual tip, but he refused it: "Those days are over now. I owe much to your family. Let's both just be glad I was able to help." Tears stood in the good fellow's eyes. He looked pale and unnerved. And just as we were about to say goodbye, there was a loud banging on the carriage door and drunken voices began shouting outside. "Open up!" "Open up, or we'll shoot!"

My poor porter turned from pale to ashen. "God Almighty, they followed us!" He rushed to open the door, and a raucous crowd of soldiers swarmed into the corridor.

"Who's this?" yelled the leader of a small gang that stormed into my compartment and hauled me out of my seat. Somewhere the porter's voice shook and trembled: "A Red Cross nurse . . . as you can see . . . her sick father's bedside. Leave her alone . . . She's earned her place here, working for you all through the war."

A soldier with only one leg and a surly voice plumped into my empty seat. "Let her stay. She's lucky I've only one leg. She can sit where the other one would be." He added a coarse joke, and the others roared with laughter. I sat down hurriedly beside him. He smiled and patted my hand with unexpected kindness. The porter seemed relieved, waved goodbye, and jumped off. The train began to move into the station.

Here another frantic crowd stormed the carriage. Soldiers tried to get in at the window. Shots rang outside. "Now then, comrades!" cried the leader of my compartment, and instantly rifles and revolvers were aimed at the window. A deafening volley blew the glass in a splintering shower onto the platform. Several answering bullets hit the ceiling above our heads. The train started with a jerk.

My traveling companions were delighted at having successfully defended their seats, and gradually calmed down. I took sandwiches and cigarettes out of my suitcase and handed them around, which added to the general good humor. I spent the night crushed into my corner, half-stifled with heat and tobacco smoke and body odors; and listening with ever-growing tension to the talk around me: would they be on time to grab land and cattle from landowners? Would the landowners resist? They'd wring their necks if they did, "those capitalists! Never fired a shot while we bled and died at the front!" And so on, and so forth, through all the long night. I thought of my parents and sister alone in the country, surrounded by peasants stirred up by clichés and propaganda, and my heart sickened. Only prayers keep one going at such moments. One must put oneself in God's hands. Still, I couldn't help shuddering at the thought that these men and thousands like them would be voting in the coming elections for the Constituent Assembly. I recalled Flaubert's remark—"Universal suffrage, that curse of the human race!"—and, looking around again at my companions, agreed with him.

At long last that dreadful night came to an end. We were approaching Kotchemirovo. I wondered how I would get out, since there was virtually no way of getting past the door into the corridor. My ruffians in uniform solved the problem for me:

"Don't worry, *sestritsa*. We'll lift you through the window." The train lurched to a stop. "Now boys!" the leader shouted, "she shared her food and tobacco with us! Give her a hand." I was lifted into the air. Somehow missing the jagged frame of broken glass, I was heaved through the window and fell. I landed in the arms of our coachman Pyotr, who had seen my perilous appearance and had run to catch me. Looking back at the toothlike shards set in the dark maw of the window and the grinning faces behind, I fell to trembling. Pyotr had to help me to the waiting carriage.

I was frightfully anxious to know what had been going on in Kotchemirovo, but Pyotr's answers were confused, vague, and evasive. I gathered that something had happened which he was afraid to speak of, which only added to my anxieties.

As we drove through the forest I tried to relax. After that ghastly night on the train, the smell of new leaves, the calls of cuckoos, and the peaceful beauty of spring all gradually made me drowsy. But when we reached the edge of the woods where cultivated land—our property—began, Pyotr sharply reined in his three black horses and raised the hood of the carriage. "It's going to snow," he said.

"What? In May."

"Look at those clouds."

Indeed, the whole sky was a low, lead-gray blanket. In a few minutes we were driving through a blindingly opaque snowfall. That in itself seemed like a bad omen. The wild cherry trees lining the narrow road on either side seemed to have exchangd their festive blossoms for shrouds. Weighed down into the road by snow, scented boughs that gave off a bitter-sweet smell brushed against me. It was a slow, heavy drive: three hours went by before the belfry of Kotchemirovo heaved into sight. The joys of past homecomings were not for this return. What was I going to find?

At last the carriage drew up at the front porch. I jumped out, and barking dogs ran to meet me, their tails wagging. That much, at least, was unchanged! I rushed into the dining room, where Father and Mother stood waiting for me. I then remembered it was my mother's birthday. Dressed all in white, she smiled at me from the threshold, her arms ready in welcome. I burst into tears.

Father came, took my hand, and kissed me. I saw at once that he had aged—new lines of worry etched his forehead and the corners of his mouth. He said little, but his eyes were full of sadness.

Sonya was there too, of course; and Alice, our Swiss governess, who had been like a member of the family for twenty-five years. We sat down to dinner around the long table, decorated with a vase full of lilies-of-the-valley. They all began talking at once: an irrational chatter of excitement that told me nothing. I noticed a deepening frown on Father's face as he tried to light a cigarette with a shaky hand. Mother saw it too, and leaning toward me, whispered, "Sonya will tell you everything later." It was only after dinner, alone with Sonya in her room, that I learned what had led up to her frightened telegram.

As I might have guessed, the troublesome village of Zaoolki was behind it all. Ever since the abortive Revolution of 1905, every unreasonable demand and complaint, every manner of chicanery and mischief, had come out of Zaoolki. Mother had disregarded it all and gone on helping the peasants of Zaoolki just as she did those of Kotchemirovo, doing her best to improve their standard of living. But with Revolution now triumphant and well-nigh out of hand, the turbulent village of Zaoolki was on a rampage. They had been calling daily meetings with the men of Kotchemirovo, at which they all drank heavily and discussed how they might grab our land and do away with us. "The estate is in your district; we'll leave that one for you." For several days, vague rumors of these goings-on had reached the house. Then, on the day before Sonya sent the wire, the footman, Ivan, burst into the drawing room where the family had gathered for tea. "The peasants! They're outside, with axes, demanding to see the master!"

Mother picked up a small icon and hid it under her cloak as she hurried after Father. The yard was thronged with peasants. Those from Kotchemirovo stood in a group apart. They took off their caps when the family appeared, but those from Zaoolki did not. The coachman, Pyotr, took one look and stationed himself beside Mother as a bodyguard.

Timofey, a disreputable peasant from Zaoolki, was acting as spokesman. He advanced upon Father, brandishing his fists: "Show us your hands, Bourgeois! They're soft and white. They've never held a plough. But look at ours! We've sweated blood and tears and worn ourselves out with work!"

Father remained perfectly calm. He spoke to Timofey with quiet authority: "Quite true. I never worked in the fields. But my hands have done work of another kind. *You* ought to know. When you had cataracts in both eyes, I sent you to a hospital in Moscow, at my expense. I paid for your operations. While you were gone I had your fields sown and reaped. And didn't I support your family for more than a year?"

"It's true," the men from Kotchemirovo shouted, "it's true, the whole world knows it!" Timofey, shamed, slunk back into the crowd. But others from Zaoolki took his place, hurling accusations.

"You feed the best meat to your dogs while we starve." "You have sacks of gold stored in the house while we're penniless." One turned on Sonya: "As for her, she's not a Red Cross nurse, but a slut! She drank champagne and made love to officers while our boys died at the front!"

Mother, who hadn't uttered a word until then, stepped forward. "Listen to me," she said in a loud, firm voice, and the men fell silent. "Say anything you like about my husband and me, but I forbid you—do you hear me!—I *forbid* you to reflect upon my daughter's honor!"

A hush fell over the yard. Even among the Zaoolki crowd, many doubtless remembered Mother as a benefactress. But their memories were not of long duration. Insults and abuse soon poured forth again, lasting until dusk, when it began to snow. The peasants gradually drifted away.

As Mother turned to go back into the house, she caught sight of a knife in Pyotr's hand. "What were you doing beside me all that time?"

"I know when there's murder in the air," he replied, shamed at the mistrust in her voice. "You might've been attacked at any moment. I was going to get my blows in first."

Meanwhile, some of the men from Kotchemirovo stepped up to Father to tell him that they would remain loyal to him. Father thanked them. But when Sonya later reminded him of this optimistic display, he only shook his head: "Yes, they were loyal today. But tomorrow who knows? The temptations are great." Several months later, my eldest brother Sasha amplified Father's thought: "Are there any peasants in the world, I ask you, who could long resist the opportunity of getting fine cattle and horses, stocks of food, and machinery—all for nothing?"

Sonya had come to the end of her story. For a few seconds we stared at each other with fear stalking in the back of our eyes. "We must leave at once," Sonya said in a loud voice, but her matter-of-fact tone sounded forced: "There really isn't any time to be lost. Our parents still don't know half of what's going on. Mother is such an idealist. Father thinks I'm exaggerating, but they have confidence in you."

Our parents, however, must have sensed more than Sonya felt they did. They needed very little persuasion to see the situation as she did. We decided to leave the next day for Moscow and take as little luggage as possible so as not to arouse suspicion. I was to travel ahead with Father. Mother and the others would follow and meet us at the Kotchemirovo station.

The next morning, I got up at dawn to make one last round of our beloved home. But others had already forestalled me: here and there I found them, gazing mournfully at the objects they loved best.

In the library, Alice stood stroking her beloved leather-bound classics in German, French, English, and Russian—20,000 books in all, of which she had compiled an admirable catalogue. "How can I ever leave them to those vandals," she sighed. A moment later she smiled ruefully: "Haven't you a Russian proverb—'When you're having your head chopped off, you don't worry about a bald spot,' or something like that? Well, it's true."

In the storeroom, I found the housekeeper Yevguenia, moaning over jars of homemade jam: "To think of all their contents sliding down those peasant throats! Horrible! Sonya says to leave them, but if only I could take a few!" With that she pulled her apron over her head and burst into a paroxysm of tears.

Strolling into the greenhouse, I ran into the gardener Artamon, in maudlin contemplation of his life's work. But for once, he was cold sober. There were magnificient Grandiflora roses and other flowers there, but he cared only for his beautiful cyclamens that rose from their pots like splendid butterflies ready to take flight. "They have done so well this year," he murmured, shaking his head, "*so* well." The slanting May sunshine flooded the greenhouse. Under the glass ceiling, there was a delicious smell of damp earth and the perfume of flowers. Suddenly Artamon clenched his fists: "And to think that that good-for-nothing nephew of mine—he's serving in the Baltic Fleet, you know—had the nerve to say, 'Soon we'll smash 'em all. Spending time over plants is a criminal waste when people are starving.' '*Who's* starving?' I asked him. 'Look at your pig's cheeks! Those cyclamens gave my son and daughter a better education than you'll ever get, you dolt.' I took up one of the pots and told him to get out before I smashed one for him, right over that fool's noddle of his! Oh God, where are we going? Kerensky talks and talks instead of sending machine guns." He scratched the back of his head dolefully: "I ought to get back to work and make an arrangement of cyclamens for the drawing room. Perhaps it'll be for the last time, but they're Madame's favorite flowers, bless her."

That gentle "Bless her" made me realize that he expected a catastrophe. I accelerated my steps to outdistance that premonition of disaster, to reach the apartment Father had once set aside for Nika and me, in which we had been together and happy.

The windows were open there, and the white window curtains billowed inward with the spring breeze. The snow of the night before was melting rapidly. I ached to leave all this behind, then repeated in self-reproof: *Habere non haberi*, possess but don't be possessed. My eyes lighted on a little Chinese vase. Nika used to put a flower in it for me every morning. With all my strength I flung it out the window and heard it smash on the gravel walk below. "There!" I thought, "No predatory fingers will touch it now."

Mother and Father were an example to us all. This was the home they had created and lived in for thirty-five years, yet I heard not a word of complaint from either of them. Mother thanked Artamon for his cyclamens. Then, calm and serene, they walked out of it forever.

Father and I left by a side road, through the linden woods. At the river a ferry awaited us, along with twelve of our gamewardens. When they saw our carriage, they took off their caps and Father got out to speak to them. The head-man saluted.

"We have come to wish you a good journey, good health, and

good luck. We'd like to tell you we'll do all we can to protect your property." He swallowed hard, and tears rolled down his thick black beard. Father was deeply moved. He embraced them all in turn: "Thank you with all my heart, dear friends." But he forbade them to take any risks in defending his property. Useless blood would be shed, since inevitably the peasants would finally get whatever they were after. "Remember, you have families of your own to think of."

Soon we were crossing the river. "Such faithfulness," Father murmured, "it does one's heart good."

His voice quavered, and of a sudden, he too was weeping. I took his hand in mine and held it tight. He laid his head on my shoulder, and thus we gained the opposite bank.

CHAPTER SIX

✦§§✦

It was a blessing to find ourselves all together again in Moscow, in the house Nika and I had taken. Nika himself soon joined us. For a while we lived under the illusion of safety, surrounded by our belongings and cared for by our staff. Yet in the streets nearby, there was constant fighting. Pockets of resistance to the Bolshevik usurpation sprang up all over town; but gradually these grew fewer in number as they were isolated, outnumbered, and viciously exterminated.

A group of cadets from the Military Academy took refuge in a nearby theater, and the Bolsheviks besieged them. During the day we heard intermittent firing. Under cover of night, we kept the brave embattled boys supplied with food carried to them in large kettles from our kitchen. But the young cadets' position grew more desperate every day. When we heard that the Bolsheviks had taken over the building, we knew that none would have survived the vengeful slaughter. Instantly our chef Filipich announced that he was going over to pick up his kitchen utensils.

"Are you mad?" Mother cried. "The Reds will kill you!"

Filipich's composure remained unruffled: "My pots and pans, Madame, are worth the risk. I won't leave them to those swine!" Amazing as it seems, he returned triumphant from his expedition, carrying all his kitchen paraphernalia with him.

Those were chaotic days of quick, difficult decisions. Fortunately we did not have to worry about Nika's family. General Avinov had died the year before, and Nika's mother and sister had gone to the United States with Nika's brother, Andrey. Andrey, now Professor Avinov, had been sent abroad as purchasing agent for the All-Russian Union of *Zemstvos*.

Our unanimous feeling was that Father and Mother should leave

Moscow as quickly as possible. The south and the Caucasus, where a White Army was being formed to fight the Bolsheviks, seemed the safest place for them. Brother Sasha and his wife Shura decided to accompany them. But Nika felt it his moral duty to remain behind and help ease the already appalling conditions in the city, which were threatening to get entirely out of control. Of course, I had to stay with him. Though I hated to part with my parents at such a time, I felt relieved that they were escaping from Moscow. A large but not merry company set off for the south: Father and Mother, Sasha and Shura, our beloved old Alice, Basil, and Filipich and his wife.

Soon after their departure, communications were cut off between Moscow and the Caucasus. Long weeks passed with no news at all. Then finally a telegram came through: Father was dying of cancer. My impulsive nature gave no thought to consequences; I insisted on going to comfort Father. For an instant I saw pain and fear in Nika's gentle eyes, but he said nothing. Instead, he went about doing what he could to help me. Somehow, through various secret machinations, he obtained a reserved seat for Sochi (a port on the Black Sea) in a special train that was to travel under military escort. "But," he warned me, "there's no guarantee for a safe return. You may never get back to Moscow again."

Typically, Nika gave no voice to his own feelings. Beyond warning me that I might not return, he never so much as hinted that he wanted me with him. He left the decision entirely to me. For days I was torn between my longing to see Father before he died, and the equal dread of never seeing Nika again. In my decisive torment, I could not sleep or eat. Natasha, unable to bear my sufferings any longer, suggested that I consult a "wise woman." Knowing my dislike of soothsayers, she tried to reassure me on this point:

"This person is more of a seer than soothsayer, Madame. She is blind and deeply religious, and the Almighty has endowed her with the second sight." I listened but still was dubious. I have always felt that our ignorance of the future was one of God's mercies. But in the end, distraught, I resorted to go to the blind woman.

Hers was a miserable cubbyhole of a room in the basement of a dilapidated house. On the floor lay a pallet, along one wall a bench, and in a corner a large icon with a lighted *lampada* in front of it.

The old woman herself was dressed as a nun, and sat in another corner fingering a rosary. When I opened the door she looked up.

"You've come . . . to ask me about your parents? And your journey . . . Don't be afraid of me. I believe in God. In my blindness, He has given me the power to look into the future, as long as I use it only to help. . . . I see a house . . . standing between mountains and . . . sea. I see your family. Your father is very ill. He . . . is in bed. Your mother is at his side. She looks much like you. There is also a young woman with them; she is not in the room. Your father is thinking of you, and longing to see you before he dies. Ah! I see the train that can take you to him. . . . But *there is no return*. I can see what will happen to those who try to come back . . . Oh, terrible—terrible!"

She fell silent, engrossed once more in her rosary, apparently no longer conscious of my presence. I was terrified but convinced: I would not attempt the journey. Two guilt-ridden months later, news reached us that the returning train had been captured by the Bolsheviks. Every passenger inside had been massacred.

Father died in 1920, without my ever seeing him again. Nor did I ever again see my brother Sasha: he died of typhus in 1918, two years before my father. But Mother, accompanied by Sonya and old Alice, somehow managed to find her way back to Moscow.

The Bolsheviks had hitherto been ostracized by the rest of Europe, but with the coming of the twenties, they became desperately anxious to renew trade relations with the West and to obtain loans to reconstruct the economy they had ruined. In 1921 Lenin sanctioned the New Economic Policy (NEP) which permitted private enterprise in certain limited fields. In 1922 (during which the Soviet Union signed the Treaty of Rapallo with the Weimar Republic) Mother and Sonya took advantage of a curious decree, unique in the annals of Bolshevism, whereby a number of prominent Russian intellectuals were to be exiled permanently abroad. Among them were the famous Peter Struve, exponent of socialism and revolution; Milyukov, leader of the Kadet Party; Berdyaev, the famous philosopher; Ilyin, a prominent professor at the Moscow University; and my cousin Prince Serge Troubetzkoy. The latter had been condemned to death for participating in an anti-Communist plot, but later his sentence was commuted to a year's imprisonment. When it was finally changed to permanent banishment, Serge was able to take Mother (his aunt), Sonya (his cousin), and Alice with him into the outer world.

Through the help of friends in the German Embassy, Nika and I were able to send to Mother one of the Novosiltsov heirlooms— a precious collection of engravings, containing works of Rembrandt, Dürer, Schohauer, and many other. The set had been originally valued at a million golden rubles *en bloc*. But when it was put up for sale, first in Paris and later in London, the market had been so flooded with the treasures of other Russian expatriates that Mother was forced to accept whatever price she could get. Even so, she realized money enough to buy a little farm near Paris, where she lived until her death in 1930. Sonya's husband, Arkady Scherbakov, died there in 1966, and Sonya lives there still.

Left alone in Moscow, Nika and I felt like two shipwrecked victims clinging to a raft in an angry sea. Every day brought new dangers; one could never be sure how to act for the best. By 1920, Nika had been arrested twice and released each time after a brief detention. The Kremlin simply could not do without him. With the mines and railways disrupted, there was an acute shortage of coal and firewood in the larger cities. Moscow was in danger of freezing. A Central Committee in charge of fuel supplies, known as "Glavtop," had been specially created by the new Lords of the Kremlin, but the problem remained unsolved. Instead of allocating their precious supplies to consumers, as they were supposed to do, the members of "Glavtop" had lined their pockets by selling fuel on the speculative black market.

The Kremlin must have been fairly desperate when they placed Nika, twice arrested as an "enemy of the people," in charge of a fuel cooperative known as "Kooperatop." Thanks to Nika's competent energies, this agency supplied far more coal and firewood than any other firm under direct government control. Kamenev and several other Bolshevik leaders preferred to deal openly with Nika's "Kooperatop," rather than with the corrupt and inefficient "Glavtop." Naturally, Nika's success aroused envious hatred, but he met the danger simply by working harder every day.

In addition to managing the "Kooperatop," Nika accepted another risky position: the presidency of K.U.B.A., a society for the mutual protection of members of the learned professions. Members of K.U.B.A. would appeal to Nika when their homes were requisitioned, when their libraries were confiscated, or when they themselves fell under arrest. Although Nika was apparently valued and even respected by several top Bolsheviks, for him to intervene in such cases was still clearly hazardous. Derzhinsky, then head of the dreaded Cheka, understood that Nika's anti-Communist sentiments were held in check only by his sense of patriotism. "We can let Avinov work for us so long as he is useful," Derzhinsky once said. "Of course, he is to remain under close watch." This was a good example of Bolshevik policy: squeeze out a man's vitality, and then "liquidate" him *when he is no longer useful.*

I lived in constant fear for Nika's life. In spite of the tacit trust shown by certain leading Bolsheviks—or rather, *because* of it—I could foresee how this precarious balance would end. When Nika's mother sent us a letter, urging us to try and join the rest of the family in the United States, I seized upon it as an aid to help settle our future. I explained to Nika that escape was still possible, that Soviet exit visas could still be bought with American dollars, and that his family would gladly provide the necessary funds.

His eyes remained as gentle as ever, but his answer to everything I said was a quiet and emphatic "No."

I felt as if I were pleading with a stone wall. In my desperation I played every trump I could: his love for his mother, her reciprocal anxiety for him; the pain he could save his brother and sister; the joys of the possible reunion. Naturally I added my own feelings: my fears for my own safety and his. His answer was the same, just as quiet and firm as before.

For the first time I felt the full weight of Nika's ruthlessness for the sake of an idea, a quality I had only sensed before.

"Nika," I cried, "can't you see? We have more than a chance to save ourselves! Before long these few escape routes are bound to be completely sealed off. You *know* that!"

He looked at me reproachfully. "Masha, the future is in God's hands. At present we have our duty to do here. We are both doing all we can for our unhappy country, and that is patriotism as I see it."

Finally, I reared in indignation: "In that case, I'm not going to be a patriot any longer! 'Mother Russia' is an unrecognizable stepmother, a mindless beast devouring her own litter. You talk the way my Father did when he squandered a million rubles on the

Provisional Government in the name of patriotism!" Exasperated by his silence, I flung his own words back at him: "You yourself told Bruce Lockhart that Communism was a contagion which would level the whole country before it could be brought under control. In the meantime, what is going to happen to you? And you might think of your own wife!" At the thought of living the rest of my life under Bolshevism, of perhaps losing Nika and remaining alone to face the whimsies of the State, I lost all self-control. "Nika," I cried, "I'm so afraid! Take me away, I demand it of you—*take me away!*" And clenching my fists like a small child, I began to weep with fear and frustrated rage.

Wrapped up in my own distress, I hadn't cared what was going on in Nika's mind. But now, as he covered his face with trembling hands, I saw that he was hiding tears. I rose to my feet in shame. With a pang, I recalled the words Mother had spoken on my wedding day: "It won't be easy, but see that you never become his Achilles' heel!"

Suddenly, with appalling clarity, I understood what I was doing: I was destroying my own husband: he, a being not entirely of this world, was about to be broken by my so completely worldly spirit, the same spirit that professed to love him more than anyone else on earth.

Swept by remorse, I kissed and hugged him: "You're right, Nika, you're right. Forgive me! I . . . we will do as you say. The future *is* in God's hands—and may He have mercy on us!"

CHAPTER SEVEN

✦❧✦

Resolved to remain in Moscow, I took stock of our situation. It was far from cheerful. Lenin's slogans—"Rob those that robbed you!" "Palaces for the Proletariat, slums for the Bourgeoisie!" "Down with Capitalists, the bloodsuckers grown fat on your toil!" —had already begun to take root in millions of minds. And of course, immediately after Lenin seized power, wanton arrests and imprisonments had become the order of the day.

At first there was no particular system to the Chekists' moves. People would be picked up in the streets and whisked away without an arrest warrant, and without even knowing what crime they were charged with. Many were guilty merely of having a "bourgeois" appearance; and what constituted such an appearance to Bolshevik eyes was undefinable. Anyone who didn't make rude noises in public was liable to be seized as a suspect.

One day both Nika and my younger brother Yuri were stopped from entering our house and marched off to prison. There seems to have been some design behind this particular arrest, for three Chekists were left in charge of the house. Their orders were to arrest anyone who called on me. This was most alarming; I knew that friends, as soon as they heard the news, would rush over to see if they could be of help to us. My problem was how to warn them. If I tried to use the telephone, the Chekists would arrest me on the spot.

I made a careful study of my three guards. Discounting their leather-bound uniforms with red shoulder straps, ignoring the red stars in their peaked leather caps, I could see that all three were young. Obviously country lads, their faces were good-natured and rather foolish; but they tried hard to seem fierce by putting on theatrical scowls. They were standing about awkwardly, hardly knowing what to do with themselves; but having dealt with soldiers and peasants much of my life, I knew how to put them at ease. "*Golubchiki*," I said (literally *little pigeons;* actually a term of mild endearment often used in addressing young people), "you must be tired and hungry. Aren't you?"

Instantly their threatening manner vanished. Ears pricked up and eyes grew eager. "You said it, Citizeness! We've been arresting people all night, with not a bite to eat since yesterday!"

"Well, you won't starve here. And you can rest, too."

My maid Natasha knew at once what I was driving at. In no time at all, she had whipped up a meal for three and poured a glass of vodka for each man. The grins on my guards' faces widened still further. They began to eat ravenously, but I stopped them:

"My boys, you are Communists and perhaps you no longer believe in God. But we are all still Russians, aren't we? No decent Russian sits down at the table with his hat on. Do me a favor and take off your caps. You see the icon in the corner?"

Without a word they obeyed. Very soon after, they had finished the last crumb, licked their plates, and loosened their belts:

"And now, how about our taking a rest, Citizeness?"

"Certainly. Make yourselves at home. Shall I get you something to read?"

Fortunately, the first book I put my hand on was very popular in Russia at the time—a translation of one of Jack London's stories. When I looked into their room a little later, two of them were fast asleep and snoring. The third—the one on duty—was avidly reading *The White Fang*.

I crept back to the drawing room and sat down beside the telephone I could not use, terrified of hearing the doorbell ring at any moment and announce a victim to be dragged off to prison. Such tension would soon be unendurable. I forced myself to put my worries aside and prayed, calling upon St. Seraphim. Before long, the door opened stealthily and the Chekist on duty thrust his head into the room. His voice was only a whisper, but what blessed relief it brought!

"If you use the telephone, Citizeness, I won't hear it."

His head disappeared, and I grabbed the receiver. In rapid succession, I called everyone I could think of. Two words sufficed: "*Don't come!*" In those days people knew how to take a hint, and during the next three days, not a soul came near me.

My young Chekists remained with me all that time. They exhausted all my Jack London novels. When at last they got ready to leave, I gave them the books for their friends. They beamed with delight:

"Thank you, thank you! We are lucky. But so are you. If you'd had Lettish troops in here—Oh oh! You'd soon know the difference. Such scum! They roll on beds with their boots on, soiling everything, and grab whatever they've a mind to. We are different, of course. We are Russians!"

As they filed out, I shook hands with each of them in turn. That same evening, Nika and Yuri came home, pale, unshaven, and worn out, yet laughing heartily over an incident they had witnessed in prison.

One of their companions in misfortune, a little man called Ivan Ivanovich Ivanov, had been utterly terrified by their grim surroundings. A fierce Commissar asked him what he thought of the Communists. "Oh, I pity them!" he blurted out. "Out, out with that idiot!" roared the commissar. "We can't waste time with such fools!" And the poor, trembling little man begged the other prisoners to forgive him for having jeopardized their lives. To his surprise, his cellmates begged him to stay: "You're a genius, Ivan Ivanovich. Help us! We couldn't find a better lawyer than you." I couldn't help joining in Yuri's laughter as I listened to his vivid description of the scene. In those days we still could laugh.

Only a few pages from my diary have survived. I burned the rest long ago as being too dangerous to keep in the house, but to me these few brief notes convey the full atmosphere of those times when every day was February.

Early April 1918. Propaganda is in full swing for the election of the Moscow Council of Soldiers and Workers. Processions bearing red banners and slogans march all over town: "Housewives, vote for List Five! [the Communist list] All avenues will be planted with potatoes! Mail, medicine, medical care will be free . . ." "Great!" I exclaim sarcastically to a man standing beside me. "I can imagine a potato-lined boulevard!" But Nika begs me not to talk to people in the street (a weakness of mine). He says it's dangerous. Hatred and envy are running high.

Later in April 1918. Watched procession going down our street: factory workmen and disheveled women carrying banners, shouting, laughing, singing. An old workman stands beside me with a grim face. "Fools!" he mutters, "Gay tunes, merry tunes, sing away! Soon they'll weep and sob to other music!" I remember Nika's warning, and refrain from starting a conversation.

May 1919. I look dejectedly at our garden. A poster is nailed to the gate: "This garden, heretofore enjoyed by idle Capitalists, is now a playground for children of the Proletariat. Children! You are free! Enjoy yourselves!"

They do. Dozens of dirty brats wrestle on the lawn, tear flowers, break down the shrubs, light a fire in the hollow of an old linden tree. They chase and capture a terrified cat and tie it up to tease it. I feel tears trickling down my cheeks. Nika comes into the room and sees my face. "What's the matter?" "Look, look what they're doing. I'm going out there. I've got to stop it!"

He takes me by the arm. "Don't, Masha. Class feelings are aroused and it's dangerous to interfere." By evening the garden is a shambles: grass trampled, flowerbeds crushed, the linden tree burned down—class feelings, indeed! I'm sick at heart and a bit ashamed of my lack of spirit.

June 1919. Our house's management is reorganized. We now have a proletarian committee. The Chairman is a notorious thief. Nika has been elected Secretary-treasurer because the others know he won't steal. Impossible to refuse the "honor"—it would be construed as "sabotage by the ex-ruling class." Nika spends hours every morning stamping ration cards and dealing with masses of intricate, useless forms.

One of the disagreeable looking new residents, a Mr. Zvensky, arrives with sheaves of papers. I ask him to wait. "My husband is on the roof," I tell him, "with the House Committee, inspecting a broken chimney." Zvensky slumps into a chair: "What a life!" He lowers his voice to a whisper: "Terrible things are going on. The Bolsheviks are now jailing Social Revolutionaries!" "Nothing terrible about that," I retort with asperity. "As Dostoevsky said, 'Let one viper eat the other'!" Zvensky turns ashen. I wonder why?

Later I ask Nika. "Oh Masha, didn't you know? He is one of the leaders of the Social Revolutionary Party." I didn't know. But I would have said it all the same.

August 1919. Rumors about the forthcoming "Week of the Poor": The Cheka is going to search every house, leaving only a change of clothes for the owners, and confiscating the rest for the "Poor." I'm boiling over with "class feelings" as I look at a trunkful of woolen sweaters, socks, and gloves—all salvaged from Mother's peasant workshop, all made of beautiful soft wool from her rabbit farm. I rush to the telephone and contact scores of friends—acquaintances, former servants, anyone I can think of. Spent the whole day giving away woolens. Felt exhausted but happy. In the end, no requisitions at our house! And suddenly I remember: in the rush, I have forgotten to keep anything for Nika and myself!

August 1920. Our beautiful Russian language is rapidly being pulled apart by the half-educated. Amazing signs are everywhere. Examples: "This shop sells children's socks and gloves made of parents' wool." Outside a butcher shop: "Meet the customer with an ample weight." Over the door of a kerosene shop: "Kerosene will not be sold to customers with narrow necks!" A long queue of citizens stares gloomily at the sign, those carrying bottles finally make out the meaning and wander away dejectedly. I can't help mourning over Turgenev's saying: "Never despair about the future of Russia. It's impossible to believe that a people with such a wonderful language could be anything but great."

September 1920. New developments occurred earlier this month: the president of our House Committee (the thief) was charged with theft. And deposed. A former general, who turned Red at the outbreak of the Revolution, was appointed in his place. Now wooden partitions have been erected in the ballroom and drawing room to form small cubicles for proletarian families. Where a dozen people formerly lived in peace, now at least ninety enjoy the benefits of Communism. Twenty kerosene burners smoke in the former downstairs pantry. The house is filled with the odor of cabbage soup and other things that are far worse. Natasha tells me that the marble bathtub in the beautiful tiled bathroom has been filled with potatoes. Pots, pans, and kettles have had to be locked up ever since an envious housewife threw a dead mouse into her neighbor's soup. Shouts and quarrels resound in the hallways from morning to night. Nika had a door put up on the stairs to keep out the noise. Now we feel at peace in our apartment.

November 1920. The House Committee ruled yesterday to take over our apartment, which will leave us three rooms. We have to clear out today. What's to become of all our furniture, carpets, and pictures? I decided to call up every available friend and acquaintance, and asked them to come before midnight. Sad, a bit nightmarish in fact, watching our tables, chairs, and rugs vanish into the snowstorm. Shall we ever see them again? I doubt it.

We move into our three rooms: a small sitting room, a small bedroom, a tiny study for Nika. He tells me I ought to get rid of my grand piano. "No," I say, "I need music to keep me going."

Later the same month. The former president of the House Committee (the thief) appeared on the stairs, shouting that Nika had stolen his ration ticket for galoshes. I lost my temper: seizing a riding crop from the wall, I ordered him out. He stumbled down the stairs, cursing. Nika was attracted by the noise, rushed out, took the riding crop from me, and pulled me back into his room. I'm afraid I raised my voice. "This is the limit! He accused you of stealing! I can't stand it!" Nika kissed me, soothed me. Finally I regained composure. And I realize how much I have to learn if I am to achieve Nika's calm and fortitude. I hope I will someday.

With this page, what is left of my diary comes to an end.

CHAPTER EIGHT

❧

Besides the house we lived in, our absentee landlord had owned three large apartment houses built around a charming garden. His agent Yegor, a capable but conniving man with an obsequious manner, had run these buildings with the help of janitors to do the heavy work. After the General became president of the House Committee, which was by then in charge of all our landlord's property, this whole system was changed. Yegor's janitors were dismissed and the tenants told they had to do the janitors' work themselves. But Yegor remained as the General's assistant, and the aroma about him had all the fragrance of a Bolshevik spy.

Shortly afterward, there was a normally heavy snowfall. But the next morning, all the women living in our block were ordered out to sweep the street and pile the snow in the garden. About fifty of us, many in coats of sealskin and mink, assembled in the bitter cold in front of the General, and asked how we were to clear the snow without sleighs and with only a few shovels among us. Our turncoat General looked down at us with an air of consequence:

"Come, come, ladies! A little energy, a little goodwill! Some ingenuity, what? You have hat boxes, haven't you? Well? There's your answer!" We spent all day scraping up the snow with our hands—wearing gloves, if we had them—and packing it into hat boxes, cartons, and other inappropriate containers. The General stood over us to inspect, looking important and urging us on.

The real purpose of his order, of course, was to provide a show for passers-by. The new Government was enforcing equality: those who had lived by the sweat of others were now trundled out in public to sweat themselves. Red Army soldiers drove by in trucks and jeered at us. Laborers, passing in the street, paused to gape and

68

laugh. But we did our best to keep up a good face, and pretended to treat the whole thing as a brisk outing in the fresh air.

That same evening the General came to call on me. Despite his Bolshevik allegiance, he professed the highest regard for Nika and me. Nika was in prison again at the time, and the General said he wanted to be of help: "Have you seen the official notices about firearms?"

I could have hardly missed them, pasted as they were, on every wall! The following evening every house was to be searched. Tenants would be executed wherever weapons were found. But I smiled confidently—we ran no risk. There were no soldiers in our family and, consequently, no weapons of any kind. The General shook his head dubiously and urged me to take a close look through every cupboard and bureau drawer. He wanted no trouble while in charge of these buildings. "And above all, dear lady, I want no harm to come to you!" I thanked him. He begged me again to make a thorough search and took his leave, promising to return at noon.

Hardly had he left when our landlord's housekeeper, who lived in the basement, burst into the room. "Oh God, what are we to do?" she gasped. "Those notices—about firearms—I looked at them and my heart stood still! We have twenty cases from the Count's property in Poland that were brought here during the war. Downstairs in the storeroom, together with the Count's other things, there are twenty cases, *twenty*, I tell you! They're completely filled . . ."

"Filled with *what*?"

"*Rifles*."

For a moment I was too horrified to speak. Like most women, I'm afraid of all sorts of trivial things, including geese when they flap their wings and come hissing at me. But when faced with real danger, it's as if someone else has taken hold of me. I believe there must be two elements in every human soul—the mortal ego and the divine spark. In moments of great danger the divine spark takes over and the mortal ego, though stricken with fright, can only obey.

I commanded the frantic, distraught woman to shut the door: "Tell Filipich and one of the other men to bring the cases up here. That will take all suspicion off of you. I'll think of something."

In half an hour, twenty gun-cases were piled in the middle of the drawing room. Inside were magnificent rifles and shotguns, revolvers in handsome leather holsters, hunting knives in pigskin sheathes, and countless boxes of cartridges: more than enough to hang us all many times over. I covered the sinister booty with a large bedspread, locked the door, put the key in my pocket, and sat down to wait. Soon the General and his spy, Yegor—"The Fox," as we called him—would both be here. At all costs, I had to prevent them from searching the house.

Years before, a gifted actor and friend of mine told me that I had missed my vocation, that I belonged on the stage. I brushed aside his compliment at the time. I had never been particularly fond of the theater and had always refused to play in amateur theatricals. "Nevertheless," my friend insisted, "you have the imagination of a great actress and the gift of changing your face and intonation to suit the mood you're in. Someday you'll discover I'm right."

I only hoped that day had come.

The doorbell rang. A servant ushered the General and "The Fox" into a small reception room off the front hall. I waited a few seconds to gather my wits together, and then flew into the room, holding out something wrapped in a white handkerchief. For a moment I stood trembling, and then collapsed into a chair with a stricken face.

The General hovered over me in alarm. Stammering, I tried to explain: "We're lost, all of us! Lost! Look what I found!"

Unfolding the handkerchief, I handed him an ancient pocket pistol with a carved ivory handle and broken hammer which I actually had found in a forgotten drawer. It dated back to the Crimean War—circa 1856.

The General smiled indulgently:

"Calm yourself. That's nothing but a harmless little museum piece."

"No, no! It's a revolver! We are lost!" I began to sob.

"The Fox" had been watching us closely all the time. Now he stepped forward: "Your Excellency—" (when alone with the General he always addressed him as "Your Excellency"; on all other occasions it was "Comrade General"): "Your Excellency, the statutes do make explicit mention of revolvers. The lady is right. If one sticks to the letter of the law, this old piece could well cause her trouble. As for the Professor"—(meaning Nika, although he did not hold a degree) "as for the Professor—well, it might land him in worse trouble than he's in already. May I make a suggestion? I'll carry this troublesome thing into the yard and throw it in the well."

The General found Yegor's suggestion "brilliant" and asked him to go at once. Following "The Fox" into the front hall, I slipped a handsome tip into his hand. He scraped, bowed, and grinned; I even thought I saw a crafty wink in his eye. To this day I don't know whether he believed me and wanted to help, or whether he had seen through my act and was after a bribe. In any case, he left with the pistol and didn't come back.

"And now," said the General, when I had returned to the drawing room, "let us search the house, shall we? Before the Cheka does!"

Outwardly I expressed nothing but mild astonishment:

"But what for, dear General? I've looked in every nook and cranny, and I only found that pistol after searching through all the other rooms. I am awfully sorry to have caused you all this trouble, but believe me, I'm grateful for your help and advice."

I don't know what else I said. Perhaps I bored him with my flow of talk. But I thought my sigh of relief could be heard all through the house when the door shut behind him at long last. I sank into a chair, exhausted.

I was still on edge when the doorbell shrilled again. I opened the door myself. But this time it was my younger brother Yuri, whom I thought miles away in his home in Tambov. "Thank God," I cried. "You're just the man I need!"

Brave as Yuri was, he blanched as I told him my story. "Masha, this means death. I've seen the notices."

We looked at each other in troubled silence. Yuri buried his head in his hands, drumming his fingers against his forehead. He finally looked up with a determined frown on his face:

"I think I've figured out your one chance. The Chief Commissar of Tambov came up with me in the train. I've known him for years. He's a decent chap, a Communist through misguided ideals—you know the type. Now then, we'll say he can have as many fine firearms as he likes. You see? It's quite simple: I'll ask him to take them away for his own use! He'd like pieces as nice as those. No, I'm sure he'll do it. Get tea ready, and a bottle of wine. I'll be back in no time."

A good cup of hot tea is always comforting. My hopes were on the rise again when, very shortly, Yuri returned with his friend. On seeing our "arsenal," he went into ecstasies.

"What magnificent pieces! What treasures! A single shotgun like that is worth a king's ransom nowadays!"

"It won't ransom my sister, though," said Yuri drily. "*One* of those little beauties could cost her her life, and her husband's as well." He coughed. "You do get the idea, don't you?" Yuri pointed at the other gun-cases: "My dear friend, do us both a grand favor and take them all away. We never want to see even a cartridge again."

But at this the Commissar paled and raising his hands in horror: "I'd do anything for you, Yuri, you know that, but do you realize what you're asking? How can I possibly get twenty of these through the streets under the noses of the Cheka patrols? You've seen them for yourself—they're down in the square, assembling for tonight's inspection. Tomorrow, yes. Bring them to my place at dawn. But tonight, Lord, no! It would be sheer madness!"

"All right!" Yuri muttered. "But what about my sister? What about her husband? The inspection starts at eight and will continue all night. There's no way for them to escape it. Is there any way the Cheka can . . . overlook this?"

The Commissar shook his head glumly. He seemed ashamed of his helplessness. "Logically, there isn't. We Marxists don't believe in Providence, as you do. You'll have to trust to luck." He gave us a crooked, half-embarrassed smile: "Or to a miracle!"

He offered his hand to Yuri. He kissed mine in the old gallant way, and when I thanked him, said, "I'm glad I can show you that a Communist can still be a gentleman."

"It's a friend we need now," said Yuri.

There was nothing more for us to do. Yuri went to bed. I sat down in the drawing room across from the ominous gun-cases, and set my ears against the sound of the doorbell. But gradually, as the night hours crept by, my senses became blurred and confused. I thought of Nika in prison. Would they shoot him this time? Would I see him again? I thought of all those dear to me, of all the things one has to leave behind when one's hour has struck. Images passed through my mind in a colorful kaleidoscope: memories of land-scapes, snatches of music, favorite poems, flowers. I did not fear death, being convinced, then as now, that the human consciousness simply passes into another sphere where all its highest aspirations may be realized. It was only the moments before death that filled my mind with terror. To conquer my fear, I prayed for guidance. I did not ask St. Seraphim for miracles; rather, I implored him to inter-cede for me, that I might be calm in the face of the final strain. I prayed for that calmness which Christ spoke of when he said, "Fear not those who destroy the body, but rather those who would destroy the spirit."

Bit by bit my fears subsided. I sat numbly, listening. Morning finally broke, dim and overcast. The doorbell had still not rung. The Cheka had not come. That day, we learned that every house in the neighborhood had been searched except ours. Was it a miracle? If so, I accepted it with humility and gratitude. That terrible night proved to be a blessed turning point in my life, during which my spirit was annealed for the thorny path ahead.

No sooner had the sun risen, than Yuri and I summoned the servants. The gun-cases and the boxes of ammunition were carried out and loaded on three sleighs. At that early hour there were few people about, but whenever anyone passed by I would call out in a loud voice: "Careful with those books! The Lenin library wants them handled with extra care." The words *Lenin* and *books* were bandied back and forth as long as a passer-by remained within earshot.

When all the cases had been loaded, Yuri mounted the last sleigh and the caravan started off for the Commissar's. I spent another hour of anxious waiting. It was a joy to see Yuri return, tired but radiant with relief. We embraced each other, smiling and laughing, and I think sobbing a little at the same time.

CHAPTER NINE

❧

Yuri's wife was a Svirbeyev and a cousin of the last Imperial Russian Ambassador to Berlin. Ambassador Svirbeyev and the Minister of Foreign Affairs, Sazonov, had urged Yuri to join the diplomatic service. There is no doubt that his mind, appearance, and manners all would have imminently suited a diplomat; but emotionally, my brother had known he was not cut out for the diplomatic life. Accordingly, he chose to stay in Russia and work with the *Zemstvo* as our father had done, perfectly content to give his time to the more humble problems of rural administration. He settled in Tambov, the administrative center of our province; bought a house, which he and his wife furnished with great taste; and soon made friends in various walks of life.

Yuri's fatal mistake was to remain in Tambov after the abominable Cheka had moved in to keep the city under control. In Moscow, he might have been lost in the crowd, but in Tambov he stood out as a conspicuous and easy target. I did my best to convince him of the Chekist danger after he had gotten rid of our "arsenal." But Yuri, loath to leave his home, and unable to believe that Bolshevik fury could reach the proportions it did, went back to Tambov to stay. My most anxious prayers went with him.

It did not take long for my worst fears to come true. After Nika's tormenters returned him to me for another brief spell, news reached us that the Tambov Cheka had arrested Yuri and incarcerated him in the great monastery in the middle of town. (The Bolsheviks had turned that holy place into a jail and "liquidation" center.) My first impulse was to go to save Yuri, without stopping to reason how. Nika, equally devoted to Yuri, encouraged me despite the obvious hazards of such a journey. I didn't allow myself to dwell on dangers, only upon doing the best thing for my brother.

My resolve was confirmed by an unexpected circumstance. Shura, my Tsigane sister-in-law, had returned to Moscow after brother Sasha's death in the south. She had the most glorious Gypsy contralto I ever heard, and had been engaged to sing in a cabaret run by the Soviet authorities for their officials. Her low notes actually sounded like a cello's. "They kill at night, and then come and shed sentimental tears over my songs," she would exclaim, not caring who heard her. But despite Shura's hatred of the cabaret and its patrons, there was no other way for her to make a living.

Now, upon hearing of Yuri's detention in the Tambov prison and of my vague plans to rescue him, she hurried to me with a note. "Take it, Masha. It's for the Prison Commandant in Tambov. I know him, he's a Gypsy like myself. But he's a traitor, as well. He betrayed my brother Dmitri, and had him shot. Now he's living in fear of his life—he knows some member of our clan will have our revenge sooner or later, and he'd do anything to placate me. Just be polite to him, show him this letter, and he'll do his best for Yuri. And may this miserable Lenin and his gang be hanged!" She spoke these last words so loudly that I had to cover her mouth with my hand to hush her. But I kissed and hugged her with tears of gratitude.

I knew that my first problem would be to find a way of getting through to Tambov. The city was entirely surrounded by a rural district in the throes of violent anti-Bolshevik revolt. A former officer of the Imperial Army had organized the peasantry of the Province of Tambov to wage war on the local Cheka. They murdered any commissars coming to their villages to requisition supplies. Bands of armed peasants made frequent sorties from their hideouts in the dense Tambov woods, burning railway stations, barracks, and telegraph offices; tearing down telephone wires; blowing up bridges; and swiftly retreating again into their forest stronghold where the Bolsheviks dared not follow.

After days of clandestine arrangements through some of Nika's dubious new "friends," I was told I could travel in the private car of a highly important commissar who was being sent to crush the Tambov uprising.

Late that evening Nika and I found the railway carriage in question on a deserted siding of the Kazan station. It looked dark and forbidding, only a faint light gleaming in the last of its long row of windows. Nika blessed me. I clung to him in sudden anguish, stricken by fears that our parting might well prove permanent. Rather than put up with such thoughts, I wanted to start, to begin immediately. Nervously, I picked up the wicker basket packed with provisions for my journey. Nika half lifted me as I scrambled onto the high step and knocked discreetly on the carriage door.

An elderly porter appeared with a lantern and helped me up the remaining steps. In the dark narrow vestibule, he raised his lantern and gave me a long searching look. Then he smiled: "I was told to expect you, but how by all that's holy was I to know you'd turn out to be a *lady*? How very pleasant! My name's Semyon, at your service."

He led me along the corridor past closed compartment doors to his own quarters. The small room was dimly lit by a kerosene lamp. It was a kind of diminutive kitchen, with a stove, a narrow bunk, a small table, and two chairs. Semyon said we had at least two hours' wait before the commissar arrived with his companion. "His sort don't have wives," he added with some contempt, "they have *companions!*"

His undernourished, sallow face showed such dejection that, in order to cheer him up, I laughed at his observation and pretended to be lighthearted: "Did you say two hours? In that case we have time enough to sup!" And when he informed me mournfully that he had nothing but hot water, I tapped my wicker basket meaningfully. I could already envision his surprise when I opened that basket. Although we were all living on starvation rations in those days, Filipich and our other servants still lived in the basement and helped us in every way they could. Now and then, through methods better left unquestioned, they succeeded in getting decent supplies for us. Earlier that day, when Filipich showed me what he had prepared for my trip to Tambov, my eyes widened in amazement:

"For Heaven's sake, Filipich, where did you unearth all that?"

"Ask me no questions I'll tell you no lies," was his brisk reply. I pocketed curiosity and accepted his illicit presents with contentment and gratitude. Such were the times we lived in.

Now it was Semyon's turn to open his eyes wide. On the table in front of him I laid out a dozen hard-boiled eggs, several dozen *pirojki* stuffed with cabbage, a large cut of boiled meat, and a bottle of red wine. It was a pleasure to see the disbelieving wonder in his eyes. He finally fell to enjoying the food and drink, although not before he had brewed some of the tea I had brought with me.

Men of his type—respectful, efficient, and talkative without being familiar—were to be found on every Russian railway carriage I had ever known. He told me stories from his past career, some of them worthy of a Chekhov. I listened with fascination. Then suddenly he switched to the present:

"To think of what was, and of what we have now! One is almost tempted to lose one's faith! Let me warn you," he continued "this Commissar and his *companion*—they are positively inhuman! They treat me like a dog. All day they eat and drink, and then throw what's left out the window. There's never a scrap for me, and if it hadn't been for you, I'd have gone hungry all the way to Tambov. I'll wager they won't even let you lie down in one of the empty compartments. They'll make you sit up all night in here!"

He groaned and swore again. "When we get to Tambov that man will begin shooting peasants by the hundreds, may the Devil smash his ugly face! I tell you, I wish Antonov [the leader of the insurgents] would put dynamite under this train. I swear I do! I'd be glad to go if that wretch went with me—that is, er—begging your Ladyship's pardon, not on this trip! Seeing as you're on board, perhaps Antonov can wait till next time." And he gave me a wink. Wine on top of a long fast was having its effect on Semyon. But he soon sobered himself.

"You'd better pack away what's left before our visitors arrive. Otherwise . . . well, you know how it is . . . 'class hatred,' they call it."

I lost no time in taking the hint.

At last the Commissar arrived: a lean man with a ferret's face and narrow, skeptical eyes. His "companion" looked rather like three pigs all rolled in a bundle and tied together with a large red handkerchief. Never have I seen a more repulsive female. She and her escort eyed me with open animosity. When I tried to thank the commissar for taking me with him, he cut me off abruptly.

"I did it to oblige a friend, not you!"

He turned his back on me and left the compartment. The woman

stepped up menacingly to Semyon, her pudgy little eyes glowering
with unspoken abuse: "Morning tea at ten. D'you hear me, oaf?
And don't be late like t'last time or you'll never be late again!"

When she was gone, Semyon let out a sigh of resigned martyr-
dom. Very gallantly, he offered me his bunk and refused to take
no for an answer: "Who d'you think I am? One of those . . . ?"
(this with a nod in the direction of the Commissar's compartment).
"No, no, lady. You're tired, you've been worried and exhausted,
and you need a good night's rest. Besides, I have an extra mattress
I can roll out across the floor." I admit I didn't put up much of an
argument. I stretched out on his bunk and slept soundly in spite
of everything.

In the morning the Commissar came to the rear of the car and
stood in the corridor outside Semyon's compartment, looking out
the window. He ignored me and never once glanced in my direction. But I, conversely, had a good look at him. I confess that the
sight of his obvious nervousness gave me some satisfaction. His
shoulders quivered, his back twitched, and his hand kept hovering
around the revolver at his hip. He was evidently expecting the
worst at any moment—a discharge of dynamite perhaps, or derail-
ment and an armed ambush. I could not resist exchanging a con-
spiratorial wink with Semyon.

The train was crossing a great plain. Bare and desolate, the land
stretched away to a pale horizon. Now and again, we clattered
past the corroded timbers of a station burned by the peasants. Invariably, the corner of the commissar's mouth would twist, and
he would mutter loud enough for me to hear. "They'll pay for
that." "I'll skin them alive!"

I have always steadfastly believed in the divine spark in every
human being, but it was hard to find any trace of it in this man. I
kept admonishing myself to detest evil, but not the man who is
merely its human instrument. The effort was futile. My aversion
and loathing only grew more intense, and I wondered if I would
ever be magnanimous enough to feel compassion for such a man.

At long last the train crawled into the Tambov station. The
commissar and the woman bundled off without saying a word. I
gave Semyon a handsome tip and what was left of the food. It was
painful to part with the good fellow. In that small compartment of
his, surrounded by his courteous attentions and sympathetic con-

versation, I had felt secure. Now I had to strike out on my own. Semyon helped me onto the platform and we waved goodbye.

First of all, I hurried to some intimate friends of Yuri's. My main tenet of hope was that the rumors about Yuri might have been exaggerated. But no: he was indeed locked in the former monastery, in a cell for the condemned. He could expect either a dark soundproof cellar and a quick bullet, or else prolonged death in an anonymous concentration camp in the Arctic wilderness. To add to Yuri's misery, his poor wife was stricken with pneumonia and lay close to death.

There was no time for grief. In less than half an hour, with Shura's precious letter folded in my pocket, I drew in sight of the monastery. The square outside was thronged with people: bearded peasants, women with small children or babies in their arms, pale young girls, and skinny, shivering boys, all of whom were carrying food parcels for jailed relatives and friends. They stood patiently in the snow, waiting for the huge doors to open, and apparently prepared to endure cold and fatigue well into the coming night.

Patience, whether saintly or bovine, was never my strong point. I all but thrashed my way through that crowd. Some of the peasants, seeing an "ex-lady" in a sealskin coat, stood aside to let me pass, no doubt hopeful that I still carried some of the influence that had opened doors in the past. And perhaps to their awe, as well as to mine, the monastery's door did swing open above me just as I started up the stairs. A man stepped out, dressed like the hero of a comic opera: sky-blue jacket, wide yellow belt stuffed with two daggers and a pair of revolvers, and high matching yellow boots dangling immense spurs. He put his hand on his hip, struck a jaunty pose, and looked down contemptuously at the upturned, hopeful faces. Was this the Gypsy whom I had to see? I gave him no time to enjoy the delights of his high perch. Waving Shura's letter over my head, I moved forward.

"Citizen Commandant! Citizen Commandant! I've come all the way from Moscow to bring you this letter from a friend."

"Come up, come up," he answered, pleasantly enough. But when I began to climb the stairs, he drew back, frowning suspiciously: "From whom this letter?"

"From Shura. You do know Shura?"

Still hesitant, he nodded. I remembered what Shura had told me,

and thought I saw a streak of fear in his eyes. But an instant later he
was all smiles.

"Come in, Citizeness, come in. This way—yes, yes, a little
place where we can talk in peace." The big door shut behind me
with a bang, and I thought I heard a faint echo rising from the
square—the sad collective sigh of a thousand disappointed souls.

The "little place where we could talk in peace" turned out to
be the monastery's former reception hall. Where holy icons had
once graced the walls, oiled rifles hung in rows. Where monks had
once glided by in silence, soldiers sat smoking and laughing over
ribald jokes. In the midst of the racket, the Commandant stood and
read Shura's letter with a knitted brow. I studied his face closely:
he was a typical Russian Gypsy, with big black eyes, a dark com-
plexion, and curly black hair. He was obviously a ruthless man but
his voice, when at last he spoke, was almost too honeyed to be true:

"So Shura, my dear, dear friend Shura, is your sister-in-law?
Well, now what do you know! And who are you?"

"The sister of Yuri Novosiltsev, a prisoner of yours." His hands
flew up as though in delighted excitement.

"Ach! But in that case, dear Shura need worry no more! Yuri is
my friend! We're buddies. We are! Already I've done a lot for
him." He lowered his voice to a confidential key. "I'll tell you . . .
You see, I've taken him out of the death-cell and put him to work
in the outer prison. Every night, you see, we have to shoot a hundred peasants. So . . . when we're through, Yuri undresses the
corpses. He sets aside any clothes that are worth saving—the Republic can't afford to waste things, you understand—and when he's
through, I join him in his cell. With my guitar, you know. And
we sing Gypsy songs together." The Commandant's voice became
brisk and businesslike: "Come! I'll take you to him. After that,
you must see the Chairman of the Cheka. I'll arrange it."

We went down a long corridor with rows of monastic cells on
either side whose doors had been replaced with grilles. From the
gloom behind the bars, pale, bearded peasants peered out at us,
like phantoms. I could hardly bear to watch their haunted eyes
follow the Commandant as he swaggered by. The one touch of
humor, nightmarish as it was, was written above their cages in
great tall letters:

"Support the Revolution that has freed Workmen and Peasants from Tyranny!"

We passed through several similar corridors, across a wide court-yard, and finally reached the block where Yuri's cell was situated. A warden rattled his keys against a lock. The heavy door swung open. And at last I saw Yuri. He still had elegance about him, even though his clothes were now crumpled and torn, and his face un-shaven. The joy in his smiling embrace was worth all the risks I had taken. Mercifully, the Commandant left us alone for half an hour, and Yuri was able to tell me in detail everything that had happened to him.

It seems that no less than the Chairman of the Cheka had headed the band that came to search Yuri's house. He had taken Yuri's five-year-old daughter Luba, held his revolver to her head, and announced that he would shoot unless all money and jewelry were handed to him at once, along with the contents of the wine cellar. Protesting or bargaining was of course out of the question. In addition, the Chekists carried off all the furniture, carpets, pictures, and linen. Even my little niece's toys were confiscated. The little girl clung to one of the soldiers and begged for the return of her favorite doll, but his rough push sent her reeling against a wall. Yuri still raged at the memory of her terrified wail: "I wanted to strangle every one of them! Oh, how right you were, Masha. I never should have stayed in Tambov!" A pathetic smile hovered at the edges of his mouth: "And now this simpleton you see before you, instead of enjoying the privileges of some embassy abroad, trudges out at night to strip the corpses of poor dead peasants and sing Gypsy songs with Ilya, their murderer. How terribly right Dostoevsky was when he said, 'Man is not a pig. He can get used to anything'!"

Our interview ended with Ilya's reappearance. "The Chairman is expecting you," he whispered to me. My heart was beating quickly by the time we reached what I took to be the Chairman's door, but once inside, I gasped. The large office was furnished entirely with Yuri's belongings. I recognized the broad sofa, the armchairs, the carpet and mirror, pictures on the walls, and even a small silver vase Mother had brought back from Florence. It cast its reflection on the heavy polished desk which used to be in Yuri's study. Now, however, the man behind the desk was a sailor with an ugly smirk on his lips and cruel blue eyes.

I was only halfway through stating my case when he interrupted with what seemed like a burst of good-natured enthusiasm: "Oh yes, yes! of course, I know your brother. A very decent man. We have nothing against him, absolutely nothing! In fact, the Tribunal will meet in three days, and I intend to vote for his acquittal."

I began to stammer my thanks, but he waved me out with a gesture of splendid magnanimity. On each of the next three days, Ilya helped smuggle me into Yuri's cell for half an hour at a time. Yuri and I were on tenterhooks, in constant expectation of the Cheka's verdict. On the third day, just as the Chairman had promised, the Tribunal sat in session. Later I learned that each of its members had voted for Yuri's release—all, that is, except the Chairman. On his personal insistence, Yuri drew a life sentence at hard labor in a concentration camp.

I remember little of what I felt when I heard the news. Perhaps the savage irony had been too refined to have its full effect at once. But I clearly recall my urge to comfort Yuri once more and to promise him we would do everything in our power to remit his sentence. I hurriedly returned to the monastery to ask further help of Ilya. But a second blow awaited me: that same morning, the Commandant had been sent to a neighboring village at the head of a punitive expedition.

For a moment I stood in a daze. Directly opposite was the porter's lodge. There seemed to be nothing else to do but go up and ask for a permit to see Yuri. I knocked on the wicket, and a coarse face peered out at me. "No permits," it roared. "Citizen Novosiltsev? He's being packed off to the Devil's back yard. Hah!" I lingered, trying to think of something to say. "Get away from here! If I see you again, I'll shoot. Can't you read the sign?"

Somehow I hadn't noticed before the large placard, warning that any person loitering without a permit near the prison entrance would be shot on sight. The wicket slammed in my face. I moved off, bitterly disappointed.

But the thought of how much Yuri was counting on me revived my courage, even to the point of foolhardy determination. Only one soldier was stationed on duty near the tall prison door, and he was reading a newspaper and paying me no attention. I took a scrap of blank paper and folded it across. Holding it conspicuously in my outstretched hand, I brushed by the guard and started down the long corridor I had walked so often in Ilya's company. I met a sentinel who must have remembered my face, since he signaled me to go on without even glancing at the folded paper. The same thing happened with a second sentinel, and a third. At last I reached the main courtyard and Yuri's block. The warden, to whom I had taken care to bring cigarettes on my previous visits, greeted me as an old friend and rattled his keys in readiness.

Yuri was overjoyed to hear that his wife had taken a turn for the better. His eyes lit up as I promised that Nika and I would be knocking at every door in Moscow to get him released. Our last farewell was a poignant one. All in all, I stayed only a moment or two before leaving, satisfied and elated. But when I reached the courtyard, I pulled up short. A Chekist in uniform was crossing it ahead of me. To my horror, I recognized him as the porter I had spoken to through the wicker. I flattened myself against a wall and tried to be as inconspicuous as possible. Fortunately, he was looking the other way. But when he entered the main building across the court and shut the door behind him, I heard the grind of a large key in the lock. I could hardly go back to Yuri's cell. I was trapped.

Frantically, my eyes swept the empty court for a place to hide. The meager pile of wood at one corner would have to do. I squeezed myself between it and the wall, and crouched as low as I could. They say that in a single moment, a dying man views the whole of his past life. Something of the sort happened to me: my childhood, my family, my happiness with Nika, Kotchemirovo and its linden trees; all swept by me in sundered flashes. Gradually the choke of fear subsided. I began to pray, disjointedly and desperately at first: "St. Seraphim, save me, or at least give me the courage to be brave . . ."

Not a breath was stirring in the yard. Snow began to fall, gently, softly, covering the woodpile and the back of my sealskin coat. Suddenly I heard a door open. In the dead silence it resounded like a rifle shot. Next I heard footsteps crunching the light snow, coming my way.

A Cheka guard leaned over the woodpile to gather some kindling. When he saw me, he jumped in surprise: "What the devil are you doing here?"

How I managed to speak at all I don't know. My throat was so parched I could hardly swallow.

"Visiting . . . my brother's . . . prisoner."

"Your permit?"

I shook my head. My whole body trembled as well.

"No permit? Then, how did you ever get in?"

His tone was more threatening than his words. Quickly I began to stammer that I knew, yes, I *knew* the regulations, but I had to see my brother, that is, just once, one last time, before they sent him away to the labor camp, for the Lord knew how long.

He looked at me, stupefied: "Are you daft or what? Who in the hell is this brother of yours?"

"Yuri Novosiltsev."

For an instant he stared at me, slack-jawed. His whole countenance changed. He stepped back, thinking to himself, and repeated Yuri's name under his breath in bewilderment. "Well I'll be! How weird . . . damnedest thing!" Taking notice of me again, he gave me a solemn whisper: "Follow me."

I got to my feet shakily, awkwardly stretching my cramped limbs. We moved cautiously, one after the other, hugging the wall, until we reached a door half-hidden in a deep recess. He unlocked it, and pushed me through. "Get lost! Quickly!"

I wanted to thank him, but he shook his head:

"No need. Novosiltsev saved my life once when the dice were rolling *his* way. I'm paying a debt."

He smiled and shut the door. The lock clicked quietly.

I then remembered that this had once indeed been a monastery; what better place for prayers to be answered with such miraculous care! I blessed St. Seraphim for Yuri's sake, turned my face away from the prison, and walked back to my friends' house through the gently falling snow.

CHAPTER TEN

❧❀❧

I tried my best to get back to Nika in Moscow, but for several days I was not even able to buy a railway ticket. The few trains that ran were packed to overflow. At last, with the help of a friend of Yuri's, I managed to squeeze into a crowded boxcar. I'd said I didn't care how jammed it would be inside, but I took it all back when I found myself the only woman among forty Red Army soldiers. The train started with a jolt, and I was scrutinized by forty pairs of eyes.

I felt very ill at ease for a few moments, until I remembered my previous experiences at the Evacuation Center in Moscow. I knew that one way to get along with soldiers was to treat them as equals. Here in the boxcar, it would have been extremely risky to appear nervous; and a joke, of course, was always the best way to break the ice. I smiled blandly: "Well, this is a relief! I feel much safer with a military escort. And thank you, friends, for letting me in." A few snorted, not enough to make me comfortable. I then looked slowly all around me: "Would anyone like a drink, or a smoke? I do have a bottle of vodka here and a few pounds of tobacco. Would that be enough for you all?" I quietly blessed the friend who, seeing me off, had insisted on my accepting the bottle: "Take it! Vodka is always useful. It opens all hearts."

This vodka certainly did. The rough, bearded faces drew closer and broke into wide, happy smiles. Their Sergeant, Fyodor, barked his orders: "Come on! Clear a place for the Citizeness. Let her sit on the sacks of flour over there in the corner. At least they're softer than the floor. And she's not accustomed to swearing, so mind your language."

"I am, too!" I retorted indignantly, "but I don't know what any of the words mean, so I don't mind."

85

My deliberate naïveté brought a round of genuine laughter.
Still chuckling, the soldiers helped themselves to my vodka and
tobacco, and soon grew talkative.

I then learned that they were returning from a punitive expedition against rebellious peasants who had refused to hand over their
land and cattle to a newly established *kolkhoz* (collective farm).
I was surprised at how brutal the reprisals had been. These soldiers
were peasants themselves, yet they seemingly found it natural to
massacre their fellows. "Today one has no choice, Citizeness,"
Fyodor explained to me. "It's either kill or be killed."

I said nothing, but grieved at the thought of what was being
done to Russia and the Russian people. Pretending to be sleepy, I
lay down on my bed of flour-sacks which had been looted from
the uncooperative peasant villages, and which Fyodor's band would
sell in Moscow at ridiculously inflated prices.

I remained on those sacks continuously for almost two days.
There was virtually no privacy whatsoever; somewhere in the car
someone was always awake. It should not be difficult to imagine the
predicament I was in. My solution was a simple one, however un-
savory. A narrow space between the sacks and the wall served me
for all purposes; so much the worse for those who would buy the
stolen flour. *A la guerre comme à la guerre.*

Toward the end of the second day, the train stopped at a station.
I managed to scramble out on the platform to stretch my limbs
and breathe deeply of the fresh air. I was hurrying back to my
boxcar when an officer jumped down from a first-class sleeper (the
only passenger car on the train) and stepped in front of me. He
was a typical Red Army officer of that period, sporting a small,
cocky mustache and dressed in a smart uniform with huge red
shoulder-knots. He was a bit unsteady on his feet, but he seized
me firmly by the arm: "Ah what luck it is to see you again! I've
often admired you in the Bolshoi Theater. You have a divine
voice!"

I told him that I was not a singer, nor had he ever laid eyes on me
before.

"What's the difference? I'm the Commander of this train, and
there's plenty of food and drink in my compartment. We'll have
fun!" His eyes narrowed to catch my reaction. From the tone of

his voice, I could tell this had been more of an order than an invitation.

Being calm in the face of death is one thing, but being at this man's mercy was quite another matter. Frantically I looked down the platform at my boxcar, three cars away. Fyodor's soldiers were leaning out and making encouraging signs to me: "Run, run; we'll help you!" But with my arm in a viselike grip, I was helpless.

Abruptly, a railway official stepped up to us and mumbled something in a low voice. Turning to answer, the Commander released my arm for an instant: I bolted. Never in my life have I run so fast as I did down that platform. Strong arms reached out of the boxcar to hoist me in, just as the Commander, red-faced and panting, caught up with me. I was lifted and dumped on the floor inside. "Give me that woman," the Commander roared. "That's an order!" He drew his revolver.

A chorus of derisive laughter flew back at him from inside the boxcar: "Come and get her!" With that, Fyodor's men started up a torrent of full-throated abuse, and aimed some two dozen rifles out the door.

The Commander turned pale. Though still trying to appear fierce and unafraid, he drew back, and the boxcar's heavy door slid shut in his face.

I was trembling uncontrollably, but Fyodor gave me a friendly pat: "Take it easy. He won't bother you again. That swine is always gorging on food and vodka, and grabbing any woman he can. We were watching out for you, and when we saw him, we knew what he was up to. But you're safe now as long as you're with us."

There were no further incidents on that trip. But when we reached Moscow, Fyodor's soldiers, each with a sack of flour on his back, insisted on accompanying me to the station exit: "You never can tell with that swine of a Commander. We'd all better stick together until we get to the street."

We parted as the best of friends. At last I reached home and closed the door behind me, much to Nika's and my own relief. I had been away almost a month, and he of course had heard no news from me during all that time. But in the joy of our reunion, we didn't forget Yuri. We began pulling strings that very same day. Nika knocked at the door of each of his dubious new "patrons," and called more than once if he felt that the "patron" in question carried real weight with the Cheka. As a result, Yuri was released soon afterward.

His reprieve proved to be dismally brief. Six months later, Yuri was again arrested and locked up in the desecrated monastery. He was imprisoned under appalling conditions in an overcrowded cell, and soon contracted cerebral meningitis. This time, the telegram that brought us the news left no hope at all. Yuri's wife was ill again, and he was alone, completely alone, and dying. Once more I packed some bottles of vodka, blessed Nika, and headed for Tambov.

By that time the peasant insurrection had been crushed and access to Tambov lay unencumbered. On my arrival, I discovered that Yuri had been transferred to the City Hospital, where the chief medical officer, a friend of his, was caring for him. It had not been easy to obtain the permit that removed Yuri from the prison to the hospital. But through sheer perseverance, the medical officer had finally convinced the Bolsheviks that even though Yuri was certainly doomed, his continued presence in prison would be a source of contamination to other prisoners.

The transfer itself had been frightful. The pain that meningitis produces is unendurable; one can hardly touch a patient without causing acute torture. Yuri was brought all the way to the hospital in a peasant's cart that jolted its way over rough roads. "For all his courage and patience," his friend said, "he screamed all the way."

I found my brother in a little room in the hospital annex. He was enjoying a rare moment of lucidity, and recognized me the moment I entered the room. Joy reflected itself in his eyes, and I heard him murmur, "Thank God. Everything will be all right now." But during the next few moments, his mind went wandering again. His speech became a tide of incoherent ramblings: scraps of literary discussions, political arguments, and economic problems; faint echoes of a once-brilliant mind. On one of my later evening visits, the doctor came to me with a pained look in his eyes. He confessed that during his rounds the night before he had seen me praying. "Please," he said, "don't pray for his recovery. If, by some miracle, your brother survives, he'll be a paralytic and an idiot for the rest of his life."

An epidemic of cholera was raging in Tambov at the time. The hospital annex was filled with patients in the throes of that dread disease. Night and day, as I kept my vigil at Yuri's bedside, I heard the sounds of dreadful vomiting, cries of pain, and the convulsive gasps of the dying. This nightmare lasted two months, for Yuri's life took a long time to be snuffed out.

Toward the end I witnessed the strange deathbed phenomenon I had witnessed on several other occasions: Yuri began to hold conversations with the already departed—our father and our brother Sasha—as though they were present in the room. Can it be that as a soul approaches death, it feels itself once again drawing close to old companions? I hope, but cannot say. I had loved Sasha dearly and I had adored Father, but it was heartrending to hear Yuri already declaring himself among their company. Now I knew that with Yuri's passing, one of the deepest roots of my old life would be torn up forever. I could only thank God that he was relieved of pain in his last hours. As he was dying, he actually began to hum, a little off-key as always, one of his favorite songs by Balakirev!

> "At the end of this desert road
> "A blooming garden waits for me."

Before my return trip to Moscow, a friend in Tambov gave me a most magnificent present: a large, thick sausage. In those hunger-stricken days it was a priceless and mouth-watering gift. But I resisted the temptation of eating it on the spot. I carried it back with me on the train, treasuring it all the way as a surprise with which to regale Nika. Upon my return home I found a telegram: DISCARD SAUSAGE STOP EXPLANATORY LETTER FOLLOWS. The letter, when it came, brought us frightful news: in Tambov, a gang had been apprehended manufacturing sausages from freshly dug-up corpses and selling them at fantastic prices in the market.

Such acts were merely symptomatic of the appalling conditions that resulted from the Communists' enforcement of their land reforms; conditions which I believe were never reported outside of Russia. During the winter of 1920–21, famine and concomitant cannibalism broke out not only east of the Volga where the land was poorer, but even in the Ukraine, that land of magnificent crops.

Even Nika, usually so self-controlled, boiled over with outrage when he first heard the news.

Finally, he grew calm and looked at me gravely: "I can't help remembering that party we gave early in 1917, when Struve gave us his analysis of Marxism." (Nika was speaking of Peter Struve, the famous Socialist who had been attracted to the Bolsheviks but had shied away upon closer acquaintance.) "Do you remember Struve's last words, that all his listeners took for hyperbole? 'Any country that is trapped by Communism will end up eating human flesh.' " Nika fell silent and stared vacantly into space. It would have seemed callous to try to comfort him. How could one smooth over this overwhelming destruction of individual dignity, this rape of the spirit of man?

"Do you recall that case of the priests who were executed in 1919?" Nika murmured. "Thirty of them were arrested and imprisoned in Moscow, and the old prison guards began treating the holy men with every possible consideration. They were even allowed to celebrate Mass for the other prisoners and the prison staff. But when the Bolsheviks got wind of the situation, they decreed a summary execution without a trial. The same night the other prisoners heard the priests being marched out in procession, singing a funeral chant. But when all thirty of them were lined up in the prison yard, still dressed in their ecclesiastical robes, the troops refused to fire. So the Bolsheviks had them returned to their cells, shaved,* and dressed in civilian clothes. The following night, they were executed by a Chinese firing squad.

"Now our dead aren't allowed to rest in peace. They are plowing up cemeteries to make room for new buildings and sports stadiums. The family down the street has been told 'if you want your dead, come and collect them.' It's no rare sight to see people dragging old coffins through the streets in their frantic search for new burial places."

Later one day, I remembered Nika's words and, although I had received no notice, I traveled to the Donskoy Cemetery to see what had become of the family plot which Grandpapa had visited so faithfully every year. Donskoy had hardly been spared. The ground

---

* Priests in the Russian Orthodox Church traditionally wear full beards.

was a morass of broken marble, uprooted trees, and raw, muddy soil. I was surprised to find the Scherbatov chapel untouched and the iron railing still intact around the family graves. But a printed broadside had been pasted to the door of the chapel:

This enclosure is the property of the National Museum of the Soviet Socialist Republics. It has been preserved to show people of future generations what former aristocratic and wealthy classes spent on their dead.

PART TWO

Genghis Khan with a Telephone

CHAPTER ELEVEN

❧

The Abbé Sièyes was once asked what he had done during the French Revolution. His response was simple: "J'ai vécu." I could give the same answer to account for my twenty years under Bolshevism: I lived; the simple task of living occupied our every thought. On going to bed at night, we were never sure where the morning would find us. Sometime during the twenties, the Cheka was renamed the G.P.U. (pronounced *Gay Pay Oo*), but its character remained the same. Our homes were being searched constantly. The investigating officials carried away anything of value they could find, even cheap paperback books. All the Commissar in charge had to do was to label an object "suspect" or in some way "subversive," and it would be confiscated. Nika and I were frequently called before the G.P.U. to pay fines for having broken some petty regulation; at the same time, new and higher taxes were being imposed constantly. Our living quarters grew smaller until they finally dwindled to a single room. As long as Nika was with me, as long as I had the support of his affection and love, I could face such harassments with equanimity; but every time the G.P.U. took him from me, I felt as if my strength were entirely gone.

Then my familiar ordeal would resume: tramping in and out of G.P.U. offices; begging for news but getting nothing but snarls. "No news for such as you. Get out!" I always felt that *this* would be the time that Nika would never return.

Between 1920 and 1933, he was arrested six times. Each time, after weeks—sometimes months—the G.P.U. released him with the assurance that his incarceration had been but a "routine checkup." No specific charge was ever filed against him. As soon as they released him, he was instantly reemployed. The answer to this paradox was that the Bolsheviks were desperately short of

competent men; Nika's services in the fuel cooperative were irre-
placeable.

Normally, we managed to live fairly comfortably on Nika's
salary plus the extra money he earned writing articles on economics;
but whenever he was taken away I had to fend for myself as best
I could. My most difficult hurdle was to find work in the field I
was best at—translation. Though I would have much preferred
translating poetry, I had to struggle instead with articles on
medicine, economics, or engineering—subjects about which I knew
next to nothing. Having always typed Nika's articles, I had a scant
but barely adequate knowledge of scientific vocabulary. In all
honesty, I believe it was intuition rather than knowledge that
helped me give an acceptable rendition of topics that I hardly understood. At any rate, questions were very seldom raised over my
interpretation of the texts.

My salary kept coming rather steadily, as long as I had something
to translate. But half the time I found myself without work of any
kind. I made the endless rounds of offices, only to be received more
often than not with an abrupt, "No work for the likes of you!"

One day, Mr. Zhuhovitsky, a good friend of mine, came to pay a
visit. He was a very well-read Jew, educated at Oxford and then
employed by the Gosizdat (Government Publishing Bureau).
When I showed him how I was earning a living, he grew indignant:
"To think that you should waste your time and ability on technical
theses that you know nothing about! It passes my understanding
how you manage to do it at all. We've got to find you some better
task than this."

He handed me an up-to-date book on Spain which had been
recently published in Paris. "I made an appointment for you for
tomorrow at the Gosizdat," he said. "They ought to let you
translate this book. Go and see them. I am *persona gratissima* there,
and I'm sure you will be well-received."

I was not wholly convinced by his optimism, but neither could I
appear so ungrateful as to refuse. At the appointed hour next day,
I presented myself at the Gosizdat. I was received in a large office
by two editors, a man and a woman. One look at them told me
what to expect. Their faces were coarse and smug, their lips pro-
truding, their expression sour, and their eyes filled with inex-
tinguishable class hatred. The woman, Comrade Topper, looked

me up and down with particular disdain. "What do you want?"

I explained that Mr. Zhuhovitsky had suggested something for me to translate for them—a most interesting book on modern Spain.

"Spain? It'll only talk about bullfights!"

I explained that bullfights were mentioned briefly, in only one chapter. The rest of the text dealt with economic problems and gave an analysis of all the existing political parties. But Comrade Topper turned to her male counterpart:

"We don't need bullfights, do we, Comrade Abramson? Do you think we need bullfights?"

"No," Comrade Abramson snapped back. "We don't need bullfights! That book has no doubt been written by some capitalist author who's thoroughly anti-Communist. No! No bullfights for us!"

"But you haven't even taken the trouble to glance through it," I exclaimed. My indignation, as it often did, got the better of me: "This is a strange way of choosing your collaborators! No wonder one of your experts took the French word for porcupine, *porc-épic* and translated it as 'the epic swine!' "

I left, feeling much better for having had my say. Zhuhovitsky was outraged when I told him about the interview, but three days later he was on the telephone again: "Good news! I think this is a real opportunity for you this time! Henri Malraux is in town— he's the brother of André Malraux, the famous French author. Henri says he's a Communist, but I don't believe him. Anyway, he's now at the Gosizdat, heading up a project to translate contemporary Soviet poetry into French. That's right up your alley, isn't it? I showed him some of your French translations of Pushkin, and he was quite enthusiastic. Please go and see him tomorrow."

The next day, I wended my way back to the Gosizdat. Upon entering Malraux's office, my nervousness was quickly dispelled. I found Henri Malraux a cultivated, charming man of the type that had become extremely rare in Russia. We fell into an animated discussion. I told him that I thought the translator of any poem should never attempt word-for-word accuracy, but instead try to create another poem with the essence of the original, but one which would appeal to the reader on its own merit. Malraux agreed with me wholeheartedly. When I added that it would be difficult for me to "recreate" poems I disliked, above all "propaganda" poetry, he gave me a knowing smile:

"I see what you mean, Madame. You shall have a free hand in choosing what you like, or perhaps I should say, what you dislike least. There's not likely to be disagreement: I'm not going to employ any others except you. *Tiens!* You should have heard some of my interviews with the translators the Gosizdat sent me! Those tyros didn't even know elementary French. They translated whole phrases verbatim, right out of the dictionary! Employing any of them is out of the question. You, Madame, can do the whole anthology if you like. Now . . . let's take this poem by Bagritsky. Begin with that one, and see what you can make of it."

Bagritsky was a gifted poet, but also an ardent Communist, ready to follow the party line wherever it might meander. When I went home to work on his long poem, I feared that it would prove a tedious and difficult task. But I found it a challenge instead, one that absorbed my interest as soon as I sat down to work. When my translation was ready, I sent it to Malraux. Four days later I went to his office to hear his verdict.

He met me in the outer office where Comrades Topper and Abramson sat at their desks, eyeing me resentfully. "Madame," he exclaimed, as he took my hand in both of his, "I must express my profound admiration. Your translation doesn't sound like a translation at all. It might have been written in French. The Gosizdat is honored to have you as a collaborator!"

I need not describe the expressions on the faces of Editors Topper and Abramson. When we were alone in his office, Malraux smiled and whispered, "Didn't I stage my congratulations before the perfect audience? I hope it teaches those two a lesson!"

He gave me all the translations I could handle. Working with Malraux was a pleasure, and when he left Russia fifteen months later, the anthology was ready for publication.* Just before he left, Malraux asked if he might pay me a visit to say goodbye and express his appreciation; but I had to discourage him in no uncertain terms. "Much as I would like to receive you," I replied, "it's out

---

* I do not know what happened to it afterward; I never saw it in print. Perhaps, in those years preceding World War II, the French were too preoccupied to give their attention to Soviet poetry.

of the question. I'd hardly want to exchange my one and only room for a prison cell! All of the comings and goings in our building are spied upon and reported to the G.P.U. For an "ex-person" like myself to receive a visit from a foreigner would be fatal."

Malraux and I bid each other adieu amidst the impersonal decor of his office. My collaboration with him had been more than financially rewarding; translations had occupied my mind and crowded out many of the gnawing speculations that came to plague me whenever Nika was away. But when Malraux left for France, my thoughts were forced to return to the round of daily worries that I had managed, so briefly, to ignore.

CHAPTER TWELVE

❧❀❧

One of Bolshevism's saddest effects was the gradual strangling of all forms of art. "The Communist Octopus," as the regime was then nicknamed, squeezed every pulse of free thought and creative expression out of the country. Literature, which had reached such colossal heights in pre-Bolshevik days, was now reduced to shameful mediocrity. The State simply hounded all fiction writers who dared to deviate from the party line, or even to write on any subject not of direct interest to the party. Painters fared no better. They were forced to devote their talents to propaganda posters whose prescribed format left no room for personal inspiration. For the unfortunate artists and writers, the choice was plain: cooperate or go without work. Nor were the works of older Russian masters exempt from State jurisdiction. Pictures of Nesterov and Vasnetsov were removed from Moscow and Leningrad galleries for being "religious," or for representing "bourgeois ideals." Beautiful paintings and statuary were saved from destruction only by the protests of some of the more discerning museum officials, who took their stand at the risk of life imprisonment.

Once, as I was passing in front of one of the major Moscow museums, I saw Trotsky's wife—then Commissar of Fine Arts—sitting grandly in her limousine while a friend of mine—a prominent painter and art critic—stood bareheaded in the rain, pleading with her. I was distressed to see his abject and obsequious manner. My friend was bitterly criticized at the time, but Russia is indebted to him for the preservation of countless treasures. Hundreds of such modest heroes put an ideal above their personal pride and safety, and fought their battles thanklessly behind the Iron Curtain. They still do.

For centuries, the Russian Orthodox Church had been the repository of priceless works of art. But when the Bolsheviks began their religious persecutions, the Church's best pieces were ransacked and frequently destroyed. During the height of this "purge," a friend of mine who was then the assistant curator of the Museum of Art in Moscow came to see me. Although still young in years, he had grown prematurely white, old, and haggard. His eyes were lifeless and dull. I felt surely some devastating bodily illness was afflicting him, but he insisted that his affliction, painful as it was, was merely of the spirit.

Every day, he told me, trucks loaded with spoils from churches and monasteries pulled up to the museum. Inside were thousands of objects worked in gold and silver; chalices, censors, icons, Bibles in gem-studded bindings; all the marvelous, inimitable workmanship of the past. My friend's duty was to select two pieces of each type for the museum, and to send the rest to be broken up and melted down. To save one medieval vestment, embroidered with pearls and precious stones, meant that a score of others had to go to the shears and the furnace. "What am I to select?" he moaned. "What am I to save? I can't sleep at night. I'm haunted by the beauty I will destroy on the coming day. And the same thing is going on all over the country. They are trying to turn Russia into an enormous gray corridor inhabited by the blind and the ignorant."

The poor man talked until he was beside himself and wept like a child. I was not surprised. I had seen the same despair in others who were struggling to preserve a shred of honor, a vestige of freedom of thought, a memory of compassionate human decency. Every one of us who refused to "bow to the Unholy One" had his share of the battle. The strong were annealed, grew stronger, and went down undaunted, with banners flying. The weak yielded and were morally crushed, but those who have not passed through mental and physical tortures have no right to condemn them.

Certainly of all the arts, poetry—that child of the spirit "that blows where it listeth"—was the first to feel the Bolshevik assault. Many poets struggled against bureaucratic pressure only to starve to death, to be shot, or to commit suicide. Blok, Gumilyov, and the gay peasant singer Yessenin who hanged himself in despair are famous examples, but there were many more, whose names are now unknown.

Pasternak, the most prominent lyric poet of the period, was

nearly hounded to death during the great "purge." His self-styled
fellow-artists reviled what they called the "counter-revolutionary"
nature of his lyrics. Most of them had glibly bowed to the party
line in order to get bread for their families, or perhaps simply to
escape prison sentences.

Even so, while plodding through officially sponsored poetry, I
occasionally stumbled upon a line or stanza that stood out amidst
the usual bombastic phrases and trite eulogies. It was depressing to
think what the author in question might have achieved if he could
have written on subjects besides "Collectivization," "Turbines," or
"The Workers' Paradise." Yet at the same time, I knew that from
such a spark of inspiration, the poet had probably drawn renewed
self-respect and a measure of strength to go on with his ordeal.

There was one famous poet whom the Bolsheviks were never able
to muffle or break: Maximilian Voloshin. His genius and extraordinary personality set him apart in the memories of those who
met him. Once during the early twenties I had the privilege of
hearing him read the poems he had written in 1917, the first year
of the Revolution.

It had already become dangerous to gather in a friend's home
for an evening of social and literary talk, but we still found the
temptation to associate with those close to us in spirit too great.
One of our favorite salons was the home of an old friend of mine,
R— M—, an elderly woman with great courage, intelligence,
and the gift of gathering diverse personalities around her in complete harmony. Everyone was welcome in R— M—'s wide, cosy
drawing room, though as time passed her courageous parties did
become fewer and farther apart.

She had lived for a long time in Paris where, among other literary
figures, she had become friends with Voloshin. One week, the poet
came to Moscow for a week from Koktebel, his place in the Crimea.
R— M— simply decided to ignore worry and to invite a number
of friends to meet Voloshin and hear him read his poetry. The
Bolsheviks had forbidden the publication of Voloshin's poetry. Only
one small volume of his, *Deafmute Demons*, had appeared during
the White Army rule in Kharkov; but it was virtually unobtainable
in Moscow. Nevertheless, we were hardly strangers to his work:
surreptitious typewritten copies circulated from hand to hand,
until most of us knew by heart at least a half dozen of his poems.

At the appointed hour, we gathered in R— M—'s familiar drawing room like conspirators, singly and in pairs, rather naïvely imagining that in this way we would escape detection.

The heavy window curtains were tightly drawn so as not to let a single betraying ray of light into the night beyond. A tea table was set in the old, pre-Revolutionary style, complete with fine silverware and china. There was very little else besides tea on that small polished table, but that was the least of our concerns. Repressed excitement was reflected in everyone's manner. Our hostess kept cocking her head anxiously and listening. At last came a discreet tinkling of the doorbell, and a moment later, our guest of honor was in the room with us.

Voloshin cut a magnificent figure. He was immensely tall, heavy-chested, and broad-shouldered. His face boasted strong oak-hewn features, piercing gray eyes, and a thick crop of curly red hair streaked with gray. Normally, at home in the Crimea, he always wore a Grecian chlamys and wound a wreath of grape vine around his ruddy-gray locks. Walking the hills of Koktebel, with a long staff in his hand, his attire seemed altogether natural. That evening at R— M—'s, however, he wore a more conventional green Russian blouse strapped around the waist with a leather belt, but he was hardly constrained: one saw at once that Voloshin was as much at home in this crowded drawing room as he would have been in his Crimean hills and valleys. He put us all quickly at our ease, and we relaxed as if we'd known him all our lives.

After tea, Voloshin turned to his poetry. I had often listened to poets and actors recite, but seldom had I felt such delight and elation at a reading. Only once, years before, had I felt a comparable transport while listening to the famous actor Kachalov, except where in Kachalov one sensed carefully studied nuances, in Voloshin one saw a free and molten expression pour forth like lava from a volcano.

Voloshin spoke so that every word sank into one's soul. He had an amazingly powerful, yet tender, voice; and natural timing that went a long way to bolster the impact of his verses. But above and beyond the grandeur of his voice and manner, the significance of what he read touched our most private memories of pain and secret confusion. He seemed to sum up all those complex emotions and confused thoughts that arise when one no longer knows which way to turn to find truth: what aspect of the Revolution to accept as ultimately constructive and inevitable; what to reject and oppose as unacceptable and vile.

As Voloshin read, we began to perceive that he was drawing from the whole of Russia and her history, from all of Russia's numerous nationalities, with their separate, conflicting, centuries-old traits; above all from Russia's soul with its depths and contradictions, its mysticism and yearnings. Listening to him, we began to realize that he was working out a synthesis, finding a pattern to the involuted labyrinth of those days. And, like the breaking of night into dawn, so much, so very much of our covert experience became visible and clear to us.

In conclusion, Voloshin read: "Russia We've Done Away With" —a poem which I cannot translate without its losing some of the Russian lilt and musical power:

We've done away with Russia! As she died,
We jeered her down and gossiped her to deafness,
Husked her skin off, swigged her down and spat new bones away;
Hawked her holy remnants through close, filthy squares;
While crying out to those who sold her too:

"Comrades! Comrades! Civic rights for barter!
Liberty and land-reform for fifteen kopeks each!"
But for the crime of seeming worn-out goods,
The people dragged our Russia to the village dump
And left her sprawled with cold cinders round her head.

Lord! God! Let loose thy wrath and crush us!
Smite us with fire and plague and what scourges you choose.
May our enemies fall like the Red Sea upon us,
And afflict us with chains and invasion again,
That we may, without ceasing, repent; in wracked subjection and
    tears,
Our Judas' sin before Thy Judgement Day!

Like a roll of condemning thunder, the poet's voice rang through the hushed room. Immobile, we his listeners sat spellbound and profoundly stirred. To calm myself, I took refuge in the next room.

Our hostess ran in after me and clasped both my hands in hers:

"Well, what do you say? Isn't Voloshin stupendous?" R— M— refused to take my helpless shakes of the head for an answer: "Oh no! Words must be found, and I know you'll find them. I'll bring Max in here and you will speak for us all. You'll tell him what we felt while listening to him."

"But he doesn't know me. Why should anything *I* say matter to him?"

R— M— only shook her head:

"You are young, that's why. We others are an older generation. Coming from you, appreciation will mean a great deal more. So be a good girl. Do as I say. Please."

I sat down in an armchair to compose myself, but I hardly had time to collect my thoughts when Voloshin entered the room. I sprang to my feet and ran to meet him, my voice a bit unsteady:

"Our friend . . . wants me to tell you what we all felt. All I can say is . . . it will be easier to die now, knowing that everything we have felt about Russia has found permanent expression in your poems."

His whole countenance lit up with inexpressible joy. "Ah, how wonderful! How wonderful that you should say that! May I kiss you?" And opening his huge arms, he gave me a mighty hug.

After an interval he resumed reading, only this time he began with an introduction to explain why my simple words had moved him so.

"The poem I am going to read now," he said, "is about a sailor-Chekist who sank the Black Sea Fleet and was, until very recently, the terror of the Crimea. He was truly a creature from hell, that man was—fearless, savage, and possessed! I got to know him well. Now, just what attached him to me I don't know, unless it was that I wasn't afraid of him and always decided to tell him the truth, straight to his face. And besides, he did have a passion for poetry and a real talent for acting. In any case, being on his good side enabled me to intercede for many condemned prisoners, thank God! And I must confess I took full advantage of that privilege.

"Well, when this poem about him was finished, I sent it to him, and I was somewhat surprised to get no answer back. Then one day an emissary reached Koktebel to tell me that my friend was in prison, condemned to death—why, I don't know. Perhaps he had overstepped even the Bolshevik bounds of savagery. But be that as it may, his message, via this emissary, was: 'I have faith in you, and I want to tell you something before I die.' The emissary was so frantic—'Hurry, hurry, Comrade Voloshin! They're going to string him up at dawn'—that I rushed out of the house without changing my clothes and literally ran to the nearby town, Kerch, just as I was—in my chlamys, you know.

"When I got to the sailor's cell, there he was, sitting doubled over on his cot with his head buried in his hands. When he looked up at me, I saw his cheeks had caved in and his face had grown almost black. But his deep bass voice boomed out, vigorous as ever —'Max! I knew you wouldn't fail me. I had to see you, Max. I had to unburden my soul and tell you this one thing before dying.' "

Voloshin paused, looking at every one of us in turn. Finally he brought his eyes to rest on me: "Funny thing! That inhuman brute used almost the very same words as did one of my listeners just now. He said, 'Max, I thank you. It will be easier now for me to die. Everything I've felt, everything I've done, you've expressed in that poem of yours. And now it seems that not all of me will die after all—Yes! Thank you, my friend!' If that isn't Russia for you! On the one hand, this compulsive killer, and on the other, this charming young woman here: two extremes. Yet they found one point in common—the magic of art, the magic of words! What a mysterious power it is!"

Our gathering parted joyfully. But the next morning, R— M—'s anxious voice over the telephone begged me to come to her at once. I found her in tears, trembling with anxiety: Max had been summoned to the Kremlin to read his poems to our new rulers. They had even sent a Cheka automobile to fetch him. R— M— was sure she would never see him alive again.

"That man doesn't know what fear is. He just smiles and goes wherever he is asked. When they hear what he has written, they'll have him shot!" I tried to console her with the point that, if Voloshin's poetry could touch a ruthless sailor, it was bound to affect the Lords of the Kremlin, some of whom were well-educated. R— M— only waved me away indignantly: "Oh, stop it! Well-educated, indeed! Would an educated man commit any of the butchery they do? They'll shoot him, I tell you, or bury him alive in Siberia!"

But that same evening, her voice was on the wire again, this time happy and jubilant: "Please come at once! He's here!"

In R— M—'s drawing room I found almost everyone who had been there the night before gathered around Max Voloshin, who sprawled in a big armchair, huge and benign. R— M— caught sight of me and turned to him: "Now's the time, Max. We're all here. Tell us everything, and don't miss a single detail!"

Voloshin sat upright and beamed:

"Well, at the appointed hour I presented myself at the Kremlin along with a briefcase bulging with poems. A guard escorts me to one of the 'Salons' of the palace. At a round table there, I find the whole tribe: Kamenev, Madame Kamenev, Bukharin, Zinoviev. We all have some tea, but the tea, you must understand, is being served in cheap glasses and chipped assorted cups that lend a more democratic atmosphere. And there is stale black bread and a few husks to chew on besides. Kamenev is playing host. He comes forward, shakes me warmly by the hand, and introduces me to all the others. All of them look just like they do on their posters. I recognize Lunacharsky. Dzherzhinsky seems pretty familiar. . ."

The thought of such an infernal gathering made us shudder. "Oh dear God, how awful!" R— M— exclaimed. But Voloshin went on unperturbed. A sly grin broke at the corners of his mouth:

"And now Kamenev is talking to me—calling me very politely, by my name and patronimic. None of that 'Comrade' business, mind you! And I quote: 'We are very anxious to hear your poetry in your own voice, which, we all have heard, is superb. Please start right away. We are busy people and have no time to waste.' So I give it to them! I read 'Russia We've Done Away With,' and no sooner have I finished, than Madame Kamenev leaps to her feet, squinting with rage. 'Counter-revolution!' she shrieks at the top of her lungs, 'Treason!' But her husband pushes her back into her chair—'Shut up! We can allow Voloshin to have his own point of view!' I swear to you, my friends, that's exactly what he said— 'We can allow Voloshin to have *his own point of view!*' " Voloshin threw his head back and roared with laughter.

"After hearing that, I was ready to read until nightfall. I almost did. I read everything, every single poem I read to you last night. Apparently I made an impression—just what *sort* of impression is another question—but they listened attentively and demanded to hear more and more. At one point I asked myself, just how is this pleasant little reading going to end? But nothing happened. Kamenev escorted me to the door and thanked me! I got into the same Cheka automobile that brought me there, and here I am, back from the lions' den!"

After a light supper we sat on for hours, listening to Voloshin's tales of his life in the Crimea. In a few words he conjured up the whole landscape: near his home was a rock known as "Bear Mountain" because it juts out into the Black Sea in the shape of a crouching, drinking bear. He described the steep slopes covered with wild grass and herds of grazing sheep.

"My house in Koktebel is a large one," he said, "and of course the inevitable happened: I was 'condensed.' A Commissar moved in with me who'd been sent from Moscow to liquidate what was left of the White Army that had been trapped on the coast. This fellow spent his nights shooting officers and soldiers by the thousands. He was large, heavy, somber, and a drunkard to boot. Every evening, drunk and surrounded by his aides, he'd stagger down the steps of my house to his waiting automobile and drive off to town. All night I'd hear the crackling of machine guns in the distance.

"For some reason or other, this Commissar was well disposed to me personally. Perhaps like my sailor friend, he was impressed by the fact that I was not afraid of him—who knows? He was always frank with me, sometimes in a rather coarse, kidding way, but never unkindly. Then suddenly he'd flop down opposite me at the table, prop his cheek in his hand, and stare and stare at me out of his tiny bloodshot eyes. Finally a heavy sigh would escape him and he'd start drinking vodka. What else could he do to blot out the darkness he must have felt weighing upon him? In every human being there is a soul that can still tremble in horror at what it has done.

"I'm not exaggerating when I say this man was a monster, even worse than a return to the primitive troglodytes. To illustrate my point—I remember one morning I had to pass by the place he had chosen for his executions. A light snow was falling over the mountains and the sea. At the foot of a great rock lay huge heaps of corpses. Women were picking through them to find their relations, while dogs slunk past to tear at the frozen bodies. To my dying day I'll carry that picture with me.

"One evening, as the Commissar was leaving my house for the field of slaughter, I sank to my knees in a corner of my room and began to pray. I didn't hear the door open or the floorboards creak, but for some reason I looked back over my shoulder. The Commissar stood on the threshold, staring at me, just staring, with a bunch of papers trembling in his hand. Finally his voice cracked through the charged silence:

" 'What are you doing, old man?'

" 'Praying.'

" 'For whom?'

" 'For those you will kill tonight, and for you!'

" 'For me? Why pray for me?'

" 'If not for you, then for whom else? You're up to your ears in blood. Your soul is black, and a dreadful weight lies on it. Who will ever pray for you if I don't?'

"Unsteadily—for he was half drunk as usual—he approached the table, flung the papers on it, and for a long while stood lost in thought. At last he turned a pair of glassy eyes on me and pointed his finger at the papers:

" 'Listen, you! Here's the list. There are one thousand souls to be shot tonight. Scratch out two hundred. I give them to you!' "

Voloshin's voice trembled: "Friends, that was the most awful moment I've ever had to live through! Which lives was I to save out of that unknown thousand? Finally I seized a pen and scratched out two hundred names at random. The Commissar left. Next morning he came to me, tired and haggard: 'I let your two hundred go. The Devil take them! Are you pleased, old man?' "

Voloshin leaned back in his chair, a thin, ironic smile playing across his face. No one spoke.

Indeed Max Voloshin's luck and pluck were uncanny. I have heard that when the Kremlin changed the name "Petrograd" to "Leningrad," Voloshin wrote an open letter to the Soviet Government:

"Lenin, undeniably, was a great man and deserves to have a great city named after him. But by the same token, I demand that all the works of Pushkin be ascribed to me."

To his dying day, the Bolsheviks never harmed Voloshin, no matter how often or how clearly he expressed his contempt for them. It was, of course, fortunate that he never had to face the conditions later to come in Stalin's day; but I still believe that his own courage and compelling personality were most to thank for his immunity. As a brilliant Frenchman once said, "In the long run, the best mask is an open face." If ever there was a Titan in the word's full sense, Maximilian Voloshin was his name.

CHAPTER THIRTEEN

❧

In 1933, Nika was arrested for the seventh time. By then the G.P.U.
had been renamed N.K.V.D. (En-Kah-Vay-Day), but was still
the same old Cheka. As always, they came by night, looked through
Nika's papers, and marched him off without explanation. I was
terribly alarmed: this time they had searched for something specific: booklets connected with the textile industry. Since textiles
was one of the few branches of Russian economy Nika had nothing
to do with, I felt there was something dreadfully wrong. Either
there was a purge coming, or else someone wanted Nika out of the
way and was making arbitrary excuses.

By 1933, the barrier had become impenetrable between the
ruling clique in the Kremlin and the rest of the country. Gone
were the days when one could appeal to a member of the Government; Stalin had put an end to that. Men who had retained a sense
of justice in their hearts, men like Yenukidze and Kamenev, had
been executed. It was against the law to have anything to do with
the relations or friends of people under arrest. Such contacts would
inevitably bring one before the notorious Commissar Nikolay
Krylenko, who was then ruling the Commissariate of Justice with
an iron fist. Merely to *obtain* an interview with Krylenko—in order
to intercede for a prisoner—was considered impossible; in fact,
anyone entertaining such an idea would be thought insane, no
matter what his party status.

Two weeks had gone by since Nika was led away, and I was
still unable to help him. Every door had been slammed in my face.
Night after sleepless night went by with me mentally searching for
any little crack that might give way under pressure. And it was
then that the name Krylenko suddenly came to mind, in connection
with an incident of ten years before.

111

In the early days of Communist rule Krylenko had been Commissar for War. Reputed to be highly intelligent, a fearlessly able speaker, and quite pitiless, it was he who had helped form the Communist Soldiers' Councils through which the Bolsheviks finally won control of the Army in 1917. This achievement started Krylenko on a brilliant career. In gratitude for helping to bring the army into the Communist fold, the Bolsheviks granted Krylenko a leave of absence, during which he went mountain-climbing in the Pamir Mountains. On his return, he published a small book about the adventures and various discoveries he had made in that little-known region.

"You know," Nika said after reading the book, "we ought to send this to my brother Andrey. After all, he's been to the Pamirs twice in search of rare butterflies, and he knows the area well. I'll ask him to write a few lines of congratulations to Krylenko. Hearing from Andrey, as head of the Carnegie Museum in Pittsburgh, Krylenko will be flattered. Who knows? The connection might be useful some day, and perhaps even save a life."

We sent the book to my brother-in-law in America. Andrey knew how to read Nika's letter between the lines. He sent an enthusiastic note to Krylenko, and a copy of it to us. The Commissar was indeed highly flattered. In his reply, he asked Andrey to translate his book into English and have it published for the benefit of the American Communist Party. Krylenko's suggestion amused us vastly at the time, but the joke had gone no further. I had completely forgotten about it, but now it came back as possibly Nika's one and only chance.

I composed a careful letter to Krylenko that would give the impression that I knew nothing at all about the previous correspondence over his book. I said that my brother-in-law, Professor Avinov, had learned of my husband's arrest and had written, urging me to apply direct to Commissar Krylenko. Professor Avinov had insisted to me that there must be some mistake, but the Commissar was a man of intelligence and integrity, and would certainly put the matter right as soon as it was brought to his attention. This advice, I said, came as a complete surprise to me, for I had no idea that Professor Avinov and Commissar Krylenko were acquainted.

I then told our faithful servant Basil to deliver the letter by hand. "I know I'm asking a great deal of you," I told him. "If he does no more than swear at you, that'll be a kind of success, but this is our only chance."

"Don't worry," Basil replied without the slightest hesitation. "I'd put up with a lot more than that for Nikolay Nikolayevich."

After an hour of tense waiting, I saw Basil return, pale but still smiling. "I've done it," he said. "It took some doing, though. You should see that man's house! First there are high walls, then barbed wire on top of the walls, and behind them in the yard, huge dogs barking. An old woman passing by chided me, 'You're going to see Commissar Krylenko, and you're afraid of dogs? God help you!'

"I crossed myself and entered the yard. All the dogs were chained up, thank the Lord. I rang the bell, and the Commissar himself came to the door in pajamas. Just as you said, he started swearing at me, but I said, 'Citizen Commissar, it's not for myself. I brought you a letter.' He snatched it from me and read it then and there. And then he crumpled the paper in his fist and shouted, 'Tell that woman to be in my office tomorrow morning at eleven o'clock!' He slammed the door in my face." Basil glanced anxiously at me. "Are you really going to see a man like that? What will you say to him?"

"My dear Basil, I shall say whatever St. Seraphim inspires me to say."

Punctually at eleven I presented myself at the Commissariat of Justice. I had decided not to resort to shoddy camouflage, and had dressed myself in my very best. There was no one in the vestibule but a porter, who looked at me strangely: "Citizeness, no one is allowed in here. Go away!"

"But I have an appointment at eleven with Commissar Krylenko."

The man's tone changed. He ushered me into an elevator in his most obsequious manner, took me up three flights and down a long corridor. All doors were closed; there wasn't another soul in sight. He pointed to one of the doors and bolted back to the elevator, evidently anxious to obliterate all traces of himself before I opened that door.

I waited until he had disappeared before knocking. Entering, I found myself in a large room where about twenty men and women were typing furiously. I paused on the threshold. The typewriters

fell silent, and from all ends of the room astonished eyes stared at
me, clearly the "ex-bourgeoise," in her tailored suit, lace jabot, and
diamond earrings. One of the secretaries stood up.

"Citizeness!" she exclaimed in shocked tones, "what are you
doing here?"

I flashed my most amiable smile: "I have an appointment with
the Commissar at eleven o'clock."

She told me to sit down. Soon, loud shouting and cursing reached
me from an inner office. The door presently flew open, and a man
staggered out, ashen and stammering, with Krylenko himself at
his heels. Everything I had heard about the Commissar seemed
true. There really *was* something of the tiger about him: the short,
sinewy body was sheathed in a tight military tunic, and the hair
cut in a brush above a now-fiery face. He continued his tirade at
his unfortunate visitor until he caught sight of me and stopped
short.

"What's this?" he finally exploded, pointing his finger at me.

"This," I replied, getting up and coming toward him with a
bland smile, "is the wife of Nikolay Nikolayevich Avinov, whom
you were kind enough to say you would see at eleven."

"What? You have the nerve to ask me for an interview, the
nerve to claim that I'm acquainted with Professor Avinov in
America? I have nothing to do with that 'White' vermin!"

How I dared, I don't know, but I put my hand on his shoulder:
"Listen, Nikolay Vassilievich, once you've heard me out you can
swear and shout as much as you please, but since you gave me
permission to come here, you ought to listen to what I have to say."
Before he could answer I quickly slipped past him and into his
office through the half-open door. He followed me and slammed
the door behind him. We were alone, facing each other across a
wide desk.

"What do you want?"

I felt neither fear nor confusion. Words in a light vein came
easily, as if someone else were speaking for me: "Nikolay Vassilievich, I know people are terrified of you. But I am not. I agree
with Frederick the Great, who said the only sort of person he
feared was a fool. He said he was afraid of our General Saltykov
because that soldier's maneuvers were so idiotic one could never
tell what he would do next. And by contrast, I do not fear you,

because you're an exceptionally intelligent man. I've never forgotten the speech you delivered in 1920 at the trial of the counter-revolutionaries. The accused were among my friends, and yet I admired you. You had courage enough to say you were glad such brave men had been spared the noose and firing squad. That proved to me that you are just and generous, despite your terrifying reputation. And why should anyone fear a just man?"

Never taking his eyes off my face, Krylenko began to smile. I continued, encouraged: "Will you kindly tell me why you called my brother-in-law a vermin? After all, he's a world-famous entomologist, a famous explorer . . ."

"I'll tell you why," spat out Krylenko. "A Russian of *his* caliber, who takes refuge in capitalist America instead of remaining at home to help us build a new communist Russia . . ."

It was my turn to interrupt: "His brother, Nikolay Nikolayevich Avinov, has done just the opposite. He could have emigrated too, you know. He could have had an easy life in America. Surely you remember my husband's reputation as an economist! Weren't you at the Leningrad University together? He has never taken part in anti-Communist plots. He has worked for the good of our country, even though he disapproves of the present Government. He has done the very thing you wish his brother had done; he has been loyal, and with what reward? This is the seventh time he's been arrested—for no reason at all! We are no children, Citizen Commissar; my husband and I realize that in these terrible times, we are suspect as ex-nobles. But to condemn a man for crimes he has never committed is, I think, unworthy of the Soviet Government!"

For some time Krylenko had been listening in silence. Now his face grew redder than ever and he roared at the top of his voice: "I know your sort—an aristocrat down to the fingertips, and a counter-revolutionary to boot! What do you mean by saying 'terrible times'? These are glorious years! What else can you call the resurrection of a country that for centuries has been ground down by Tsars and capitalists?" I don't know how long he would have gone on in this vein if a pretty young blonde, presumably his secretary, hadn't come in to see what the commotion was about.

Krylenko turned to her immediately: "See this woman, this idiotic ex-aristocrat? She's come here to make a scene, to accuse *me*—!"

Instantly I took his cue, turned to the young woman, and pointed back at Krylenko. "And the Commissar," I cried, "why is he insulting me? Just because my husband, Nikolay Nikolayevich Avinov, has done exactly what the Commissar admires, only to be thrown into prison for the *seventh time!*" I spread my hands in mock bewilderment: "What am I supposed to do? The Commissar and my husband are both loyal Russians, but which of them is right? Whose side can I take?"

Krylenko laughed at my parody of his own rhetoric.

"Well, what do you want *me* to do?" he asked at length.

"Please look through my husband's dossier. You will see for yourself that he is innocent of any crime. That's all I ask you to do. I rely on your intelligence and sense of justice."

"Very well." He slowly leaned across the desk and brought his face close to mine. "I will. But I warn you . . ." His small yellow eyes bored into mine. "If I find any evidence whatsoever of counter-revolutionary activity, your husband will get what he deserves, and I'll pack *you* off where you won't be back in such a hurry."

Somehow, I felt not the slightest intimidation. A will stronger than mine had taken over. My face broke into a smile quite naturally, as if his threat were a half-jesting argument in a comfortable drawing room.

"Nikolay Vassilievich, a woman fighting for her husband is afraid of nothing. Exile me to the North Pole if you like, but I will not fear you. So come; accept my thanks for hearing me out, and let's shake hands. Whatever the outcome, I will bear you no malice."

Krylenko smiled: "I'm glad to shake hands with a brave woman. You will hear from me."

We both rose to our feet. As I reached the door, he began to call down thunder on Andrey's head, for the obvious benefit of those secretaries in the outer office who might have been listening at the keyhole. Even top chiefs of the Communist Party lived in dread of compromising themselves.

Back in the lonely corridor outside, I came close to collapsing. Leaning against the wall, I felt my knees weaken and my head swim. I had but one desire in mind—to get home, to lie down, and to be far away from that face, that voice, and those eyes.

Two weeks went by. I was sitting alone one evening when an old friend dropped by to cheer me with a bouquet of flowers.

The street door had been left ajar. As we two were talking, I heard it shut. Then we both heard steps coming up the stairs. The next thing I knew, Nika laid his hand on our friend's shoulder. It is moments of such intense joy that manage to compensate our sorrows.

After heartly congratulations, our friend left, and I had time to take full notice of Nika's appearance. His beard had grown long, his clothes had split their seams, and to my horror I saw that one of his front teeth was missing. His other strong, white teeth made the dark gap all the more conspicuous. He tried to convince me he had not been beaten, but lied so badly that he gave up:

"Don't give it a thought. What matters now is that I'm back again and free." I told him of my interview with Krylenko. He gave a toss of his dark eyebrows: "Aren't you the one! You turn pale at the sight of a broken tooth, but you're brave as a lioness in the face of real danger!"

"How else could it be?" I cried. "One can't pray for guidance when a tooth has already been lost, but when one's faced with real danger, or rather, when *you* are faced with it, my whole soul goes up in prayer . . ."

"Yes, yes, I know—I have felt that way myself." Again his sad smile revealed that dreadful black gap.

To explain the reasons behind this particular arrest, I must go back to before World War I when, as a young woman, I used to go riding in the Moscow Riding Academy. In the afternoons there I often met a charming young man, L—, who owned a number of cotton mills. Like many other rich manufacturers of that period, he had been to England to learn methods of modern production. I got to know him well, but only in the riding school. He never visited me at home, and after the outbreak of war I saw him no more.

Five years later when the Red Terror was in full swing, I met him by chance on a miserably wet day in Moscow. Rain was mingling with snow, and the neglected streets were filled with half-frozen ice. My *valenki* had been carried off in one of those "drives for the poor" the week before, so I was splashing through the slush in an improvised pair of overshoes made from old green carpeting. L— was overjoyed to see me, but I noticed the startled look he gave my feet. I laughed, but he did not conceal his look of outrage:

"You always used to be so impeccably turned out! I can't bear to see you this way! Please let me make two pairs of *valenki* for you and your husband."

It turned out that L— had once taken up shoemaking as a hobby. Now he lived by it. I tried to refuse, but he looked so pained that in the end I gave in. He came to our house to meet Nika and measure our feet. Ten days later L— returned with two precious pairs of felt and leather *valenki*. Although we invited him to stay for a cup of tea on both occasions, we never saw him again. Yet on the very first night of Nika's seventh arrest, this matter of almost ten years before was brought up in detail.

"I was given hour upon hour of interrogation by some official from upper Bolshevik echelons. After reviewing my whole life, the man opened a thick folder with my name on it. He opened it and read in an unctuous voice. 'You are accused of having taken part in a plot to sabotage and wreck the textile industry of the U.S.S.R. You advised and guided Citizen L—, leader of a group of former factory owners. Citizen L— is dead, but you won't slip through our fingers this time for lack of evidence!'

"Believe me, Masha, I drew a blank. I listened to this gibberish without comprehending a thing. I told my interrogator I'd never even been remotely connected with the textile industry and certainly hadn't known any L—. He called me a liar and read again from his folder, 'In such and such a year, on such and such a date, Citizen L— went to Avinov's house and stayed an hour and ten minutes. He returned ten days later carrying a big parcel, which he left after staying an hour and twenty minutes.'

"It was then that I suddenly remembered those *valenki*! The whole accusation seemed so ludicrous that I burst out laughing. 'Yes, yes,' I cried, 'I remember now: it's true that my wife knew L—. He made us two pairs of *valenki* and brought them to our house. I saw him only twice—once when he measured our feet and again when he delivered the goods. I'd simply forgotten all about it.' At this my inquisitor leaned forward, 'That's a bit too thick! Forgotten! D'you expect me to believe such tales? I'm surprised that a man of your standing should descend to such lies!' "

Nika shut his eyes for an instant and sighed wearily: "This went on, Masha, hour after hour for three consecutive nights. In the end, instead of a hearing, they gave me ten years hard labor in the Ural mines—à propos des bottes, as the French would say. I was right there in the mines, breaking stones, when of a sudden they picked me up and put me on the train back to Moscow. It was then that I was petrified. I knew that Vyshinsky was presiding over purge trials. I wondered whether I was to be taken to prison, or called as a witness, or tried in court. I never could have guessed that they were sending me home to you."

His dark eyes were shining with happiness, but in my mind's eye, I kept seeing what they must have done to him, and tears began to roll down my cheeks. "Masha, you're thinking of that wretched tooth again! You're like that lady in the French Revolution. They said a gale couldn't knock her down, but a puff of wind blew her over."

I began to cry: "That's not a puff of wind, Nika, your tooth knocked out! It's an outrage! What's going to become of us?"

He put his arms around me and held me until my own heart had grown quiet again, until my whole mind turned to the bliss of having him home.

Like many others during Stalin's purges, Krylenko came to a violent end. After Yagoda, former head of the N.K.V.D., was executed along with many of his subordinates, Krylenko realized what lay in store for him. He prepared himself. When the secret police came for him, they found him locked in his study. They broke down the door, only to be attacked by those ferocious hounds that once confronted Basil. Krylenko himself stood behind his desk with a loaded pistol in each hand. They say he killed a dozen or more before he was finally shot down. Krylenko was indeed a man who knew no fear.

CHAPTER FOURTEEN

❧❧❧

Life under the Soviets continued to be highly inconsistent. In 1934, barely a year after Nika's release from the Ural mines, the N.K.V.D. appointed him head of the Economic Planning Department of the Ridder Combine in the far Eastern Altai Mountains. Characteristically, this assignment was made in the form of an offer of a purely voluntary nature: Nika might take it or leave it. Yet we all knew that a refusal would lead to prison and perhaps even to death. Even on principle I did not want Nika to refuse, for in its way, this would be a worthy and most challenging position.

I could have gone with him to Siberia, but after a long sifting of pros and cons, we both decided against it. First off, my departure from Moscow would inevitably entail the loss of our room and our last possessions. We couldn't take them with us, and greedy Bolshevik hands were always ready to confiscate on the least pretext. Moreover, we agreed that my presence in the Combine would only handicap Nika: I always appeared drastically out of place in a proletarian milieu. Before long, workers in the Altais would sneeringly refer to "Madame Avinov the aristocrat!" or to "Madame Avinov's Salon!" Heartrending as it was to part with Nika for three whole years, we decided it would be far wiser for me to stay behind in Moscow.

Nika was allowed to write to me. Of course, our correspondence would have to pass under the eye of the N.K.V.D., which scrutinized and weighed our every word. As it turned out, he was also allowed to send me money, but the little he was able to spare proved insufficient to live on. Everything had become frightfully expensive; and besides, I had to help my brother Yuri's ailing widow, and his growing daughter Lyubochka who was staying with me at the time. I also had to feed my faithful former chef Filipich and my maid Natasha, both of whom were grown too old to work. I feared they would perish without me, yet before long, they were all to have to shift for themselves. Soon after Nika's departure, I was graced with what I had dreaded but long expected—a midnight "visit."

Two N.K.V.D. men searched my room, tearing sheets off the bed, ripping the mattresses, and emptying drawers and cupboards while I sat collecting my thoughts and preparing myself for the worst. My mother had always said, "In difficult moments, pray. Never think of yourself. Think of others, and how to help them." All had seemed so clear and easy then, but now that the moment had come, how was I to put her advice into practice? Who were those "others" I had to think of? Why, other prisoners of course!

I remembered a recent conversation with a cousin who had just been released from prison. She told me that gloom and boredom had become agonizing after months in a crowded cell where other half-deranged women brooded, wept, quarreled, and bickered all through the day. Her depressing account was hardly a spur to courage. With a heavy heart, I glanced at the two N.K.V.D. officials. I forced myself to ask the fateful question:

"Must I take my things?"

"Yes. Get ready. We're almost through."

In those days everyone kept a packed suitcase under his bed for just such an emergency. I dragged mine out, opened it, and added ribbons, bits of lace, cambric, thread, and needles to the clothes; tea, sugar, and cigarettes I had already packed. All women like to sew, I thought to myself; all women, even prisoners, are interested in finery. Perhaps these odds and ends would draw their minds away from themselves and their misfortunes. My mother's advice, prying my thoughts away from my own misfortune and concentrating them on the unfortunates I was about to join, helped me over that last difficult half-hour. I even felt calm and composed as I followed the two men to the black N.K.V.D. car waiting at the corner.

Dawn had not yet broken. Through the slats across the car window I could see empty streets under a waning moon. During our ride, I continued to peer out at the sleeping, tranquil city. I still felt undisturbed. But when the car passed through those heavy, forbidding iron doors that slowly screeched open and then clanged closed behind us, my heart began to pound. We had entered the dreaded Butyrka Prison.

"Get out!" The command was gruff. The butt of a rifle made it emphatic.

Dragging my heavy suitcase, I followed an armed soldier down a few steps to a damp corridor. He opened a padlocked door and pushed me into a large dark cell. A nauseating stench hit my nostrils. By the weary light of a small electric bulb high up on the ceiling, I distinguished groups of figures lying on shelves and benches and on the concrete floor; their limbs crumpled in strange positions, snorting, snoring, and moaning in their sleep. Suddenly a head arose. "What? A new one? But there's no room! Lie down there in the corner by the door."

In the corner stood the communal toilet, known in all Russian prisons as "Parasha." It exuded a dark and evil-smelling fluid through a crack in the floor. Was I to lie in that? I braced myself, and arranged my suitcase flat on the floor, so as to cover as much of the wetness as possible. While I stood over it, still hesitating, a small white figure rose from a bench in the opposite corner and beckoned to me so as not to attract attention.

I had to thread my way among prostrate bodies—strangely postured corpses they seemed to me—in order to reach her. I then saw that she was a nun, clad in white, with a very pale face and enormous dark eyes. "Let me bless you," she whispered. "Don't be afraid. God is everywhere."

Tears welled in my eyes as I kissed her hand. "Not afraid, not afraid," I muttered, hardly knowing what I was saying. "But it's the first time I . . ."

"Yes, my dear. There is a first time for everyone. Now go and rest." I returned to my corner, lay down, partly on my suitcase and partly in that foul dampness, and fell into an exhausted sleep.

Next morning, cramped and cold but somehow rested, I awoke to a reality that made me long again for sleep. The postured corpses of the night before were sitting up now, stretching, scratching, and shouting at each other. The cell door clanged open. Two women grasped for the heavy pail of steaming water and the few loaves of stale black bread the guard pushed in at them. "Get up! Tea! Tea!"

As the last of them came awake, they noticed me, and jeers broke out from all sides: "Look! Look at *her*. We don't know her—no. A new one! Ah! an aristocrat! Her ladyship with the enormous suitcase! A landowner, no doubt, come home from her estates—" Hostile glances raked me and more derisive laughter split the air. It all hurt—hurt unbearably. But then, just as I thought I might break down in hysterical sobbing, another voice reached me.

"Shut up! What do all of you know about aristocrats? I know plenty! I used to work for them. She's one of them all right! And you want to know how I know? None of *you* would've lain down in that foul mess she slept in without squealing your heads off and waking us all up. But she did! I watched her. She crossed herself and lay right down in it without a whimper of complaint."

My unexpected champion was a plump old woman who grinned at me pleasantly. With a gesture of her hand she invited me to sit beside her at the table, where an angular woman with a determined jaw—Katya, the cell leader—was pouring hot water into tin cups. Despite the older woman's friendliness, I felt dazed and timid, and very nearly ashamed of my good clothes and heavy suitcase. In the hopes of redeeming the impression I had created, I took some tea and sugar out of my suitcase and went to the table.

Jibes and jeers rang out again. One woman squinted at me venomously, "Accursed capitalist!" she hissed. "Sugar! Even tea?"

"May I offer you some—?"

Her coarse answer, with "Lady Bountiful" added to it, was worse than a slap in the face. Women laughed. Women made faces at me. Women stuck out their tongues. In the midst of the clamor, the echo of my mother's voice came to me—"Masha, Masha, control yourself"—and I struggled to get a hold of myself.

The nun in white rose to her feet and again beckoned to me: "Come here, my dear. Please give me some of your tea, and a bit of sugar. It will be a nice treat."

I went to her, unable to speak. If I'd said a word, the tears would have started. She patted my hand, while searching my face with her beautiful understanding eyes: "Don't be afraid, dear. Everything will be all right."

I saw now how old she was. She was a tiny woman, with a face that seemed carved from ivory. Her large dark eyes, inherited from her Georgian ancestors, could melt into sweetness or flash with scorn, but always with an indomitable spirit shining in them.

This was the famous Abbess, Mother Tamara. Her brother, high up in the Communist hierarchy, had pulled strings in her behalf so that the wardens treated her with a certain deference. Two other nuns—slender young girls with mother-of-pearl complexions—had been allowed to remain with her. They hovered near the reverend mother like two seraphs ministering to her needs. In one corner of the cell, they had spread white sheets over the dirty boards, and there the Abbess sat all day, reading the Bible, praying, or receiving "visitors," as she called her cellmates. All were anxious to have their chat with her—the strong-jawed cell leader, the hysterical brilliant Jewish actress, the peasant woman, the intellectuals, even the prostitutes. She had a gift of approaching each woman in a special way and radiating such light and kindness, such faith and wisdom, that everyone in the cell worshiped her.

My first evening there, I sat beside Mother Tamara in her corner. The white sheet was spread neatly under us, and her belongings were neatly arranged to one side. It was an oasis in the midst of squalor.

"Do you feel better?" she asked me with concern. My affirmative answer must have sounded dubious, for she quickly added: "You had quite a shock this morning. It's understandable."

"But what, please, *what* is understandable about it? I came here with an open heart. Why did they want to throw insults and laugh at me? Aren't we all in the same predicament?" My voice broke. I was close to tears again; but Mother Tamara's quiet voice was soothing:

"My dear, I come from the same world as you. I know just how you feel. But life has taught me many lessons. You're not in the same predicament that they are. Not yet. You've been educated into a privileged position, not only of wealth but of the old traditions of nobility, faith, and goodwill. From childhood you've been taught that your duty lies in sharing whatever you have, in helping those who are not so fortunate. And you no doubt brought out your tea and sugar from motives of philanthropy."

"Oh," I protested, "I hate philanthropy. I hate everything it implies. There's something mawkish and false about that word."

"Wait. Let me put it this way. Say you are traveling in a comfortable sleeping car, through an impoverished country where people have to travel on foot or in rickety carts. You see life through a polished window. You are sorry for those people outside; you rightfully want to help them. Perhaps you even do so. But however good your intentions, you still have to step down from your sleeping car in order to help. And people resent condescension. You yourself have noticed that philanthropy never breeds real gratitude. Verbal thanks, perhaps, but not the real bond that should exist between giver and receiver."

I nodded in agreement, remembering Grandpapa's home for old ladies and my own discomforting term as manager. Mother Tamara went on, with her dark eyes fixed upon me:

"It has all been quite natural up to now. This morning, you were a privileged outsider, trying to be kind. But in their eyes you were not one of the downtrodden and humiliated. They judged you at your face value, as a Lady Bountiful, a superior being. All these women, even the harlots, murderesses, and thieves, carry a deep misery within them. They hide it under a display of arrogant rudeness and contempt, just as you saw them do this morning. But remember, they are—all of them—suffering, just as you are. And when they feel that you're suffering with them, that you're their equal, so to speak, everything will be changed. You will easily find ways to be of comfort to them."

But I shook my head in dismay: "I've read about such wretched people . . ."

"Oh, books!" Mother Tamara shrugged her thin shoulders. "Life is the best and the most revealing book. But one must have the golden keys to unlock its binding—love and faith. I'm sure you must already have both in your heart."

Despondently, I shook my head again: "My terrible handicap is my love of beauty and my equal hatred of ugliness. These damp gray walls, those awful faces, dirty clothes, and tangled hair— everything here simply crushes me and makes me feel sick. I've never understood the point of Dostoevsky's 'digging for diamonds in refuse'! Why bother to, when life can be so beautiful!"

I buried my face in my hands for an instant. When I looked up again, there was a far-off look in Mother Tamara's eyes.

"There you were wrong. Dostoevsky was a genius. He knew the strange and honest depths of the human heart. But I wasn't thinking of him—I had someone else in mind. Before I took the orders of the Holy Church, I was a young and high-spirited girl—much too high-spirited. I loved music and the arts, above all else. There was a saying of Leonardo da Vinci that much impressed me then— something about finding beauty everywhere. What was it? Oh, how sad to be so old and be forgetting things . . ."

My face brightened: "That must be his famous advice to his pupils: 'Learn to look at monsters and hideous objects, at patterns of dampness on old walls, and you will find many beautiful things, *cosi molti belli.*' Oh, how wonderful that you still remember that saying! I wrote quite a good sonnet about it once."

Mother Tamara smiled: "If you've been able to write sonnets, you'll be able to put our maxim into practice. Find the hidden beauty."

"But where?" I whispered. "In that prostitute over there, for instance, where is it?"

"Have you forgotten that a memory of its Creator remains in every human soul? Find *that*. Approach people in the right way. Choose the right tune for the instrument you approach: what is written for the piano often doesn't suit the violin. You are in new surroundings now. You must adapt yourself. Do what God intended you to do in this life on earth. You'll learn, you'll grow; and that should be the aim of every soul that still has flesh around it."

Despite the note of sternness in Mother Tamara's last words, I fell asleep comforted that night. When I awoke next morning, she called me to her side again: "Prepare yourself for a shock. We are all going to the bathhouse."

"The bathhouse? Why should I be shocked, Mother?"

"You will soon find out. Don't worry now. I just wanted to prepare you, so hold yourself well in hand."

When the order came to prepare for the bath, I saw with surprise that the other women began packing everything they owned. Someone explained to me that the cell must remain empty. During our absence, it would be cleaned and disinfected with a torch to kill off lice and bedbugs.

Mother Tamara and her two seraphs led our procession. The rest of us followed in pairs, laden like camels. We filed out into an immense courtyard. The March snow was melting, and ravens flapped their thin wings amidst the bare branches of dark trees. We tramped past high, gray walls with heavily barred windows, and down into a basement where the damp bathhouse awaited us, smelling of sweat and disinfectant.

The bath's ground plan was in the shape of a letter T: first was an antechamber where prisoners undressed (the left arm of the T), then the bathhouse proper (the base of the T), then to the right, a back chamber in which the prisoners dressed again. The Abbess passed directly into this last room. She had been given permission not to disrobe in front of others, as this was against the rules of the Orthodox Church for persons of her standing. But the two young nuns had to go with the rest of us.

I was one of the last to enter the antechamber. I stopped aghast, rooted to the threshold. No wonder Mother Tamara had given me that warning! Stark naked women were handing their clothes to four young soldiers who stood at the open door of a disinfection room. Quite unconcerned, the women laughed and joked with the grinning guards. "Hurry! Hurry and take your clothes off," they shouted to me. "The boys are about to shut the door." I shrugged, obeyed, and followed the others.

The sight reminded me of the *Walpurgisnacht* scene from Goethe's *Faust*. The bathhouse was filled with clouds of steam through which naked women ran, jumped, and danced. Here they were shrieking at the top of their lungs; there laughing and singing to the melody of clanking pails, splashing water, and hissing steam. Here were models for all the nudes I'd seen represented in art, reveling in brisk activity after the cramped quarters of our cell. There were lush Rubenses with reddish tresses, lean Goyas dark and swarthy, hideous Dürers with bony limbs and sagging breasts; and of course, the pre-Raphaelite nuns with their loose golden hair. It was a sight to be locked in one's subconscious, only to be let loose in raucous nightmares.

After half an hour, a fat, elderly man with a grinning, clean-shaven face bustled into our midst. "Quiet," he squawked in a falsetto voice, "and out with you! The next batch is waiting." This benevolent eunuch herded our whole flock toward the back chamber, joking and slapping at naked buttocks. No one seemed to mind him. The women wrung out their drenched hair, over-turned buckets, and ran giggling past him to the door.

The back chamber was a large room with benches lining the

whitewashed walls. Mother Tamara was moving up and down making signs of the cross to dispel any devils that might be lurking about. The walls were covered with scratched or penciled inscriptions: "Curse you Communists for sending me to Siberia!" "Life, love, hope, goodbye forever!" "Vengeance! Some day you'll pay for my misery!" and so on. Mother Tamara suddenly grasped my arm: "Look, oh look! I don't know how to bear it, it's terrible!"

I followed her eyes to an open door where four young soldiers were now handing out our disinfected clothes. In front of them stood the two young nuns, their naked bodies gleaming like rosy shells, their eyes modestly averted from the men's appraising smirks. From their manner, one would think they were in church. Mother Tamara's usually serene face was trembling with indignant repulsion. The scene did seem sacrilegious, but at the same time, ludicrously ribald. Before I knew it, I was speaking through fits of stifled laughter: "Dear Mother—don't b–be distressed—it's not their fault—What can they do? It's their only chance in life to have their bodies admired."

It was disgraceful of me. Even as I stroked her hand to comfort her, I feared I had lost her friendship. But a whimsical smile passed across her strained face: "Well, perhaps. Perhaps you're right. It's better to laugh than cry, only I'm an old woman, you know, and a nun."

She remained my friend and mentor throughout my stay in that cell.

One day we had a newcomer: "Ophelia." She floated in a vision of ethereal beauty: tall and slender, with golden hair falling to her waist and enormous, shining violet eyes. This was Princess Varenka. I had often seen her in Moscow drawing rooms, surrounded by enraptured admirers. Later, working in the British Embassy where visitors raved over her beauty, she received many offers of marriage. She could have married anyone she chose, and by now, could have been living safely in England. But instead, she fell in love and married a somewhat shady Russian. Shortly after, she was arrested for having been a "spy" in a foreign embassy. I knew there had been strains of insanity in her father's family, and that many of her relatives were afflicted with strange idiosyncrasies. Varenka's was a morbid fear of insects. Now she stopped in the middle of the

cell and, seeing a crawling procession of vermin making its way
down the wall, she dropped to the floor in a dead faint.

We laid her down on a shelf in the corner. She recovered her
senses, but refused to eat or drink and would not sleep. All our
ministrations were to no avail. She even refused to speak. Lying
motionless, she simply stared at the floor for three days. She
literally began to fade away before our eyes. Katya, our cell leader,
entreated to have Varenka removed to the prison hospital, but the
officials scoffed: "Nothing the matter with her! She's faking."

Finally we all decided a unanimous hunger strike was the only
effective way of influencing the prison authorities. Katya had just
called for the strike when, as luck would have it, the guards came
to deliver our food parcels from home. These were our source of
provisions for days and even weeks to come, but undaunted, Katya
decided on the only practical plan of action:

"We will eat everything we have tonight, and start our strike in
the morning!"

"Look at this beautiful ham," moaned one woman. "I haven't
seen any ham in ages . . ."

"See these eggs, these hard-boiled eggs," sighed another.
"They'd've sustained me for a whole week at least . . ."

A third woman, Marya by name, was counting her meatballs
meticulously. "No, really, Katya, this strike is idiotic." She gave an
arrogant snicker. "It's everyone for himself in this ugly world, I
say. If we stick together, we'll only wind up starving."

Katya glanced at her with contempt: "Shame on you! Solidarity
is our only weapon. What happened to Varenka over there could
happen to any one of us. You aren't always so totally sane either!
Suppose a few more of us get deranged; where will we be then?"

Marya stared back at her furiously: "I know where we'll be
tomorrow. In the dungeon, on bread and water."

"All right! So let's gorge ourselves tonight," laughed Katya,
through a mouthful of sausage. The rest of us, chewing hard, joined
her in her determined feast.

In the morning, the female guard who brought hot water and
stale loaves of bread was met with shouts: "Go away! No bread!
No water! We're on a hunger strike!" She stood glaring at us from
the threshold, and an empty tin can bounced off the door, some

inches from her head. Amid shrieks of laughter, she turned and fled, slamming the door behind her. One of the former prostitutes who'd been standing near the door snatched up a piece of bread, but Katya seized her, tore the bread out of her hands, and threw it into the toilet:

"None of that! Solidarity, remember?"

Dinner time came. Large kettles of the food that we normally despised were pushed through the door. That evening, the smell seemed delicious. "Take it away, take it away," shouted several hysterical voices. Tin plates were thrown down and battered on the floor. Lynx-eyed Katya searched the benches and shelves for scraps that might have been concealed, but there were none. Without food, we soon began to feel the cold, and shivering, we drew together and waited for something to happen. We didn't have to wait long. Outside in the corridor, heavy footsteps approached our cell. We heard keys rattling, and the door flew open. The Prison Governor himself stood on the threshold. This man, Adamson by name, was renowned throughout Moscow as the brutal "Scourge of Butyrka." He was a broad-shouldered redhead with a fiery mustache. One hand was ready at the revolver on his hip, and his bloodshot eyes surveyed us, waiting for someone to speak. Katya faced him without flinching.

"Chief—." Her voice was drowned in his roar:

"You shut up! The rest of you, you tell me—what's the meaning of this hunger strike? I'll show you; I'll teach you a lesson you'll never forget!"

Katya bravely stood her ground: "But Varenka is mad. She's dying. It's inhuman to leave her here. She ought to be taken to the prison hospital!"

"And who are you to tell me that? You're a slut! Are you a doctor too? I tell you she's as sane as I am! She's nothing but a malingering make-believe . . ."

A general gasp silenced him. Exquisitely, slowly, Varenka rose from her bench, stepped down from it, and came toward him with a vacant stare. Her curls hung loose over her pale, drawn face pierced by her enormous violet eyes. Falling on her knees before the scowling Governor, she stretched out her hands in a gesture of supplication. In the awed silence that enveloped the cell, her soft voice could be heard by everyone: "I am the greatest sinner on earth. The Communists—above all the N.K.V.D.—are saints. Holy, holy saints!"

For a long moment, Adamson stared at her. Then he stepped back and murmured over his shoulder to a guard: "Yes, I see. She *is* mad! Take her away."

Once Varenka had been removed, he turned to us and again raised his voice to a roar: "You! I'll teach you to behave! All of you! I'm going to disperse you all into different cells, and no more food parcels for two weeks! As for you, Katya, you're going to the dungeon for a week of bread and water!"

We packed our belongings sadly, kissed, and bade each other goodbye like lifelong friends. Mother Tamara blessed us all. Brave Katya marched off to the dungeon with her head high.

With its two tiers of sleeping shelves, my new cell was larger and brighter than the old one. At first sight it seemed cleaner too, and its inmates more refined. They sat in groups, talking in low voices. When I entered with two other newcomers, they nodded and welcomed us with smiles: "We'd advise you to sleep over here." "There's still a good place near the window."

I sat down between two women and leaned back against the wall. The younger one to my right, dressed in gray, had a thin, intelligent face framed in black curls; the older, to my left, had wonderfully slender hands and bright blue eyes. They had been engrossed in an earnest conversation on Theosophy when I joined them. Now the younger one resumed the thread of their discussion, but the older one interrupted her:

"Wait a minute." She turned to me: "Don't lean against the wall, dear. The bedbugs—see, there's one on your shoulder already." She brought a bit of paper from her pocket, deftly caught the insect, crushed it, and dropped the folded paper on the floor.

The younger woman eyed these proceedings with contempt. "We must live on a higher plane," she said, and would have said more if I hadn't interrupted her with a forced smile:

"Do you mean that even an insect has a right to live, as St. Francis or some Buddhist monk might say?"

The two women beamed with delight: "Oh, so you've studied Buddhism? How wonderful!"

I told them I had read a good deal about Hinduism and Theosophy, adding that one of Russia's leading Theosophists was a good friend of mine. At this they all but clapped their hands with joy:

"Oh, what luck! One more of us! We will make a real Theosophist out of you!"

"I hope not!" said a sharp voice that cut through their exultations; and a hand brushed my hair to catch a crawling insect.

Standing over me was a woman, with a white kerchief on her head and a face that might have come from an ancient icon. She looked at the two Theosophists with disapproval. "I hope not!" she repeated forcefully, and looked down at me: "These are kind women, kind but erring. Don't listen to them. Everything your soul needs is to be found in the teachings of our Holy Orthodox Church. Anything else is one of the Devil's snares. Beware!" she repeated, and brushed another insect off my neck.

I wondered whether she was referring to the Devil or to the vermin. Body lice and bedbugs seemed to be everywhere. The walls were streaked with brown and red lines, like an animated map! The sight of it made my skin crawl. The younger Theosophist saw my discomfort. "Pay no attention to them," she said with a condescending smile. "Everything in life is *Maya*—illusion. Only the lotus growing in your heart is real."

"These are all too real!" I cried, trying to brush more creeping bugs from my skirt. "Oh, God, what are we to do?"

"Pray!" said the woman in the white kerchief. "This is the way of the Cross," she added, in a quiet voice.

I spent four months in the Butyrka Prison before I was told it had all been a mistake. I was released without a trial. Luckily, I still had a "home" to return to. My niece Lyubochka had been visiting me at the time of my arrest; and she had been allowed to stay on in—and thus preserve—my room while earning a living copying mechanical blueprints.

Nika had not learned of my imprisonment until a month afterward, when my great friend Nadya Shipov (of whom I will have much to say later) managed to write him about it. She assured him she would try to get me released through the influence of her friends, but she had had to couch her optimism in the most patriotic terms. Letters were treacherous things, since all of them were being censored by the N.K.V.D. When Nika wrote to me after my release, he could express little beyond the nature of his work and the interest he took in it; while I, similarly, could mention nothing of the trials I had just been through.

Of all my problems, the chief one was to find work again. I could hardly have lived off my niece's salary for more than two weeks. Making the rounds of countless offices, I was everywhere met with the familiar rebuff: "Get out! Nothing for you here!" Then one day, as I sat disheartened in my room, the telephone rang and a stranger's voice greeted me:

"Citizeness Avinov, do you need work?"

"Who's speaking?" I asked, breathlessly.

"Never mind. Come to my office tomorrow morning." My caller gave me an address and hung up.

The large office I entered next day was located in the Commissariat of Agriculture. The man behind the desk seemed to be a grim, typical Bolshevik. He greeted me with a curt nod:

"How many foreign languages do you know?"

"Three: French, German, and English."

"Good. Do you know anything about cows and milking machines?"

Before the Revolution, my family had owned a large herd and a model dairy farm. I used to make my own butter and had been awarded a gold medal at an international exhibition. All this I told him, and again he nodded:

"Excellent. Now look at these magazine articles in French, English, and German. Tell me if you can translate them."

I leafed through the three articles. "To be quite honest," I said, "these three articles about milking machines are identical. It would be a waste of money to translate each one separately."

"That's none of your business. Do as you are told—translate each one separately, and you will be paid at the highest rate. I wish you to be properly remunerated."

"Thank you, but—may I ask the reason for your kindness?"

A rather charming smile touched his lips: "Don't thank me. I'm paying a debt. Many years ago your husband did me a great favor."

I wrote Nika to ask him who this mysterious Comrade Vassilyev was, and what Nika had done to earn such gratitude. But Nika's answer only sidestepped the mystery: "I have met so many

Vassilyevs, Ivanovs, and Petrovs in my life that I have no idea who this one is."

Thanks to this covert benefactor, I was given regular translation work. Although money was no longer a problem, those midthirties were dreadful years. Even now I rankle to think of the heartrending frustrations; the longing to be with my Nika; the endless, exhausting hours of work; and worst of all, the ever-present anxiety. Danger lurked everywhere, spoiling for a pretext. Communists did their best to deprive me of my room because I was the wife of an "enemy of the people." I had to fight this charge personally to avoid being turned out into the street. No sooner had I silenced one accuser, than another would try to take over my room or even my possessions. And these perpetual harassments only seemed the lowering omens of some final, crushing blow.

At one point, I fully believed that blow had fallen. It was the week when income tax agents were scheduled to make their assessments. Each vied with the other to extort the maximum from former intellectuals still holding jobs. Three such agents inspected my room and asked me insinuating questions: Did I ride in automobiles? Did I go to the theater? Did I buy new clothes? What did I eat? They asked me what sort of translations I was doing, how many pages a day I could finish, and how much I was paid. I knew that the maximum I should be assessed was from ten to fifteen rubles. But after putting their heads together, they filled out a form and showed me the total: ten thousand rubles!

"But that's preposterous," I cried.

They simply smiled: "You must pay in full on Monday. Failure to do so will mean the confiscation of everything you have, right down to the last handkerchief."

I held myself very erect. "Very well," I said, "we shall see!"

"Yes, we shall see," they grinned back, and departed.

I fell sobbing on my bed. Even if they let me keep the room, Nika would find it bare when he came home—even his priceless books would be gone. Worse still, there was virtually nowhere to turn for help: it was already Friday, and all government offices would be closed for the next two days. Those agents had clearly known what they were doing!

Anna, an old friend of ours, stopped by that afternoon. She had once worked for Nika, and was now a secretary to the Commissar of Finance. Anna listened to my story, aghast: "But this is crazy! You could never raise such a sum even if you did have the time!"

"No! And there's nothing we can do about it!"

"Oh yes, there is! We can fight! Where is your courage and faith? Even better, where are your friends? Get on the telephone, and tell them to come here and carry away everything they can for safekeeping."

Those close to us came to the rescue *en masse*. Men filled dispatch cases with priceless family icons and weighted their pockets with silver and valuable bibelots. They put on Nika's clothes under their own, while the women wore my blouses, skirts, and underwear over or under their own dresses. Before long everyone began to look like a distended caricature of himself, and we were all dissolving into hysterical laughter. We waited for dusk. Then each of them stole away separately into the night, for of course Communist lodgers in the house were on the lookout. Later still, Anna returned, beaming: "The Lord be praised, you're saved! It's a miracle! Wait until I tell you!"

After leaving me to call my friends, she had returned to the Commissariat of Finance. The Commissar had been about to address a meeting of the Finance Committee, but seeing the anxious look on his secretary's face, he came to find out what was the matter. Anna told him of my plight. He appeared incredulous; he told her he knew of Nika and, moreover, of Nika's magnificent job of handling the Ridder Combine. "Who committed this outrage?" he asked Anna, and her reply was brief: "Your agents, Comrade Commissar."

The Commissar grew quite red in the face, "The Committee is waiting for me. You stay here. When you see me give you the sign, go into the next room and pick up the telephone."

Anna said she waited there in the large conference hall, praying all the time. After the Commissar had finished his address to the Committee, she saw him go to a telephone and speak quietly. At a quick sign from him, she rushed into the next room and picked up a receiver. A man's voice at the other end answered:

"The Commissar's secretary? All right, take this down . . . By order of the Commissar, Citizeness Avinov should be informed that her tax assessment is ten rubles. The three agents who called on her are to be dismissed and jailed."

It was truly extraordinary how, time and again, I came to be helped by the affection and respect Nika had inspired in the most unlikely quarters. Yet he himself was never able to benefit. The term of his "voluntary" mission to the Ridder Combine had expired long since, and still he hadn't returned home. I inquired at the N.K.V.D., and was told that his return was no concern of the Central Bureau. The N.K.V.D. of the Altai District would have to make arrangements. It was clear to me that Nika had been unable locally to obtain his clearance and release. I decided to request an interview with Vyshinsky the Attorney General.

This was the same Vyshinsky who was later to serve as Soviet Ambassador to the United Nations. He was a truly sinister man who had attained his high position thanks to Stalin's Purges. In order to satisfy his bloodthirsty Premier, Vyshinsky had condemned many hundreds of people to be shot for crimes they had never committed. His road to power was literally paved with human lives, but in the United Nations he was received with the personal admiration and honors due an Ambassador. Pushkin's bitter verse comes to mind: "O pitiful race of men, worthy of tears and laughter: high priests of the impermanent, worshipers of success . . ."

I don't recall how I obtained the appointment with Vyshinsky. I seem to have had no particular qualms about it, but when I actually entered his office, my hands grew cold with apprehension.

He sat behind an enormous desk about ten or twelve feet wide. It must have served as a precautionary barricade between himself and his visitor, although I can't imagine how a visitor could have done him much harm after being so thoroughly and unceremoniously frisked by Vyshinsky's guards.

Vyshinsky had a strong, handsome face and very cold eyes. Impeccably dressed, he reminded me more of a pre-Revolutionary pillar of society than of a Bolshevik nabob. He heard me out politely, without interrupting; and when I was through, answered in a level voice:

"You did well to come to me. The N.K.V.D. in the Altai has no business detaining your husband beyond his rightful term. I know Avinov's reputation. He's an honest, talented man who knows his métier perfectly. He has been extremely useful to us."

As usual, I could not repress my bitterness: "If he has been honest and useful, then why has this honest, useful worker spent half his life in prison?"

Vyshinsky shrugged: "That is neither here nor there. You may go. I will issue orders, and he'll soon be back."

The future diplomat, I must say, did keep his promise: ten days later, Nika was back with me for the first time in three years.

CHAPTER FIFTEEN

❧§❧

Before coming to Nika's eighth and final arrest, I would like to add a few strokes to the image of him I have tried to recreate. He was at times difficult to live with, but even more difficult to be without; a man tenderly loving, but so detached that part of him seemed always to slip through my fingers. Perhaps a few brief episodes will give an insight into the selfless modesty that was so much a part of his nature.

During our earlier married life, Nika labored for two whole years over a book on political self-government. But instead of having it published once he'd finished it, he gave it to a young man who needed to submit a long political thesis for his master's degree. Being young and terribly ambitious for Nika, I of course grew indignant. "You did all the work, and now he gets the reward! That book would have won you such honors in the literary world!"

Nika only smiled: "Dearest, I don't *want* honors in the literary world. For me, the reward lies in the work itself, and besides, this book will start my young friend on his career."

Before the First World War, the Tsar visited Moscow to inspect a *Zemstvos* exhibition. Nika was selected as the guide to escort Nicolas II. "Aren't you nervous?" I asked Nika, "about having such a long tête-à-tête with the Emperor himself?"

A boyish smile lighted up his whole countenance: "No, I'm delighted! Of course he is the Emperor, and I'm his loyal subject; but he's also a man like the rest of us. I've heard he has a very engaging personality, and is rather shy."

Later, I was told the Emperor spent a whole fascinated hour at the Exhibition. Afterward, he said to one of his staff: "This Avinov is a brilliant man. He has such a charming manner, too; very natural and simple. I felt quite at ease with him."

In all the years I shared with Nika, only once did I hear him speak with pride of his own achievement. In 1917, by commission of the Provisional Government, he prepared the electoral law that was to choose the Constituent Assembly. The Assembly, of course, was only one day old when Lenin kicked it out of existence, but Nika's electoral law remained on file. In 1919, the Weimar Republic adopted it as the basis for the Reichstag elections. "My law!" Nika cried when we heard the news.

"They took it just as it stands, with no amendments, without a single paragraph changed. Coming from the Germans, that really is a tribute!" His dark eyes shone with happiness. I was delighted for his sake, though I personally shared Flaubert's view that universal suffrage could be a curse. I hated to imagine drunken soldiers, ignorant workmen, and vengeful peasants deciding the fate of my country.

After the Revolution, when Nika was in charge of the Kooperatop (fuel cooperative), he worked harder than ever. He rose at seven and wolfed down a large breakfast, since he seldom had time enough for lunch. My old maid Natasha came to me one morning in a state of indignation.

"Imagine, Madame, this morning your husband was up at *six* to pile a cord of firewood onto a sledge. Then he went and dragged it through the streets himself. Think of it, a man of his position, known to everyone, doing such labor! It's disgraceful!"

I asked Nika why one of his men couldn't have done the job, and he said: "That wood was for old Madame Duvernoy, the former professor at the Conservatory. Poor soul, she's been freezing in that miserable room of hers. If one of my men had pulled the load over there, it would have looked like charity. I felt it would be more of a respectful tribute to her if I did it myself."

During the periodic weeks or months he spent in prison, the most disreputable looking visitors would appear suddenly at my door. They would knock just to say, "I came to thank you for your husband. He was my guardian angel when we were in the same cell . . ." During Nika's long absence in the Altai Mountains, I was called to the telephone one evening. "Citizeness Avinov," a stranger's voice said, "I have just returned from the Ridder Combine, and I want to tell you that your husband is in good health and is doing a splendid job." After a slight hesitant pause, the voice added: "I want you to know I'm grateful that fate has brought me into contact with such a man."

There was a note of authority in that voice that couldn't have belonged to an ordinary Bolshevik official. "May I ask whom I am speaking to?"

"It doesn't matter." The wire went dead.

A few weeks later I heard a possible solution to the riddle, when one of the workers at the Ridder Combine came to see me. He told me how much Nika was doing to improve the plant's efficiency. "And he's so popular with the management and the miners. As a specialist, Avinov of course gets an ample allotment of clothing and food, but he gives it all away. 'Imagine!' one of those unfortunate miners said to me, 'He gave me his waterproof boots, when he could have sold them for a fortune! It's hard to believe such things still happen. God bless him!' " Giving me a few moments to fight back tears, my guest added: "When Comrade Kirov, the President of the Leningrad Soviet, came to inspect the plant, he insisted on Avinov showing him around in person."

I told my visitor about the mysterious telephone call. "Could it have been Kirov?"

My guest nodded vigorously: "That's just the sort of thing he would do. Despite his adherence to Communism, he's a high-minded and just man. Stalin hates him, you know."

My visitor's fears for Kirov's life soon came true. He was assassinated, supposedly by a "White" officer, but the N.K.V.D. was actually responsible. Immediately afterward, Stalin liquidated every one who had been in on the secret, including their chief, Yakoda.

It was on a dark night in November of 1937, during the very first days of Yezhov's—the new N.K.V.D. head's—infamous purge, that Nika and I had our last midnight awakening. There came a loud knock on the door, and in stepped a policeman (the police force had been amalgamated with the N.K.V.D. some time previously). He was followed by our janitor, Ivan Petrovich, with hot, fright-

ened tears glistening in his eyes. Instantly I realized that he knew
something we didn't about this particular arrest! I heard the policeman saying, "Citizen Avinov, come with me."

Nika remained calm and self-possessed. He got up at once and
stood tall and erect. He looked much the same man I fell in love
with thirty-one years before. There were only a few lines in his
face, and a few streaks of gray in his dark hair. I had heard it said,
when the worst misfortune strikes, one feels no pain at first: I found
this to be true. I felt nothing but a gradual tightening around the
heart. I glanced at Nika, and his look seemed to convey all he might
have said: Goodbye; be strong, God bless you. . . . He didn't
utter a word as I kissed and blessed him. A moment later, along
with Ivan Petrovich and the policeman, he was gone.

CHAPTER SIXTEEN

❧

For me, there was no knocking on doors this time—there were none left to knock on. I had a dual and secret task: on the one hand, I kept alert for any force, good or evil, that would set my husband free. On the other, I probed into myself to seek an ever-stronger spiritual link with Nika. Again and again I turned to his picture on my desk as to our icon. His absence strengthened the bond between us, and I clung to my solitary life and tried to live up to the enduring faith he had placed in me.

Three months went by in this fashion. Fortunately I had typing to do, which brought in a modest living and occupied my mind for at least a few hours each day. Friends, trying to boost my morale, told me I should consider myself lucky: other wives whose husbands had disappeared in the Great Purge had been arrested. After three months, I could consider myself out of danger. And one morning, as I sat in my warm wrapper drinking a cup of tea, my heart did give a skip of selfish joy at the thought of such luck—but only a moment later, as I was moving across the room to my typewriter, there came a loud knock at the door.

How well I knew that very special knock, that did not ask but demanded admission! After hearing that sound, no one in Russia would dare keep his door locked, and on opening mine I found what I had expected. A soldier with fixed bayonet was stationed in the corridor. A tall man in gray with the inevitable dispatch case in his hand stepped into my room: his insignia indicated he was a high-ranking official of the N.K.V.D. Of a sudden, I felt as if I might faint, but the spell of giddiness passed. I looked closely at this intruder. An old man he was, with stooping shoulders and a deeply lined face. The skin around his half-closed eyes was heavy and wrinkled; he looked tired. His voice sounded almost gentle:

142

"Sorry to disturb you, Citizeness, I see you're about to get to work. But I must ask you to come with me."

"I quite understand. I'm ready."

"I don't think you are." His slow eyes traveled wearily around the room, resting first on the empty teacup, then on my wrapper: "You will want to pack a few things before we go."

"Oh, everything is packed. I have lived for the last twenty years with a packed suitcase under my bed!"

"I see . . . But you *will* want to dress. So with your permission, I will withdraw for fifteen minutes. The guard will remain outside your door. Please don't try to escape."

I stared in amazement as the door shut very slowly, very quietly, without even a click. I had seen many Bolshevik prosecutors—stern, distant, ominously civil and formal—but never one like this. There seemed to be a touch of pre-Revolutionary courtliness about him.

I dressed swiftly and hurriedly swallowed another cup of tea. The prosecutor returned, bowed me out of my room, then pad-locked the door and sealed it with red tape. We descended the stairs to the street; the soldier followed, treading heavily on the steps above us. I felt as I had when my father and I left Kot-chemirovo for the last time: never again; this must be the end. . . .

It was the last week in March. A tang of spring and thawing earth hung, bittersweet, in the air. As we drove swiftly through the streets, patches of melting snow glistened under the mild sun, and bedraggled little boys stood on street corners selling nosegays of mimosa. Greedily I took in those last glimpses of outdoor Moscow: they would haunt me for days to come.

The car stopped at a side door of the Lubyanka, headquarters of the N.K.V.D. Its magnificent facade inlaid with yellow marble belied the interrogation chambers and execution cellars within. The building was near the spot where in the sixteenth century Ivan the Terrible had built his own prison, complete with vast dungeons in which Chief Warden Malyuta Skuratov tortured and killed the enemies of his Tsar. Muscovites believed the Lubyanka to be haunted and avoided walking that street after dark.

An elevator brought us to the third floor. Courteous as ever, the prosecutor motioned me to a chair in front of his desk, sat down himself, and produced a file. "Your husband," he said, "has confessed his crimes to our chief, to Comrade Yezhov himself. So now, will you please tell me how he committed them. Tell everything you know about his criminal activities." He spoke in a flat and colorless voice, without looking at me; as if repeating a lesson by rote.

How strange our reactions can be! I felt wholly indifferent as to my own fate, but intensely intrigued by that tired old man. I was always saddened and a bit embarrassed to see someone lie, and I wanted to make this prosecutor understand that I pitied, but did not despise him.

"Citizen," I said. "You are getting on in years and I'm no longer young, either. We both know why I have been called here. Let's not, then, waste your time, but instead look at things as they are. I realize that you are obliged to bring up these lies, but I'm equally sure that you know my husband is innocent."

Before the prosecutor could answer, another officer, who must have been listening at the door, stormed into the room. This was a more typical N.K.V.D. official, in regulation red breeches and blue tunic. His heavy face framed a pair of cruel eyes; his torso was muscular and thick-set. "How dare you speak like that?" he shouted at me. "We always arrest the right person. We never make mistakes!"

At that point, I had nothing to lose but my temper.

"You never make mistakes, do you? How about your former chief, Yakoda, who tortured and killed for twelve years before getting shot by your own N.K.V.D.! If you know anything about history, let me tell you that the Borgias were angels compared to him!" He opened his mouth to say something, but I was furious: "In any other country, my husband would have been an honored citizen, but here he's arrested and jailed, over and over again, without proof! For no reason at all! You send cognac, food, and radio messages to Papanin and his crew on their iceberg near the North Pole because they are 'heroes' who can advertise your government, but you have no mercy or even justice for quiet men like my husband. Shame on you! *Shame!*"

The N.K.V.D. official had a point or two to make, but the prosecutor put an end to our interview with a voice of cold authority:

"Comrade Gorin, go back where you belong."

Reluctantly, Comrade Gorin turned on his heel and stomped out of the room. When the door had banged shut behind him, the prosecutor lit a cigarette and shook his head at me:

"You shouldn't talk like that. It will do you no good."

"I know. I'm sorry to embarrass you, but I'm glad he heard some of the truth for once."

He gazed at me for a while in silence, sizing me up with those tired eyes of his. "I see you're an idealist," he said at length.

"By that, do you mean someone who believes in God, in truth, nobility, and beauty? Yes, I am. And I hope to be one until I die!"

He heaved a sigh. "You are fortunate to have any faith left. I have long since ceased believing in anything."

"What, not even in your work? I pity you!"

He stared for an instant into space, and then quickly changed the topic. "I would imagine you refuse to sign this?" He pushed a piece of paper toward me.

"I do."

"Have you any cigarettes?"

"No. I forgot them at home."

"Money?"

"Yes. I took every kopek I had—why?"

I thought I saw a smile at the corner of his mouth: "Give it to me. I will buy you cigarettes and exchange the rest for prison chips in your name. Otherwise, it will be a long time before you can buy anything at the Commissary, and you know what prison food is like."

Incredible as it may seem, he escorted me downstairs, gave me the chips and ten packs of cigarettes and, with a kindly "Good luck," handed me over to a guard. For a moment I remembered Nika's saying that such people are meant to show that kindness can be found even where one least expects it. A wave of intense happiness swept through me; I said to myself, This cruel new road may lead me back to Nika. But I lost him again in the long corridors of the Lubyanka, as I plodded along with my heavy suitcase behind the armed guard.

That same evening, I was transferred to the dark and now all-too-familiar Butyrka Prison, where I was to spend nine months.

During the first week of my imprisonment I passed through a terrible moral and spiritual crisis. The quarters were unbearably crowded—about a hundred of us were packed in a cell designed for thirty. With all my roots torn up and Nika lost, perhaps forever, life seemed hardly worth the effort. Even more than on my previous detention there, my spirit was crushed by the ugliness, the dirty damp walls, the barred windows, the foul smells and haggard faces. I felt literally forsaken.

There is a German saying, *"Der Mensch ist was er isst,* Man is what he eats."* Our daily diet was boiled corn without fats or seasoning, coarse black bread, and one tin cup of hot water with a sugar lump. At first the food made my stomach turn. Later, it undermined my physical strength, then my nerves, and finally my spirit. For hours on end I trembled and wept in the dim light, struggling against an overwhelming despair.

In the end I managed to escape madness only by grasping at the firm memories that floated in the turmoil of my thoughts. I remembered the saying of great teachers and saints: "If one can no longer pray with the heart, then say the sacred words with the lips." I did that, and persevered. And gradually, faith in the Wisdom which shapes our lives, and gratitude for the breath of life began to sprout in me again. And again those words of Leonardo da Vinci returned to me, as cited by Mother Tamara: "Learn to look at ugliness and you will find many beautiful things, *cosi molti belli."*

My personal grief and pain, my egotistical self-centeredness, ebbed away. I began to put out feelers and was amazed at the results. Women who had seemed unfriendly, alien, and forbidding now came to me to unburden their hearts. Most were ardent Communists, and I came to realize that they, having put the State above their conscience, now had nothing to keep themselves going but their faith in the Party—a faith which Stalin had besmirched and finally shattered. No better lesson in anti-Communism could have been found anywhere else in Russia. I slowly understood how Stalin had negated all of Communism's appealing aspects. By deforming and twisting the doctrine to serve his own ends, he had wrung out of it every redeeming trace of human feeling. He was now the undisputed Autocrat of the Proletariat, that very same "Genghis Khan with a Telephone" whom Leo Tolstoy had foreseen.

Among the hundreds of women to whom I spoke during those long months, several distinctive figures stand out in my memory.

One, the wife of a high-ranking "Red" General, had fought like a man beside her husband throughout the Civil War and had earned the most distinguished military decorations. She was now a tall, spare woman with tortured eyes in her energetic face. In a hushed voice (we all had to speak very low to keep the din in the cell from becoming insufferable) she told me the story of her life. Her eyes shone and her voice swelled with pride as she described battles, Red Army raids, and the execution of "White rebels." But once she clenched her fists and groaned:

"Oh, what's the use! For all his medals, my husband is in a concentration camp, and it'll be the same with me. We gave our youth, our faith, and our blood to the Party, the Party that is no more! Now there's nothing but a Tsar Despot ruling Russia!" Ashamed and fearful, she glanced at me furtively: "It's strange that I'm so frank with a stranger like you," she said in an almost pleading whisper. "Don't give me away."

I reminded her of Dostoevsky's words: "Where there is sorrow and pain, the soil is sacred." "Here," I said, "we all have sorrows, therefore we are all sisters." She kissed me, with tears running from the eyes that once had calmly watched the execution of hundreds.

Another neighbor was the wife of the director of a famous automobile factory. A handsome woman of forty, she was dressed in smart foreign clothes.

"I bought them abroad," she told me. "I used to travel with my husband to France, England, and America. He called me his 'right-hand man.' Together we studied foreign automobile plants, and then organized our own, the best in Russia! Our plant was a model of efficiency, with all our workers well cared for. The Party rewarded my husband many times. . . ." She smiled bitterly: "But you see, we were too busy to give the children much of our time. They scarcely ever saw us. We left them to be brought up in Communist schools. Now they would never believe that actually, envious men denounced their father as a saboteur, and that he was tortured to make him admit he was a Trotskyite. All they know is that their parents are in jail, accused of treason. . . . With their upbringing, all three of them probably despise us as a disgrace to the Party."

Sons and daughters weighed heavily on the minds of these unfortunate women. In the evening they would tell me stories about

their children and later at night, I would hear their smothered sobs.
But of all the grieving mothers, there was one who left me stunned
and shocked. She was thirty-year-old Anna Abramova, an intelligent, lovely woman with black wavy hair and lustrous eyes. She
was a doctor by profession, and her husband held some important
position in the Commissariat of Health. She never mentioned his
name to me but spoke often of her son.

"He is my greatest love outside of the Party—I did everything I
could to give him the kind of education that would make him a
first-class Communist."

One day she was in a confidential mood: "From his earliest days,
Alexey was so clever and high-spirited! I could only reproach him
for one weakness: he was much too soft-hearted. You couldn't
take him on a walk without his finding some person or animal to
feel sorry for and brood over. I knew someday this had to stop. So
I got together about two dozen puppies and kittens in a deep
laundry basket, and told Alexey to carry them down to the lake
shore. Once we got there, I told him to drown them, every one.
He burst into tears, but I made him do it! He had to be strong and
ruthless to fight the enemies of the Party. There is no room in us
for pity, compassion, or any such bourgeois weaknesses."

I could hardly believe her: "Don't you understand what you've
done? You've tried to ruin that which was most precious in your
son! Now he's been taught to torture and kill whenever he's told
to. If you've succeeded, well, all right! Soon you'll find some well-
trained youngster to treat *you* the way you taught Alexey to treat
those puppies and kittens."

She had apparently never considered that eventuality. She sat in
front of me, now shocked herself, and deathly pale. Leaping to her
feet, she stumbled over others, and staggered like a blind woman
to her place, where she lay down with her face to the wall. With me
again next morning, she was outwardly calm, but her eyes were
red with weeping.

"I understand now," she murmured. "If I'm spared . . . if they
let me go home, I will try to undo what I've done. I promise
you!"

"Go home? That seems a pretty large sugarplum to wish for! But
perhaps your boy has realized a few things for himself." And I
prayed that this might be so.

As time went by, new prisoners came, bringing us news of the outside world. I remember two women, claiming to be of Lettish descent, who arrived late one night. They were well fed and dressed in foreign clothes; to my unaccustomed eyes, they looked positively opulent. Both were seething with hatred and misery, and repelled all friendly advances, preferring to crouch together in a corner by themselves. I finally decided to speak to them; perhaps I could comfort them in some way. When they found I could speak English, they broke down completely. To my consternation, I learned that they were Communists from America. They had sold their nice little place on Long Island, they told me, and had rushed to see this "splendid land of true democracy and freedom."

"And look at us now," they hissed; "we were arrested after three days, and brought to this lousy hole!—Accused of *spying!*"

I must say my Christian charity deserted me. I turned away, satisfied that they would now have time aplenty to study and evaluate the Paradise they had longed for. Shortly afterward, they were each condemned to ten years in a concentration camp.

My closest neighbor was Sophya Vladimirovna, a famous Jewish prosecutor and president of a revolutionary tribunal, who in obedience to Stalin's almighty policies had sent hundreds to their deaths. Forceful and energetic, she was accustomed to leading, and tried to bring some order and "Communist discipline" into our cell. By that point, however, the nerves of the other inmates were so raw that even small incidents provoked them to screaming, howling fights. Sophya Vladimirovna would go about scolding, shaming, and upbraiding. I regarded her with interest and a certain admiration, for despite everything, she had remained faithful to her standards. Moreover, I fervently shared her desire to preserve some decency in this wretched crowd. Once, after a particularly dreadful brawl over a missing lump of sugar, Sophya Vladimirovna jumped onto a bench.

"Comrades!" she shouted, "are you Communists or wild beasts? Where's your training? Where's your discipline? I see only one true Communist here, and I want you to behave as she does." She pointed to me. "I mean Comrade Avinov!"

In the hush that followed this curious pronouncement, I began to laugh. "My dear Sophya Vladimirovna, I'm neither Communist nor Comrade!"

"Hush your mouth," she shot back. "I know the beliefs you claim as the source of your 'Communism,' but you're a good example all the same, so be quiet!"

When left to myself, I would turn to what poetry I could remember, translating various poems by Pushkin into French. To do so without pencil or paper required great concentration, inasmuch as I had to immediately memorize what I'd translated as I went along. But without those strenuous mental exercises to help blot out my surroundings, I do believe in the end I would have gone mad. And yet, my mental discipline failed completely when it came to food. Desperately hungry as I was, I simply could not bring myself to stomach our vile rations. I subsisted on black bread, garlic, and an occasional glass of tea in place of plain hot water. Of course I began to grow weaker with every passing day. At last I fainted and was taken to the prison hospital.

The hospital was a haven that every woman in my cell dreamed of. It had slightly more palatable food, narrow iron cots, thin hard mattresses, and a total lack of compassion on the part of the staff. At that time, naturally, I had not yet heard of the goings on in Dachau, Belsen, and in the Soviet concentration camps in Siberia, and today, I feel almost ashamed to speak of my own hardships. Next to what others had to undergo, the Butyrka was child's play.

Somehow, one hardly expects kindness from a jailer or a prison guard, but it is appalling to recognize brutality in a doctor or a nurse. In this hospital, the nurses would wake us with a sound slap. The doctor was always attended by an armed soldier when he made his rounds, and never spoke directly to a patient. He gave me orders through a nurse or through his bodyguard; "Tell her she can have water but nothing else. Tell her to remember she's a criminal in prison!" With that, he would pass on to the next bed. The doctor told me I had come down with malaria, though I don't know where or how I possibly could have contracted it. I was shaken intermittently by dreadful chills and burning fevers. When my teeth were chattering with cold, I was refused a blanket. When the fever was high, I longed for some sour drink and begged for some vinegar in my water; I never got it.

The night, a quiet time of rest and comfort in any normal ward, was for us in the hospital, a ghastly and infernal time. The prosecutor's offices were on the floor right over our heads. Prisoners were grilled up there every night, starting about nine. All night long I'd listen to the screams and shrieks of tortured, beaten men. My convulsive chills and dreadful thirst, the moans of sick women around me, the howls of agony from the floor above, all blended into a fevered and exhausting nightmare that lasted for twenty-three days. It still remains a puzzle to me why I didn't die.

Giddy and trembling, I was released at last. The doctor's final advice was the height of irony: "Tell her to beware of cold, and dampness. She shouldn't get her feet wet. Tell her to have a good rest and take nourishing food."

I was too weak to laugh, but I felt fully compensated for my long recovery when I returned to my cell. All the inmates rushed to meet me, hugging me and laughing, and escorted me to my corner, which the dear souls had saved for me in my absence. They had even arranged a surprise there: cigarettes, sugar, and tiny bits of sausage, all bought with their few pennies and stored up for my return. Weak as I was, I burst into a flood of joyous tears. They stroked my hands and patted my shoulders, telling me they were certain that I would soon be released. They begged me, whenever that day came, to look up their children: "Gather them around you, and teach them what you have taught us. Tell them what really matters in life. Open their eyes. Will you promise?"

Touched as I was by such affection, I couldn't quite visualize myself in my little room, holding a crowded Sunday School for children of all ages and trying to pierce through the total uncharitableness of their Socialist creed. I was amazed, though, that my cellmates should be so sure of my eventual release.

"Why," I asked, "should I go free, when you, who have been good Communists, are being sent off to concentration camps?"

"That's just it," was the reply. "We *are* good Communists, but the regime has changed. We know too much, we have seen too much. We remember Lenin. But you, what have you done?"

In a corner, an old woman nodded her head knowingly. Once a close friend and collaborator of Lenin's, she had been deported many times in the days of the Tsar. Later, under Lenin, a beautiful mansion in Moscow had been requisitioned for former political deportees, where this woman and other members of the Communist

"Old Guard" had enjoyed comfortable retirement. But Stalin had closed the mansion. Its old inhabitants were being shipped off to the same Asiatic wastes they'd been banished to in their youth. As I looked at this bent woman and pondered her wrinkled and resigned old face, I knew there was no room here for a complaint from me.

CHAPTER SEVENTEEN

❧

The fateful day came at last when our cell's heavy door swung open and a voice called out, "Maria Avinov, collect your things and follow me!" No prisoner could ever forget that call. It meant the close of a period of suffering, and an opening into a new unknown.

My hands were trembling as I packed my belongings. The other women crowded around me, kissing me, weeping, and pressing small gifts of bread, sugar, and cigarettes into my bag. The guard at the door threatened them with dire punishments if they didn't behave, but no one paid him the least attention.

I stumbled after my guard. We passed along endless corridors, past locked doors guarded by Mongolian girls in uniform, trained in jujitsu and able to cope with the strongest man. The silence was oppressive. Our footsteps echoed loudly along the hollow walls, and my heart sank with every step. To distract myself, I began a little guessing game: if, at the end of this long corridor my guard turned left, it would mean freedom; if right—banishment, slavery, or death. This little pastime soon became depressing, and I decided that one way was as good an another, if only I might find Nika at the end of it.

We continued through a prison yard and through gate after gate, until we finally reached a large, dismal court rockbound on all sides by walls faced with hundreds of barred windows. It was a place of silence and darkness. Far, far above twinkled a few dim stars. Straight ahead, rising shadowy and sinister, stood the Pugachov Tower, assigned to those condemned to death. The guard led me in. I realized that if this was my sentence, then they must have already done away with Nika! My knees gave way, and I supported

153

myself against a wall, praying. The guard fumbled with a key and opened a door.

Dazed and trembling, I saw rows upon rows of women huddled in a wide, low cell. Surely, I thought to myself, even in this place they would never be executing this many! The women stared blinking back at me. Suddenly it dawned on me; the Tower must have been reassigned to prisoners awaiting deportàtion. Was that to be my road, I wondered, and the road taken by Nika before me?

In silence, I followed my guard to a cubicle near the door. "You will now hear your sentence," he said. Unfolding a paper, he read distinctly and slowly, enunciating every word. In the state I was in, I could hardly understand what he was saying, but somehow I gathered that as the wife of a "political criminal," I was condemned to three years of "Free Deportation."

"Free . . . ?"

"Yes, free deportation. In central Asia! A strange verdict." he shrugged. "But it's none of my business. Yours must be some kind of a special case. Congratulations!"

I stared at him without understanding: "But what does 'free deportation' mean?"

"You'll find out; it's not for me to explain. Into the cell with you now!"

I spent several weeks in that gloomy tower where, as legend has it, the famous Pugachov spent his last days for having rebelled against Catherine the Great. Here, I was reunited again with some of the women who'd left my former cell before me. They were still waiting for a train to Siberia. I was deeply touched when they rejoiced over the good fortune of my verdict; they seemed to have no consciousness of their own sad fate. They told me "free deportation" meant that I would be living in some out-of-the-way place and reporting once a week to the local N.K.V.D. office. The term "free" implied that I would be free to starve, if I found no local employment and no friends to send me money and food parcels. It was hardly a rosy prospect, but the word "free" still sounded good to me. I felt happier, and lit a cigarette.

Early one cold, snowbound December morning, I and some two hundred other women were packed into a few ill-smelling motor vans known as "Black Ravens." I could not tell which railroad station we were driving to, since there was no opening in the walls of the van. Finally the doors opened on the Kazan station—the same station from which my family used to embark each spring for our beloved Kotchemirovo. I couldn't help smiling at the contrast between then and now.

Rifle-carrying N.K.V.D. men lined us up on the slippery station platform. We certainly were a motley throng of deportees with only our gender in common: former noblewomen shifted their weight from foot to foot along with thieves, intellectuals, and prostitutes. More than half our number were wives, legitimate or otherwise, of Party members fallen victim to Stalin's purges. This Communist "elite" stood apart, with a defiant air. We stood there for an hour or more until our legs felt weak and our knees wobbly. One woman fell. A guard gave her a hard blow with his rifle, and she shrieked. There came a gruff, reluctant reprimand: "Easy there! What's the good of beating her?"

I found myself coupled with an "ex-lady" in her seventies, who had been a noted musician and a friend of Rubinstein, Tchaikovsky, and other famous composers. She had been arrested the past July while strolling in a Moscow park, and hadn't been allowed to return to her room to collect any belongings. Now she stood shivering in her thin shoes, with a ragged and bloodstained army coat wrapped around her once white summer dress. In her hands she clutched a tiny suitcase, that she had somehow obtained in prison. I offered to carry it for her.

"Oh, no, thank you," she said in a nervous whisper, "it's not at all heavy. All I have in it is an old ivory fan."

"A fan?" I repeated incredulously.

"Yes," she added in the same hurried whisper, "yes, you see, I had it with me when they arrested me. It was such a hot day, that day was. Now it's all I have left. I'd hate to lose it."

For what seemed an eternity, we kept waiting on that platform. Several more vanloads of prisoners arrived and were lined up behind us. Thieves and prostitutes quarreled and swore; many others wept quietly. I felt sorry for the Communist "ex-ladies" who were trying to appear defiantly aloof. We others, at least, didn't have to pretend this was all the fault of some official blunder.

We looked like a herd of ragged cattle about to be shipped to a somewhat less green pasture, and when the train finally crawled in, the analogy became even stronger. As we were driven into the railway carriages, I decided that we would have probably been more comfortable if we *had* been cattle. The carriages were all alike, each with a passage running its full length. On the one side was a row of tightly sealed, whitewashed windows, and on the other—where one finds the compartments in a sleeping car—a row of wire cages. In each cage, there were three tiers of wooden bunks, four bunks to a tier, with so little space between bunks that the occupant could never sit upright. The boards were hard, but it was blissful to be able to get off our feet and lie down.

In our car, the last three cage-compartments were occupied by male prisoners. We caught glimpses of them as an armed guard escorted us on our way to the washroom. We were forbidden to look around while passing the men's area, and had to keep our eyes fixed on the floor ahead of us. The heart of every woman faltered as she went by: her own husband could possibly have been in there. One night, I thought I heard Nika's voice when a man called out for water. The sound of blows followed. Then a scream: "You have no right! There's nothing against the law in what I said!" From the sound of things, the beating went on. I shut my eyes and stuck my fingers into my ears. Was this the way Nika had lost his tooth? Soon afterward, the guards dragged their victim through the corridor to the end of the car. Later still, we learned that he had been stripped and thrown naked into a small, unheated cell. At this news, one of the women in our cage began to sob aloud. The commander of the guards flattened his nose against the iron partition. "Do you want to join the gentleman?" he asked in an ominous voice. The woman fell silent.

This hellish journey lasted a fortnight. Our daily ration was some black bread and two cups of tepid water. I had not fully recovered from malaria, and in the stifling atmosphere, my thirst became a torture. From the corridor where our guards sat smoking, whiffs of tobacco intensified my craving for a cigarette. One evening I became slightly delirious and began to moan for a drink of water—an offense that called for the little cold cell.

Two young cage-companions of mine tried to comfort me as best they could. Both had been singers in the Moscow Grand Opera, before their husbands had been arrested and "disposed of." Now the talent and energy of these lovely young artists were destined to be buried in a forced-labor camp for the next ten years.

I saw one of them creep to the wire partition. She called out in a soft voice.

"Comrade Chief! Oh, Comrade Chief! Would you care for a little music? We're well-known singers, you know. We've been applauded by Comrade Stalin himself, and now we'd like to sing for you and your men."

There fell a prolonged silence, during which a slow, collective smile crept over the faces of the guards and ended in a broad grin on their commander: "Well, perhaps, just one or two songs . . ." Putting their rifles aside eagerly, they all crowded in front of our cage.

Whatever their backgrounds and political shadings, Russians love music and have a soft spot for artists. That night, in the stifling heat of the rumbling train, under the ecstatic gaze of the N.K.V.D., I heard a most amazing performance. First a crystal-clear, enticing soprano rose in the "Habanera" from *Carmen*. I had often heard that lovely melody, but never as I heard it that night. One of Rubinstein's duets followed, then my favorite Schubert, *Der Wanderer*. Boisterous applause broke out from every cage-compartment. The Commander reeled around as if awakening from a dream.

"Stop it! Quiet! Shut up! And you, Comrades, back to your places!" The men dispersed. Lights were lowered. But presently a hand pushed a cup of water into our cage and a rough voice said, "Eh, you singers! Here's your reward. Now keep quiet!"

As I lay in my bunk, shaking with thirst and emotion, that cup of cool, refreshing water was pressed into my hand.

"Have a drink, my poor dear," whispered a gentle voice. "We sang to get it for you."

At last the train reached Alma Ata in Kazakhstan. But no "free" deportation awaited me in this place. Instead, I was marched to the local prison with the rest of the women, only to be told that the cells there were full up"! All day we sat in the snow, guarded like a flock of sheep by Kazakh soldiers and their watchdogs. Night fell, and still we remained, shivering. Suddenly we heard the loud shuffle of many feet. An abrupt flood of light revealed two hundred prisoners being led from their cells, who knows where to, to make room for us. Almost of their own accord, my eyes searched those drawn, anguished faces—was Nika's among them? Was I still on the same road as he, and only a little way behind him? For a few moments, I had the sensation that his smile had enveloped me. But I remembered how alone I was when the guards led us into a gloomy one-story building full of dampness and decay. Layers of old whitewash were peeling off the walls. The long corridors were lighted intermittently by tiny kerosene lamps. I saw heavily padlocked doors right and left; and underfoot, slippery and ill-smelling slime.

The chief warden, an exotic figure who had been leading our column, stopped in front of one of the doors. His peaked fur cap, high cheekbones, and slanting eyes reminded me of the Asian warriors in Vereshchagin's famous painting by that name. He opened one door, and a light cloud of rancid steam billowed out at us. From inside anxious voices cried, "No, no! no more! We can't take any more!" A tall, white-haired woman came to the doorway, pleading: "You can't, Chief—we're a hundred already in here. We've nowhere to sit anymore. Even those who faint remain standing!"

"So what?" he said with a grin. "You'll get used to worse. Move back."

The wall of sweating, outraged faces receded a little, and some fifty of us were shoved inside. We stood crushed, one against the other, until around midnight when the door opened again and a few women were taken away. Now, from time to time, one of us was able to crouch on the floor and enjoy a brief respite from aching feet and the warmer layers of tepid air. The windows to the outside were barred but otherwise open. Snowflakes drifted in; and all night long persisted a ceaseless hum of voices, numbing and exasperating by turns. Thus we spent our first night in Alma Ata.

When morning came, many women were found in a dead faint, and a number of them were removed to other quarters. This left the rest of us room enough to huddle on the floor. I took stock of my new companions. Only one stood out—the gaunt cell leader whom I had seen the night before, standing at the door to protest the overcrowding. Elena Ivanovna was a good psychiatrist who had formerly practiced in Moscow. Her husband and two sons had been shot during the purge, and she herself now looked forward to a long term in a concentration camp. I recognized in her a typical product of the Russian intelligentsia: a brilliant, disinterested unbeliever with a noble, loving heart. I felt instantly drawn to her, and she, too, seemed to single me out. In a low voice she told me who was who in our cell, and at the same time, dropped a few useful hints:

"That group you see there consists of prostitutes and common criminals. Those others, as you see, are nuns. These over here are the Communist "aristocracy," picked up in the last purge. And those nearby are no-party women—students, actresses, and of course, the Asiatics. They fight, all of them, the whole day long. I tell you, I have my hands full! . . . And let me warn you about the food: it's vile! They serve it on unwashed plates straight from the adjoining cell, where the riffraff of Alma Ata have licked them clean. Some of them have unspeakable diseases." After that, I never dared touch the gruel they served us on those plates. I lived on bread and hot water, as before.

Day after day, Elena Ivanovna struggled with her wretched task as cell leader, trying to argue with the authorities and keep the women quiet. Savage fights would erupt over nothing; women clawed each other and tore each other's hair. Dreadful catlike yowls sounded from one corner where two women rolled on the floor, biting each other over a lump of sugar. A blood-curdling scream came from another girl hit with a bottle; blood gushed from the victim's head as other women rushed in to scratch at the aggressor. Elena Ivanovna ran from one to the other, entreating and threatening in turn. In all my prison experiences, I'd never seen a cell in such bedlam. Next to it, the Butyrka seemed like a haven of peace.

My admiration for Elena Ivanovna grew all the more when I saw that she was obviously a very sick woman. One day she was seized with a dreadful fit of coughing, and her handkerchief was soaked in blood. She noticed my horrified glance:

"Yes, I know. Consumption. I haven't long to live. I'll welcome the end, but as long as I'm alive, I must do what I can for these unhappy creatures. This terrible regime may be a thousand times worse than any Tsar's, but even so, I feel lucky! I was supposed to be sent to a concentration camp long ago, but the chief warden here heard I was a psychiatrist. He kept me on to maintain order. So I am here, trying to do the best I can."

I desperately wanted to be of help to her, but couldn't think how. I racked my imagination and even prayed for guidance. Then one day, after a prostitute had nearly strangled another over a piece of stolen bread, and Elena Ivanovna had spent a good half hour tearing them apart, I had a sudden inspiration.

"Elena Ivanovna," I whispered as she turned to me, still panting after her strenuous exercise, "would telling these women some stories keep them quiet, do you think? I'm considered a good story-teller, and I know quite a few."

"Stories!" she exclaimed. "How marvelous!" She glanced at me dubiously: "Are you sure you can, though? You seem so awfully weak, and your voice, my dear, is only a hoarse whisper." I told her I could manage, if only she would get the cell quiet enough to hear me. Quickly she climbed up onto a rickety box: " Com-rades! Hush, please! Listen to me! We're about to have some entertainment! Mrs. Avinov has offered to tell us stories. She tells me she remembers many. D'you want to hear them?"

The room responded with loud applause and eager assent, but Elena Ivanovna eyed them severely: "If your answer is yes, then you must be very quiet. If you don't behave, I'll stop the story-telling at once!" And again, a chorus of voices rang out with promises to be good.

That is how I became, as I laughingly called myself, "The Scheherazade of Cell 26." From my perch on the same rickety box that Elena Ivanovna usually used as her podium, I saw a hundred pairs of eyes fix on me, and a hundred hollow-cheeked faces light up in eager anticipation. I wondered if even Cicero had ever com-manded such a grateful audience.

I began with *Around the World in Eighty Days*, and Jules Verne captured everyone's attention from the very start. Even the nuns stopped mumbling their prayers; and the Communist "ladies," who at first had tried to appear indifferent, listened intently. My voice was starting to falter when a small lump of sugar was passed from hand to hand and finally given me by one of the prostitutes:

"Dear Storyteller, it's small because others have sucked on it, but it'll soothe your throat."

I thanked her, tucked the sugar into my cheek, and went on. After Phineas Fogg had won his bet, I chose a love story—*Jane Eyre*. My listeners were as quiet as could be. When I came to the end, and my voice faded away from sheer exhaustion, sighs of contentment filled the cell.

Every day thereafter, for several hours a day, I told stories. At night I'd lie awake preparing my next day's repertoire: *Ivanhoe, The Three Musketeers, The Lady of the Camellias, Call of the Wild,* and so on. What I had forgotten, I filled in with improvisations of my own, and gave silent apologies to the authors whose tales I mutilated. Jack London and Arthur Conan Doyle were everyone's favorites; any humorous passage of theirs always elicited a boisterous laugh. It was well worth the strain and fatigue to hear such merriment within those dismal walls. The women's gratitude was touching: poor threadbare rags were placed under my head at night, and I often received small onions—great treasures in prison. Most happily, Elena Ivanovna was able to maintain order effortlessly. At the smallest outbreak of bickering, she had only to say "Stop at once, or no stories!" That threat never failed.

One day while I was in the midst of a story, the door opened to reveal our magnificently barbaric chief warden posed on the threshold. He waved to me to go on, and so I finished it up while the warden listened with interest. I don't remember which story it was, but it must have had a funny ending. The women broke into shrieks of appreciative laughter, and even the warden joined in, his white teeth flashing. Finally, he raised his hand for silence.

"Women," he said, "when you came here, you were the worst bunch I've ever seen! Now you have become the most orderly cell. I'm going to reward you—there'll be more bread and sugar for everyone, and tomorrow you can buy cigarettes."

Wild cheers! He turned on us savagely with a fierce "Shut up!" but as he left a smile still lingered beneath his wild mustache. The bolting of the door sounded somehow less emphatic.

Later that day, in response to a general request, I began telling Arthur Conan Doyle's *The Brazilian Cat.* The women sat enthralled. I had reached the point at which the hero's diabolical host invites him to see how the cat is fed and then locks him alone in a room with a ravenous black panther; but just then, my voice broke. I felt too weak and dizzy to utter a sound. Elena Ivanovna laid her hand on my shoulder and announced a recess:

"Comrades, to your places. Mrs. Avinov is tired. We will hear the end tomorrow." Like wind over a wheat-field, protest rippled

through the cell; "No, no!"—"Not tomorrow, today."—"Please!"
But Elena Ivanovna remained adamant and, crestfallen, my listeners
shuffled back to their places.

I was lying in my corner, not merely exhausted but feeling half
dead, when Lucy, a prostitute and murderess, crept silently up to
my side.

"Dear Storyteller," she whispered, "I was sent to scrub the floor
in the chief's office today. A guard there told me that I'm on
tonight's list. You know what that means—they'll be packing me
off tonight, to a concentration camp. Before I leave I must, I
simply *must* know—is he going to be saved?"

I roused myself from my stupor, trying to make out whom she
was speaking of. "The hero!" Lucy whispered anxiously. "The man
in the panther's cage. Oh, I'd be so much happier if he escaped.
Please, will you whisper the end in my ear?"

Her simplicity touched me, almost to tears. In a trembling, hardly
audible voice, with a treacherous lump still rising in my throat, I
whispered the end of the story. Lucy listened intently, and then
gave me a rapturous hug: "Now I feel better! Everything is all
right, then! Thank you, thank you!"

A few minutes later the door opened, and the chief warden
reappeared holding a typewritten list. Slowly, he read off the names
of those who were to go on their last dreadful journey. Among
them was Lucy, just as she had been told to expect. She filed out
with the rest, but on the threshold she suddenly turned around,
smiled, and blew me a kiss.

CHAPTER EIGHTEEN

❧❦❧

"Maria Avinov, collect your things and follow me!" Once again I heard that fatal call. Again an armed guard on the threshold; again touching farewells. Elena Ivanovna burst into tears.

My guard pushed me into a closed truck that was waiting in the prison yard. It was very dark inside. The truck started with a jerk, and I landed across someone's knees. I heard a sputtering laugh.

"Lucky Fomeech!" exclaimed a croaking voice, "only one woman, and she falls right into his lap!" I felt an arm slip around my waist and a nose squash itself against my back.

"All right, dearie," said Fomeech, "stay where you are, but please don't move. I'm sitting on a broken crate!"

As my eyes accustomed themselves to the dim light filtering through a hole in the truck's roof, I began to distinguish my companions: twenty ragged, dirty, unshaven men, all sitting in a muddle together on the floor. No "politicals," these. I could tell from their secretive whisperings that I was among criminals—thieves, pickpockets, speculators, rapists, and perhaps murderers. Their faces, speech, and mannerisms were exactly those I had once paid five rubles to see in the Moscow Art Theater's realistic production of Gorky's *The Lower Depths*. Now I was seeing the real thing for nothing, with myself as a part of the cast.

We clambered off the truck at a long lonely railway siding, in the outskirts of Alma Ata. It was dusk. Streaks of crimson still lingered under a darkly purple cloud on the western horizon. For once there was no delay—a cattle train stood waiting for us. The cavalier whose lap I had shared turned out to be a puny little man with small, shrewdly twinkling eyes and a nose like a ripe, puffy strawberry. His loose clothes were worn to rags and barely covered his skinny frame. We formed ourselves into a marching

163

column, two abreast, with Fomeech and myself in the lead. Instinctively I kneaded my faded Parisian beret to a more rakish angle. I didn't want to appear dejected or, worse, to be taken for Fomeech's "companion."

Our group was herded into the last freightcar, the door behind us slid shut with a sharp bang. The entire car was lit by a single candle fitted precariously in the neck of a vodka bottle, and the air was heavy with the odors of coal, grease, and stale sweat. Near the roof, the narrow slit-windows had been boarded up, but benches had been installed along the walls for our convenience.

Dropping their bundles, the men charged the narrow benches, elbowing and punching one another for a good place. They finally settled down, each hunched or slouched into his hard-earned space. Their hollow-eyed faces loomed, goblinlike, in the flickering candlelight. Free at last from the enforced hush of prison life, they let go a profane volley of oaths and curses, slapped their thighs, and squealed with laughter.

For a moment I felt panicky at being alone with twenty men who hadn't been near a woman for months—but again, experience drove out my fear. Soviet life had taught me the sovereign value of tobacco, the last thing any smoker would give away. Perhaps, if I shared my precious supply with them, they would treat me as a friend. Plucking up courage, I managed to raise my voice above the din:

"Comrades, we are all in the same boat, so let's make the best of it. Here, I have some tobacco. You are welcome to it. A smoke will do us all good."

Avid hands came shooting forward, and I carefully measured a little tobacco into each dirty palm.

"Thanks, little Mother."

"God bless you."

"That's a woman for you."

"My first smoke in months!"

"God be with you always!"

And then came a voice with the unmistakable note of authority: "Give her the best place, there under the window, and make some room on the bench so she can stretch out. And mind your foul manners, you punks. She's a lady!"

Good-naturedly they made room for me. Tobacco smoke rose in the air, and everyone began conversing with his neighbor.

"How free is 'free' deportation?" I asked the man next to me, who again happened to be Fomeech.

His voice was like the grinding of coffee beans: "It means they'll throw you out in the desert somewhere. For your sake, let's just hope they pick a spot that's near a village. In the desert proper where the Kazakhs live in dugouts, the only way a woman can survive is by being a prostitute. And those filthy natives are all putrifying away with galloping cases of . . ." He gave a cautious sidelong glance. "Of the you-know-what."

"Shut your fat mouth!" shouted the voice of authority. "You're going to frighten this good *barynya*." Then, addressing me: "Don't you fear, lady. You'll land in some village. Not that that'll make it any easier, but at least you have some friends, don't you? Or relatives, who can send you food and money?"

"Oh yes, of course. And I'm sure they'll help!"

Fomeech turned his toothless grin on me: "Hah! *Of course*, my hat! When a man's in trouble, where do his friends go? My own wife don't even lift a finger any more to help *me!* And as for her nephews that I raised with the sweat of my own brow, those s.o.b.s . . ."

"Once and for all, shut your foul trap," roared the voice of he who was still protecting my womanly sensibilities. (Strangely, for the life of me, I cannot recall what that man looked like.)

Conversation gradually died away until at last, the rumbling of the train and the intermittent snores of the men were the only sounds to disturb the night. The hot air settled around me like an evil-smelling blanket. I shut my eyes and fell into a remembered daydream. I found myself occupying a comfortable compartment in a first-class sleeping coach. A porter in his brown, gold-braided uniform was making up the bed, and putting oranges and cigarettes on the night table. The silver fittings of my dressing case glistened in the glow of the electric lamp, and I caught a whiff of lavender on the air. Nika stood in the doorway with an anxious frown on his face.

"You'll be all right, sweetheart. I gave the head porter a good tip."

And I, amused and touched by his almost childish fears for my well-being: "Oh, darling, I'm not off to Timbuktu, you know! Only an overnight ride to St. Petersburg."

But I stopped myself: to think was to remember; to remember was to weep. At last, I fell asleep.

With a loud screeching of brakes, the train came to a stop. I awoke on the floor and clutched frantically at my bench. Men raised their heads, stretched, scratched, cursed, and yawned. Then a pregnant, uneasy silence fell upon us all. After a while the car door slid open and a man's voice called out two names—mine and Fomeech's! My companions of the previous night shouted "Good-bye," and "Good luck," as my red-nosed friend and I scrambled out of the dark, reeking car into a clear, cool dawn.

For a moment I paused transfixed before the splendor of the countryside. A snow-covered, rose-tinted steppe stretched out for level miles, before rising to a range of mountains that shone and glistened against the pale horizon. After so many dismal months of confined squalor, the beauty of God's universe took my breath away. Such space; such light and invigorating air; such a superb sky, serene and formidably blue! How ardently I still loved life! If only Nika were not too far away!

Two men stood in the snow waiting to meet us: a very young soldier, holding his rifle in clumsy readiness, and a swarthy N.K.V.D. officer with slanted Mongolian eyes. The Commander of our train handed this local dignitary some papers which he signed, using the side of a freightcar as a prop. He gave back the papers and exchanged a brisk salute with the train Commander, who jumped on the step of the only passenger car and signaled with his arm. The locomotive let out a shrill whistle. Bumpers clanged. And slowly the train moved away across the sparkling plain and disappeared beyond a bend like a quick, gray snake.

But where were we, Fomeech and I? I could see no station, no buildings of any kind. On the road leading away from the railway stood a dilapidated carriage driven by an old gray nag, but a wide ice-coated ditch separated us from the vehicle. In my thin clothes I shivered at the sight of it.

"Jump!" said the N.K.V.D. officer who was standing beside me. "And look out, the water is deep."

I could envision myself taking off at a run and landing with a frigid splash. "Oh, come now, officer," I pleaded. "Have a heart. I'm not a circus artist."

"So what d'you expect me to do? Carry you? Go on, jump!"

I looked to his companion. The young soldier had the promisingly boyish face of a none-too-bright village lad.

"Have you a mother, *Golubchik*?"

He grinned sheepishly: "Sure! Far away she is, in the village of Krasnoye, Kharkov District."

"For your mother's sake then, help me. First throw my bags across the ditch. Then you jump across yourself and stretch your gun stock back over to me here."

The soldier looked to the officer for approval, who smiled and turned away. He did as I asked him. Then, with my beret pulled well down and skirts flying, I performed the longest, if not the most graceful, jump of my life and landed on all fours on the hard, dry earth. But poor Fomeech was not so fortunate. No one lent him a hand, and he climbed into the carriage beside me, drenched to the waist and shivering miserably.

After a long, jogging ride we came to a village about ten miles distant from the mountain range we had seen from the railway. Here in the middle of nowhere, I was delighted to find that the village was surrounded by thick groves of acacias and poplars, and bore a close resemblance to Shideyevo, Nika's beloved home in the Ukraine, two thousand miles away.

As I learned later, a large Ukrainian community had emigrated to this part of Asia some eighty years before, and had settled in Addis Ada. *Chinaras*, enormous trees of great beauty, lined the main street. Their branches would bear dark canopies of foliage in summer, but were now covered with hoarfrost. Except for these Asiatic trees, all other rustic, local touches seemed to have vanished. I saw nothing but whitewashed cottages in the midst of carefully arranged orchards. It was like a second homecoming to a new Shideyevo. But back in the Ukraine Nika and I, a bride of a few weeks, had been merrily welcomed on all sides by neat and hospitable peasants. Here in this "New Ukraine," there was no immediate welcome at all for Fomeech and me.

Our old carriage rattled to a stop before a large one-story building—the local office of the N.K.V.D. The front door was adorned by a lithographed portrait of Yezhov, and beside it, a wide red flag drooped limply in the clear, still air. The officer who had met us at the train led us in to be interviewed by the Party chief. This local "boss" sat behind a plain kitchen table. Apart from a kerosene lamp, some papers scattered on a shelf, and the inevitable pictures of Bolshevik worthies on the whitewashed walls, his office was completely bare.

The Party chief quickly thumbed through our papers. "Your sentences," he said, "are three years of free deportation each, with ten months of prison deducted. That means you will each have to live here for two years and two months. If you attempt to escape, we'll catch you, and skin you alive. You may go now."

I felt so cold and tired that I longed to lean against his table. "Where am I to go, Comrade Chief? I have no money. Where can I find a room?"

"Find a room in the village."

"But where do I look for work?"

"That's none of my business. Now *get out!*"

Crestfallen, Fomeech and I went out into the snow-covered street.

Huge poplars loomed like black candles against a luminous sky and slippery snow crunched underfoot, as I wandered with Fomeech through the big sprawling village in search of work and shelter. All I had left was one ruble, and Fomeech was totally penniless. We kept walking all day, making inquiries of anyone who was willing to listen. People looked askance at us—a pair of ragged, shivering deportees obviously without funds—and their answer was always the same:

"No one has a room to spare. As for work, in the summer perhaps, but not now."

Late in the afternoon we knocked at a door. The woman who came out had a kind face. "You poor dove," she said to me, "a deportee, aren't you? Nothing but skin and bones, you poor soul."

Her sudden compassion was too much to bear. Something snapped in me, and tears came streaming down my cheeks. All I could manage to mumble was, "Please, hot water . . . Please?"

She ran into the house and returned with a cup of hot water, a lump of sugar, and a slice of black bread: all of which I shared with Fomeech. Standing in leaky shoes in the snow, we took turns gulping down the water as the rising steam warmed our faces. The woman watched us, her eyes melting with pity, but in answer to my question about a room she shook her head.

"Ah no! I'm full up! I'm afraid you'll never find a place in winter. In summer, yes, it will be easier then."

We could hardly wait six months to find a room, but I said nothing. In silence I kissed her, and trundled on, followed by Fomeech. Before turning a corner, I glanced back and saw her still on her front step, watching us mournfully.

Fomeech and I continued our search, jumping over ditches, climbing through hedges, stumbling over frozen cabbage patches and through snowbound orchards. We had finally made the round of the village and had walked for a good many miles, all for nothing. I could hear Fomeech whimpering a few steps behind me. Then, of a sudden, I heard him gasp, but when I looked back he seemed to have disappeared.

As it turned out, he had slipped on the ice and fallen into a deep, snow-filled hole. He was wriggling and bouncing in it, trying with all his might to get free, but the more he struggled, the deeper he seemed to sink. Finally he gave up, leaned back, and began to curse God. Never in my life had I heard such blasphemy!

"Be quiet," I shouted at him. "Have you no shame? God is our only hope—our only protection!"

"There is no God!" he retorted at the top of his lungs. "God was invented by the priests to bleed poor suckers of their last kopeks. But I know better—I don't fall for that sort of muck. If God does exist, why he's a scoundrel, a dirty *louse!*" Fomeech menaced the sky with his clenched fist. "Yes! You up there! You and Your wicked, filthy world with its wicked, filthy people who won't let us into their wicked, filthy huts, and who leave us out here on this filthy plain to die! The pox on you, the *pox!*" With that, Fomeech let go an interminable string of the vilest words I've ever heard.

My throat was dry, my knees were trembling, and I felt faint with hunger and cold. Fomeech was still ranting. "All right," I said wearily, "if you want to be that way, stay in your hole. I'm leaving."

He gave a long plaintive cry, strangled by a convulsive sob. "No, no. Don't leave me. Please! You are God's own angel! I'm coming with you. Wait till I get out of this wicked, filthy hole."

He finally crawled loose, with me tugging at his arms and

shoulders. Then I went on as before, marching ahead with a forced determination while Fomeech lagged a few steps behind.

It was almost dark when we finally retraced our steps to the N.K.V.D. building, only to find the door padlocked and every window dark. A small groan escaped Fomeech at the sight, and slumping to the ground, he burst into tears. I felt so sorry for the little man, that wretched bundle of rags, that I pulled out of my pocket my last ruble.

"Here Fomeech, take this. It will buy you a drink in the *chay-hane*, and perhaps they will let you sleep there." I was referring to a disreputable eating place we had seen, where no decent woman would have dared enter.

Fomeech looked at me, wild-eyed. But then he clasped both his hands to his heart and rolled his head from side to side. "No! No! The last money you have in the world! I couldn't accept it! I can't!"

Despite my fatigue, I couldn't help smiling at such histrionics. "Don't argue, and take it. You don't have any faith in God, so here's something to provide for you."

He seized my hand and kissed it. But before I could say or do anything, Fomeech had snatched away the ruble and was off like a streak around the corner.

Not knowing what to do next, I stood alone in the middle of that dreary road. Night was closing in fast, and a thick fog was rolling up to muffle all sound and haze over the lights in the surrounding windows. A strange, supernatural calm came upon me. This is the end, I thought: Saint Seraphim, help me. There is nothing more I can do but sit down on the ground of God's earth and wait for death.

But I was given no time to even bend my knees. Out of the fog a dark figure emerged, coming toward me. Almost at once I saw that it was a woman. She stopped and peered at me suspiciously.

"What are you doing here alone? It's dangerous."

Once again I had to tell my story. She listened attentively until I was through. "Well," she said, "I know a woman who'd take you in, but she lives three miles away. *You'd* never find your way there on a night like this. And I'm sorry I can't help you. I have to cook dinner, and I'm late already. The family's waiting."

She was just about to turn back into the fog when we heard

footsteps approaching. She turned to see who it was, and then seized me feverishly by the arm:

"What incredible luck! Of all people! That's the very woman's daughter-in-law!" She ran to meet the newcomer, spoke to her in low excited tones, and then returned to me: "It's settled. Nyura will take you back to their place. Oh, how glad I am I met you! God and His saints must be on your side!"

To many, such gratuitous strokes of luck might have seemed like lucky coincidence, but to me they were a source of grateful consolation. And my surprises for that day were not quite over!

About an hour later, sitting in a clean white cottage, I was introduced to the woman who was to be my landlady for over two years. My composure was indeed somewhat shaken, but my faith bolstered, when I learned her name: Seraphima.

CHAPTER NINETEEN

❦

Hers was a typical Ukrainian cottage, just like the ones I used to know in Shideyevo, with a thatched roof, whitewashed walls, and tall poplars just beyond the door. The wide room in which Seraphima lived, cooked, and slept was spotless and pristine. Dried herbs hanging from the walls and the rafters gave their clean and subtle smell to the surrounding air: sage and garlic hung even among the icons. There was a huge Russian stove at one end of the room, a large double bed at the other, and several bright home-spun rugs on the earthen floor. The walls were hung with framed family photographs, one of which caught my eye: a robust young father in his Sunday best was seated like an idol, his big hands spread over broad knees, his eyes popping at the effort of keeping still. Behind him was his young wife, prim and proper, one hand planted on his shoulder, and the other tucked under her chin. On the floor, their two grinning children leaned against their father's shiny knee-high boots.

The group had been photographed not ten years before, yet already it was hard to recognize the plump, round-cheeked house-wife of the photograph in the lean old woman now spreading a clean tablecloth for our supper.

Actually Seraphima was in her mid-forties, but her stern face and broken teeth made her look old. She was a hard-bitten, reticent woman, but as I was soon to learn, she had a warm heart for those she loved. Even as I watched her on that first evening, I was struck by the brightness of her gray-blue eyes, which made a striking contrast to her thin, deeply lined face, as did the little movements of her broad shoulders, her straight body, and her still-abundant hair drawn into a tight bun at the back of her head. She

172

moved with a poise and dignity characteristic of Russian peasant women. Watching her, I remembered the words of Churé, author of *Les Grands Initiés:* "An aristocratic stance is found only at both ends of the social ladder, never in between."

That first evening, as we sat at the table over boiled potatoes and sweetened hot water, Seraphima's eyes never left my face. She was frankly probing, scrutinizing me, and trying to decide if she had done well by taking me in. As I told her my story, her expression softened.

"My poor dove," she said, "think no more of prison. Climb behind the stove now, and get a good night's rest. We're all in God's hands, and He will watch over us."

I climbed onto the large overledge at the back of the stove. It was so warm and cosy there, that I soon felt good all over. What's more, for the first time in God knows how long, I had a pillow under my head and a homespun rug to cover myself with. I had the further, exquisite relief to know that no one would disturb me during the night: the constant waiting for something to happen had been perhaps the worst torture of Soviet prison life.

From my vantage point I watched Seraphima clear the table with swift, deft movements. She then undressed, put on a shift, and knelt before the icons. After crossing herself devoutly, bowing to the ground, and whispering prayers, she blew out the tiny kerosene lamp and got into her bed. Moonlight falling through the small windowpanes splashed silvery-blue patterns across the floor. The determined chirping of a cricket somewhere behind the stove seemed to swell rather than break the silence.

I lay motionless, listening. The cricket's chirp went on and on. . . . Only it was another cricket now, chirping in a faraway nursery, where four of us children are tucked into our white beds, and Nikitishna, our nurse, sits darning stockings under a shaded lamp. Shifting her spectacles, she glances angrily into my warm, dark corner. (She never did like crickets; she thought they brought bad luck.) The cricket's chirp goes on and on . . . But now it's another one, sounding off in my mother's boudoir, while Mamma in her dressing gown of fawn-colored velvet writes letters at her marquetry desk, oblivious of the cricket and of me in my corner. Her shapely hand guides the pen, and the rings on her fingers sparkle . . . A soft thud, and the cricket falls silent.

Green eyes—Seraphima's cat—shone at me through the dark, pulling me loose from my reverie. Loneliness, the past's sole residue, rushed in upon me with an almost physical pang: Father, Mother, and my two fine brothers—Dead; my sisters unreachable beyond Stalin's impenetrable Curtain; our home burned to the ground; and he—for so many years the mainstay, joy, and center of my life—gone, dragged away to some bleak camp in Asia. Repressed sobs strangled me. No! I oughtn't to weep, oughtn't to think, oughtn't to cry—rather, think of others and how to help them. If the Lord is our stronghold, as Seraphima had said, then He might send His angels to set my Nika free. In the meantime, after all, I was in the security of Seraphima's home, and I *was* free!

To test my freedom and the better to savor it, I slid off the stove, tiptoed across the room and opened the door, standing back from the cold. All traces of fog were gone. The moon, sailing in a cloudless sky, kindled sparkles from the ice on frozen trees and shrubs. The night was so brightly lit and clear that I could distinguish the reddish glow on the last two leaves still clinging to the copper beech in the yard. Far beyond the gray fence, mountain peaks loomed cold and remote on the horizon. Somewhere far, far out on the steppe sounded the mournfully drawn-out cry of a jackal. I stood there, breathing in the clean wintry air. Then I saw a dark line undulating slowly along the road in the direction of the village—a train of camels. Yes, I was indeed in Asia.

Next morning Seraphima's greeting gave me a shock: "Come and have tea, *Babushka*."

"*Babushka?* Grandmother? Seraphima, how old do you think I am?"

"I would say about seventy." My incredulous expression seemed to puzzle her: "Well, if you aren't, you ought to be. Just look at yourself in the mirror. You must be seventy, at least."

I moved to a chest of drawers and snatched up a piece of broken looking-glass. Aghast, I stared at my own reflection. Surely this haggard creature was someone else! The chalk-white face and strands of wispy gray hair couldn't be mine! Foolish, bitter woman's tears welled up in my eyes.

"But I'm barely in my fifties," I cried.

"It's the prison, dear," said Seraphima soothingly. "The hunger and the hardships, that's what's done it. But you'll be yourself again, once you've had the proper rest and food."

Unconsoled, I sat down to a frugal breakfast consisting of a glass of hot water, a lump of sugar, and boiled potatoes. My mind was still on that dreadful image in the mirror, but finally, I had to laugh —my problem was still one of survival rather than looks. Leaning forward, I told Seraphima that I'd simply have to sell something at once, in order to get the money to wire friends in Moscow.

"What have you got to sell?" she asked.

Out of my battered suitcase I brought two towels and a pillow-case of fine linen. Embroidered with princely crowns, they represented the last remains of my mother's rich dowry. Seraphima fingered them, shaking her head in wonder.

"What beautiful linen! . . . much too good for the people here. It will be difficult to find a buyer, very difficult . . . but after all, this is market day!" She persuaded a neighbor of hers, Annushka, to go with me and help.

My fellow bargainer, a garrulous young woman with red apple cheeks, led the way through the soft snow. As we neared the marketplace, I was surprised to find that for all my tramping the day before, I hadn't seen all of Addis Ada after all. In my misery and haste I had entirely missed the native quarters. But I didn't have to ask questions about them, since Annushka was handing out information as fast as I could absorb it:

"That over there is the Kazakh community. When our grand-fathers emigrated here, they were careful to build our neat, white village well away from *them*. We don't like mixing with them, those black heathen devils! Phoo! They're dirty and promiscuous, and they hate all Russians!" As we wended our way through the Asiatic settlement, we were followed by the suspicious, slant-eyed glances of dark-skinned women in immense white turbans.

"Those headgears! Have you ever seen anything like them? And have a good look—their clothes can wear to shreds, but still they stick that white stuff on their empty noodles, as much as they can lay hands on. Sometimes they use up twenty yards, or more." Naked children ran around playing in the snow, and great, mangy dogs snarled at us viciously.

"Watch out for those dogs. No one ever bothers to feed them, so they hunt in packs, like wolves. Don't run when they snarl or you'll get torn to pieces. The other day, a woman got scared and started to bolt, and—well! They used a breadbasket to gather what was left of her after the dogs were through."

Silently, I digested this grim bit of information, but I had to exclaim my delight when I saw the marketplace perched on a hill-top above the village. In the art galleries back in Moscow, I'd often admired such scenes in Vereshchagin's paintings. The real thing was splendid and vividly bright under the sun and snow.

We elbowed our way through a dense, milling crowd; past little donkeys loaded with sacks twice their size; past camels with great sloe eyes, standing or lying in rows but always chewing hay. Shouting and bickering all around us were women—Russians in old shawls, Kazakhs in once-bright velvet coats—each bargaining in a high-pitched, quarrelsome voice. All manner of cheap goods were for sale: old crockery, knives, heaps of rags, corn and cabbage in wide woven baskets. On a tree stump stood the magnificent figure of an Asiatic huntsman who towered above everyone else. A hawk with a tiny hood over its head perched on his outstretched arm.

"They hunt foxes and gazelles with those birds," Annushka explained with a disdainful sniff. "Hold your nose, they all smell bad!" She brushed by the huntsman and kept on cleaving her way through the frenetic bustle and commotion of the market.

In the midst of it all, I stationed myself to proffer my two towels and my pillowcase. It seemed I was taking part in an incongruous dream, devoid of sense and reality. A few Asiatics paused, looked at my crested linen, then shook their heads and went on without even asking the price. Next, a leather-jacketed Bolshevik official planted himself in front of me and began to upbraid me in loud harsh accents:

"Have you lost your senses, Citizeness, all your shame and decency, to be showing people things with crowns on them?" He pretended to spit: "Tfu! They're fit for the garbage! They're relics of an accursed past!"

"I'm a relic myself," I said.

He scowled, wished me a derisive "Good luck," and sauntered on. My knees shook, and a lump rose in my throat. Seeing what a state I was in, Annushka took over and told me to wait under a tree she pointed out to me. From my new post I watched her expertise as she raised the towels and pillowcase over her head and called people together at the top of her voice. When a large enough crowd was gathered round her, she began inducing them to bid, one against the other. At the end of half an hour, she triumphantly handed me thirty rubles.

Without the slighest hesitation, we both made a straight tack for the butcher shop—a great, open shack where bulky chunks of pork lay scattered or heaped on shelves. After months of prison, my craving for meat was such that I eyed the display like a hungry leopard. Clutching my money in one first, I realized that I could now afford one of those gorgeous hams, and that tonight, there would be a succulent borsch for me and for Seraphima's whole family! The florid, mountainous butcher said nothing, but he studied me closely with a distinct twinkle in his eye. He took my order in silence. As he was chopping up the meat, he decided to start a conversation.

"You know, I look at you and say to myself, there's an agreeable lady! Citizeness, won't you marry me?"

Annushka went into peals of laughter. I stood gaping for a moment, convinced I hadn't heard him right.

I had.

"You'll eat as much ham as you like," he promised. "And ach! What a beautiful, nice time we'll have!"

I answered as demurely as I could: "Thank you for the honor, but I'm married already."

"Naturally you are! Who'd jilt a woman like you? I figure you must be one of those 'ex-people.' . . . Husband in some concentration camp, eh? Oh well, that's all right. Until he returns, you can wait with me. I'll take good care of you—I'll feed you. You look as if you could do with a little extra food."

I was seized with a wild desire to laugh in his face, but presently a boost of ego eclipsed my indignation. This man didn't see me as a septuagenarian *babushka!* He found me attractive and even wanted—oh, no matter what he wanted! I felt all the better for his attention. I smiled in appreciation but declined his kind offer. Although the humor was lost on the lovelorn butcher, for the fun of it I repeated the words my Great-grandmother had used to reject an Emporer's advances.

"I'm listening, but I don't hear a word."

Like the Emperor a century earlier, my new admirer didn't seem to mind this rebuff, and we remained good friends. Whenever I came to his shop, I got the best meat available, often with a small extra chunk thrown in.

On our way home from market, I sent a telegram to my oldest and most trusted friend, Nadya Shipov. Confident that Nadya would let nothing stand in the way of her aiding me, I returned to Seraphima's house in a cheerful, almost elated state of mind. One would have thought that money and food packages had already arrived. That evening, without a care in the world, I sat down to a true gourmet's delight: thick, fragrant borsch spiced with onions, tomatoes, and red pepper. Around the table, Seraphima, her two sons, her daughter-in-law Nyura, and Annushka were beaming and gobbling up our feast. The poor souls had almost forgotten what meat tasted like. And I knew that having spent my first money on her family would endear me to Seraphima. Kind and compassionate as she was, money was an all-important factor in her life. Anyone who shared it with her would stand high in her estimation.

My optimism was soon rewarded: next day I got an answering telegram from Nadya; and three days later, three thousand rubles. I now had means to furnish my new home. Seraphima had rented me the whitewashed cottage in her orchard. It was outwardly a tiny replica of her own, complete with thatched roof. Inside, the floor was of hard-beaten earth, and there was no ceiling under the bare rafters. Even so, I was permitted to have only one of the cottage's two equal rooms. Seraphima had reserved the other for her greatest personal treasure—a cow named Mashka. Thus Masha and Mashka settled down under the same roof.

"She'll be no trouble," Seraphima assured me. "If she kicks the wall at night, give it no thought. She's a good cow, such a good cow! I once killed a man for her sake."

It took some time for her last sentence to sink in.

"Oh yes," she nodded, in a matter-of-fact way. "It was soon after these godless Bolsheviks took over. Thieves and murderers were prowling all over the countryside. One night Grigory—he was my husband, Grigory was—he heard someone moving outside, near the shed. 'They're after our cow!' he whispered, so we each grabbed an ax and stole out of the house. Grigory saw one man and chased the thief half way to the village. But as it turned out, there were two of them. I saw the second one trying to creep along in the shadow of the cottage wall. A Kazakh, of course! He was tossing bits of meat to the dog to keep it quiet. I crept after him, and followed him; right into the shed I followed him. He couldn't hear me because of my *valenki*. And once inside, I gave it to him, straight from the shoulder. His head cracked in two like a watermelon." She shrugged. "What else was there to do?"

Amazed, I stared at Seraphima's unperturbed countenance. Here was a typical Russian peasant, I thought, prepared to fight savagely to protect her possessions. She was just like the millions who had perished fighting collectivization. She proudly killed the man who had tried to steal her precious cow, and yet she would share her last crust with a hungry stranger.

Later, when we two began spending our long winter evenings knitting by the light of a tiny lamp, we got to know each other better, and she began to unburden her heart to me. I then learned what a bitter struggle she'd had after her husband's untimely death. She had only her cow, the orchard, and the small vegetable garden to provide money for herself and her two sons. Our long talks gave me a profound insight into peasant life, better than any amount of reading could have done. Two emotions dominated Seraphima's heart: her fierce love for her sons and her property, and her equally fierce hatred of the Bolsheviks who had changed her simple, uncomplicated world. I was happy to realize that, in a way, my coming was a godsend to her. The modest rent I was to pay during these many months brought a considerable increase to her otherwise scanty income.

With Nadya's money safely in my pocket, Seraphima and I went to buy furniture for my half of the cottage. It turned out to be a rather bizarre shopping expedition, since there was only one shop left in Addis Ada, and that one had hardly anything to sell. On our way there, Seraphima maintained a steady flow of bitter complaints:

"When decent supplies arrive, the Kazakhs grab them! We Russians don't stand a chance. A Russian woman tries to venture into the crowd, and she gets a needle jabbed into her back. It happened to me once. I've never bought so much as a yard of cotton since!"

Gradually, her mind shifted to memories of sweeter days: "You should've seen this place before the Revolution. It was a paradise!

Just imagine, seven hundred shops! And each one full of everything one's heart desired. The food market alone—oh holy Mother
of God! Why, with one ruble you'd buy enough to last the whole
week. The best meat, marbled with rich fat, cost only a few kopeks.
Addis Ada was the center of the cattle trade in those days, and the
Kazakhs used to drive thousands and thousands of sheep and steers
to our market. Then, when they'd sold them, they'd go on such a
shopping spree as you can't believe, simply buying everything that
caught their fancy. You've seen their women wearing their threadbare velvets and silks? Well, before the Revolution each one of
them was magnificently dressed! And our seven hundred shops
used to be always full of customers and thriving! Yes, that's how
it was."

She pointed to a large area behind the market place that looked
like the ruins of Pompeii. "That's where those seven hundred shops
used to be. Each had its own yard full of flowering shrubs, with its
own little pool, and round each pool, cages hanging from boughs,
and a singing nightingale to every cage. . . . And the fat, good-
natured merchants from Tashkent sat around in the yards, sipping
tea and playing chess while an apprentice took care of the customer.
Yes, that's how it used to be!"

"But what became of all the shops?"

The Bolsheviks, she told me, had confiscated the Kazakh herds
and had slaughtered them for food. Shops had been looted, burned,
and smashed. "And now the only merchant left is this magnificent
creature you see here."

She pointed to a dirty, disheveled merchant sprawling on his
counter behind a grime-encrusted window. I peered at him and his
dismal wares—earthenware jars, thick drinking glasses, and pieces
of crockery lying about on sparse, dusty shelves. But in a far
corner I spied a bed. "Look!" I cried. "Is that for sale?"

Seraphima shook her head: "His Foulness won't let you have it.
He'll be saving it for some special crony. They're all the same, they
stick together like lice on a dog's back." Noticing my determination
she shrugged and added: "All right! There's no harm in asking.
You do have a way with you, and maybe even that fat pig can be
charmed. But don't be disappointed if you don't succeed."

The slovenly merchant hardly raised his head to look at us when we went in. He grunted and settled his bulk more firmly over the counter. When I said I wanted to buy the bed, he raised himself on his elbow and stared at me arrogantly. "No! That's for a worthy customer of mine, a Kazakh!" With some surprise, he noticed that I hadn't budged: "You heard me! A Kazakh, I said! He'll be in tomorrow to get it."

"And has he paid you?"

"No, but he will tomorrow."

"Well, I'm paying today!" After twenty years, I decided it was about time for the Communist system to do me some good. I raised my voice threateningly. "If you refuse me, I'll go to the N.K.V.D. I'll tell them all about how you discriminate. This is a Communist State, and all citizens are equal. First come, first served!"

He was on his feet now, startled and a little amused by my effrontery. But the dreaded name of the N.K.V.D. had its intended effect. He puffed, grunted, swore at all women in general and at me in particular, but took my money. The bed was mine now. Seraphima and I picked it up and dragged it to the door; but just as we were about to stagger out, I noticed a number of cobwebbed brown sacks on one of the top shelves. I paused, pointing to them: "What are those?"

The merchant snorted disdainfully: "Stuff nobody wants!"

"Show me."

To my astonished delight the burlap bags, when he unwrapped them, turned out to be filled with unground coffee beans—a commodity worth its weight in gold back in Moscow. As a way of thanking Nadya for her help, I would be able to send her coffee! Best of all, I was able to buy the whole lot for a song: such were the surprises and incongruities of Communist economy.

But now, these pounds of coffee added to the weight of the bed made more of a load than Seraphima and I could handle between us. I looked around helplessly, and caught the merchant's malevolent smirk, clearly insinuating that my greed had been too much for me. I was fully prepared to fling him at least a mild insult, when joyful cries of "Benefactress! Benefactress!" made me turn around sharply.

Fomeech appeared in the doorway, his arms outstretched and his small nose redder than ever: "What's new, Benefactress? Need any help?"

Seraphima gave a narrow-eyed look at the sly, toothless mouth that grinned out of the depths of an unkempt brown beard. She shrank back in disgust. "Who's that?" she sniffed.

"My *sputnik*, Fomeech. We traveled together."

Seraphima visibly stiffened. "A born crook if ever I saw one!" But she did allow him to hoist my bed on his back, while she and I divided the bags of coffee between us. Our weird caravan returned home to the cottage.

After he had installed the bed in a corner of my room, Fomeech looked around in dismay. "But there's no other furniture," he cried.

"That's how things are," I said. "I'll have to make do with what I've got."

He swore and then said, "A lady of quality like yourself, with nothing but a bed—what will people say?"

With that, Fomeech spun around and galloped out the door. Seraphima was still bristling. "The less we see of that little stoat, the better."

But for the next ten days we were to see him with welcome regularity. He appeared at frequent intervals, always bearing a gift: one day came a table; then a day or two later a couple of rickety chairs; then a shelf for books; than a pail, a kitchen knife, cooking ware, and other things that were impossible to buy. Every time he lumbered into the yard, Seraphima would spit venom: "He's here again! The thief!" When he brought frying pans she actually spat on the floor: "He's found himself a woman! The whole village is agog about it. Just fancy—that runt winning a girl's affection! He's probably robbing the poor demented soul!"

But I pretended deafness and refrained from asking Fomeech any questions. Whatever his sources of supply, my room was getting furnished: for the *ruble* I had given him, his gratitude was limitless. Every time he came in triumph to deposit a new article in my room, I'd give him a glass of hot water with an extra lump of sugar. Then he left, followed by Seraphima's habitual invective: "Swindler! Scoundrel! Crook! Don't you dare show your dirty face here again!"

I believe she became a bit jealous of him, for one time, out of her own meager belongings, she gave me two homespun rugs. The expression of her face was clear: "There, it's not only the thieves who are good to you!"

Ater a while, Fomeech disappeared from sight, although not before my room had been made livable to the point of being almost cosy. To make it even more comfortable, our kind neighbors brought me potted plants for my window sill, including a begonia of the *Semper Florens* variety, which I had always loved. And best of all, Nadya's letters began to arrive regularly from Moscow and, little by little, I began to reestablish touch with whatever was left of my old world.

CHAPTER TWENTY

❦

Although I now had modest comforts, Addis Ada was still far from being an Earthly Paradise. The first question to arise was the old, familiar one of unemployment. As a deportee, I couldn't find work, since the N.K.V.D. refused to issue me the necessary permit. My health was poor: prison had undermined my stamina and I suffered recurring attacks of malaria. If it hadn't been for the money and the medicine which Nadya sent me, I doubt I would have pulled through. In addition to those vital kindnesses, every six months Nadya made the then-incredible sacrifice of coming all the way from Moscow to visit me. Her first visit came as a bright ray of light across a dark plain.

Nadya had announced the day she would arrive, and I had been at my wit's end over how to meet her. The railway station lay more than four miles away over a winter road deep in snow and slush; I could find no vehicle of any kind to be had for hire. Seraphima and our few other neighbors only sighed and shook their heads. I had to be reconciled to the fact that poor Nadya would have to walk all the way and handle her luggage as best she could. I didn't sleep a wink the night before her arrival, and I was up pacing my room like a caged lion at the first glow of dawn. When I heard the gate creaking, I rushed into the yard as I was, in my nightgown and barefoot. There stood Nadya, a familiar, slight figure in a modest black coat and hat. But I was distracted from her shy, tentative smile by the astounding sight behind her. There was Fomeech, leading a horse hitched to a cart filled with Nadya's luggage.

"Fomeech!" I cried. "Are you an angel or a wizard? How did you know that Nadya was coming, and where did you get that horse and cart?"

By then Seraphima had joined us. "He stole them of course," she hissed.

"I bought them, you silly old witch!" Fomeech shouted.

She bolted off to make sure her precious "Mashka" was still in the cottage.

Fomeech turned to Nadya, his chest puffing with pride: "Don't listen to that peasant! Fomeech has a heart. Fomeech never forgets. This noble lady gave him her last ruble when he was down and out. What else can he do but serve her?"

Nadya, dividing her stare between Fomeech and the vanishing Seraphima could make neither head not tail of this declaration. Indeed, we never did learn how Fomeech had heard of her arrival in the first place. With a smile deep in his beard, his nose like a tiny scarlet monticule, he carried Nadya's luggage into my room and hurried off without waiting for his usual recompense of sugared hot water. I'm ashamed to say I hardly even thanked him, flustered as I was at the sight of Nadya's dear face. I seemed to catch a breath of my former life with all its latent happiness.

Nadya Shipov was the only girl among several boys in a most distinguished family. Her father had been a man of lofty ideals and great personal charm, a prominent member of the *Zemstvos* and founder of the liberal Octobrist Party. Her father's favorite, Nadya, shared his deep religious faith and his conviction that life's only worthy aim was service to others.

Her mother was conventional to the very roots of her hair. As the French say, *elle n'avait pas inventé la poudre*—she had not invented gunpowder—in short, she was not overbright. Resentful of Nadya's devotion to her father, her sole ambition was to make a good match for her daughter. When Nadya did fall in love with an excellent young man, her mother quickly pointed out that he was not of the nobility, and worse, that he entertained liberal ideas. She somehow contrived to eliminate him altogether from Nadya's life. Season after season, poor Nadya was dragged to receptions, balls, and dinners. She became a dejected wallflower whose sad expression and appalling gowns (ones her mother had chosen for her) conspired to discourage romantic interest. But success could have been hers: although never pretty in the strict sense of the word, she had magnificent long hair, large blue eyes, and a lovely figure.

Friends of ours could never understand why we were drawn together. The arts, which played so important a role in my life, meant nothing to her. But that was understandable: as Paul Bourget wrote, good taste needs the soil of beautiful surroundings, in which to flourish. Nadya could have found little beauty in her mother's drawing room, whose sky-blue walls were hung with enormous oil paintings of buffaloes wallowing in the swamps of the Roman Campagna, where the worst Victorian furniture was upholstered in bright red and bright blue plush amidst a cluttered ambience decorated in garish colors by Madame Shipov.

What is more, Nadya was calm, levelheaded, and very obstinate, whereas I, as should be obvious by now, was erratic, passionate, and hot-tempered. But I felt an immediate sympathy for Nadya's constant struggle between loyalty to her mother and love of her father. According to her, ours was the only "patrician" house she liked to visit, because it alone had an atmosphere of freedom and gaiety. Her stubborn prejudice against "high society" refused to acknowledge the many delightful upper-class families in Moscow. I admired her character, outspokenly sincere and honestly obstinate as she was.

In our youth we went to lectures and courses at the University, and discussed what we had learned for hours on end. This too deepened our friendship. But when we came of age and could do as we pleased, I chose marriage to Nika, while Nadya plunged into all sorts of educational activities and won renown from the very start.

Undoubtedly it was the Revolution that brought out Nadya's true mettle. When her father and three brothers were arrested, she worked at two different jobs in order to provide for her mother. Late at night she cooked food and packed it in parcels which she carried to the prison. A friend of ours who'd shared a cell with the dying Mr. Shipov, later told me that to the very last, the old gentleman had kept his eyes on the door, hoping that Nadya would walk in.

Nadya finally obtained an unheard-of personal interview with Yagoda, the infamous head of the N.K.V.D. She talked him into giving her the needed visitor's pass, but when she reached the Butyrka Prison, her father was dead. Nika, who had always been devoted to Mr Shipov, obtained a coffin and sled. All by himself, he dragged Mr. Shipov's remains to a cemetery several miles outside Moscow. After we had buried her father, Nadya took me aside.

"Masha," she whispered, "I will never be able to repay Nika for what he has done!"

I threw up my hands in indignation: "What a dreadful word— 'repay'! One doesn't repay friendship and love!"

But Nadya did in the end.

In 1937, when Nika had been arrested for the last time, Nadya moved in with me until I recovered from the shock. When I was deported to Kazakhstan, she took charge of the parcels Nika's family was sending me from America. She flatly ignored the danger of helping a declared "enemy of the people." Her sole precaution was to make one of her pupils wait for her outside the Customs Office.

"If I'm not back in half an hour or so," she would say, "you will know that I've been arrested. If so, then go and tell our friends."

At the time, Nadya was earning her living by tutoring high-school children after school hours. According to Bolshevik law, this was as heinous a crime as private speculation, but Yagoda was apparently impressed by her abilities. Whatever the cause, he issued an order that Nadya should not be molested in any way. Even after Yagoda was assassinated and replaced by the still more blood-thirsty Yezhov, she continued to give private lessons. Of course, she by then had an added protection in the form of the tutored pupils themselves, who were always at the top of their class. The compliments went directly to the school authorities who were, accordingly, all in hearty favor of Nadya's enterprise.

Nevertheless, her fees were small and left her no margin for herself. While living with me, she took in laundry and went to the washtub and ironing board every night after dinner. She continued as a part-time laundress throughout the three years of my exile. The only breaks in her routine came when she left Moscow to visit me.* Though third-class fares were not expensive, Nadya was nevertheless often obliged to sell some of my few belongings left in Moscow to buy her ticket. But her visits meant far more to me than even the most precious trinkets.

* Later we figured that in all, she had traveled 30,000 miles!

Shortly after one of her visits, Nadya actually saved my life. No sooner had she left for Moscow than I fell seriously ill, probably with typhus. There was no doctor in Addis Ada to diagnose the the case, let alone to supply the necessary drugs. Faithful Seraphima kept a constant vigil at my bedside, but of course wasn't able to do much. For a week I lived on vodka and water and grew steadily worse, until at last I realized that I was very close to death. In the face of my strict injunctions, Seraphima finally sent Nadya a sparsely worded but urgent telegram. Nadya dropped everything and immediately returned with food and medicines. When I regained consciousness one day I found her bending over me, and for a moment thought I was already in another world. In the years to come, whenever Nadya's patience was strained by my flashes of extravagant impracticality, I was to tease her that she must have saved my life as a penance for her sins.

The time finally came when my "free deportation" was over, when I was able to leave central Asia. The ominous year of 1941 was upon us, though no one yet suspected what was to come. Had I been allowed to remain in Moscow, I might eventually have gained some inkling of the situation developing outside Russia's borders. But directly upon my return, the N.K.V.D. paid a call to confiscate the little I had left. As a bonus, they informed me that, as a former political deportee, I would have to find a place of residence at least three hundred miles from the capital. They granted me a period of three days' grace in which to clear out.

Nadya could go or stay, as she chose, of course. But by that time, she'd had quite enough of walking the tightrope of daily existence under Stalin. She decided to come with me and share my fate, rather than face Moscow's snares and pitfalls by herself. In order to settle my affairs, I blatantly disobeyed the N.K.V.D.'s orders and remained in hiding for ten more days. It was cruel to subject Nadya to such a risk, but fortunately no one informed on me. We were not apprehended.

For our place of future residence, Nadya had suggested Zubtsov, a small provincial town situated close to the Soviet Union's western border. She knew a man there who she thought might be of help. But I was dubious at first, and balked at moving in the opposite direction from where Nika was likely to be. Yet at the same time, I nourished an unformulated hope that some power would intervene to set him free. Already across the border, close to Zubtsov, stood a formidable section of the German army. That much I knew; or should I say, that's how *little* I knew. I envisioned those rumored but invisible hordes as an avenging host which might descend on us as if in answer to Voloshin's poem; whose power would crush the Bolsheviks and liberate the millions they had imprisoned. In the state of mind I was in, even a cataclysm appeared merely as a possible path back to Nika.

In the end I agreed that Zubtsov would be a good choice for us. In May of 1941, Nadya and I took the little we had and left our native Moscow. Only one month later, German troops were to come pouring across the border, and my search for Nika was to take yet another direction.

PART THREE

❧⟨⟩❧

Portals to a Dead End

CHAPTER TWENTY-ONE

❧

That blind naïveté which let one misconceive of Hitler as a potential liberator was not an uncommon affliction. The vast majority of my compatriots had also been kept in ignorance of what was going on in the outside world. The Soviet Press had always slanted its foreign news items to such a degree that we had grown accustomed to believing the reverse of whatever we read. But just how accurate this method was, no one could rightly tell.

As the world crisis of the late thirties grew, news items became so blatantly self-contradictory that they left us hopelessly confused. At first, the Nazis had been "Brown Devils," "Fascist Bandits," or "Scum of the Earth." After the Hitler-Stalin pact was signed, we were to understand that our gentlemanly allies were reluctantly participating in the rape of Poland. Certainly my prevailing knowledge was even less than average, inasmuch as during my three years of exile I had been completely cut off from all news. Stalin's monstrous reign had crushed not only my patriotism, but also whatever interest I might have had left in current events. I had reached a point where I didn't care what happened to Mother Russia, and having little news at all to ponder on, my speculations had been reduced to the single concern of Nika's welfare.

Zubtsov, as it turned out, was a small town deeply mired in its own provincialism, a place reminiscent of Gogol's village of Mirgorod and its eternal puddle. But in the green flourish of that spring of 1941, seeing it from aboard the ferry carrying us across the confluence of the young, narrow Volga and the Vazooza, we thought Zubtsov friendly and even rather cute.

Nadya's friend, Zahar Kuzmeech, was an old gentleman who lived up to all she had led me to expect. He knew everyone within a radius of a hundred miles, and before our first evening there, he had escorted us to a little house on the outskirts of town. Our hostesses were two maiden sisters, exquisitely clean and tidy old souls who dressed in faded cotton dresses and white aprons. Evdokia, the eldest, greeted us.

"You are welcome since Zahar Kuzmeech recommends you. He is such a faithful friend! Ah yes, in our youth we spent many a summer evening in the garden with him, listening to the songs of nightingales!" She looked up lovingly at her aging beau, who returned her glance with a cocky little smile.

The little house was immaculately clean, with carefully polished floors and white curtains. Pots of geraniums lined the windows, and an icon hung in the corner of each room. Beyond Evdokia's small garden of bygone romance began the forest which stretched uninterrupted to the western border. That "garden" itself was an exuberant tangle of lilac, jasmine, and raspberry bushes; all overrunning something that had once passed as a large apple tree. Natalia, the younger of the two sisters, explained to us why it was still standing.

"Our father, God rest his soul, picked that tree as his very favorite. Every day in the summer you could find him sitting in its shade, reading his paper. Then he died, and later on, the tree too; but we were never able to bring ourselves to cut it down. It holds too many memories." On the same afternoon of our arrival we were served tea beneath this arboreal skeleton. Of course, hot water with a tiny lump of sugar passed for tea in those days, and on this occasion, dried potato peels took the place of biscuits.

Not satisfied with providing us with a lodging, Zahar Kuzmeech found us a provider as well. "For you I would do anything," he said to Nadya. A few days later, he appeared with Darya—a stout, good-natured peasant woman who lived in a village five miles away.

"Darya comes to the town market regularly to sell her produce," said Zahar Kuzmeech. "She has promised to supply you with potatoes, cabbage, and whatever else she may have in the way of vegetables, providing you let her have some tea and sugar in exchange." (The news had quickly spread that Nadya had arrived with a sizable supply of both commodities, which she'd accumulated over years of abstinence.) Zahar Kuzmeech kept his large, rolling eyes on Nadya, and Darya's knowing wink made me realize how irresistibly naughty the old boy could be. It was all I could do to keep from laughing, but Nadya was a bit shocked.

"I'm afraid," she said when we were alone, "my friend Zahar Kuzmeech is a sort of a local Don Juan."

"Yes," I teased, "and you could easily play first fiddle in his harem."

Surprisingly, Nadya was quite embarrassed by my remark. Perhaps it was just as well that Zahar Kuzmeech left for Moscow a few days later. We never saw him again.

We found it easy to settle in with Evdokia and Natalia. The two old spinsters cleaned and scrubbed all day, and Darya supplied us regularly with potatoes. For a brief spell, we enjoyed real peace in that quiet little home on the edge of the vast forest. But no one could tell exactly what lay on the other side of those trees. My attitude toward a possible German attack, was *tant pis, tant mieux*, but Nadya, always the true patriot, deplored my lack of concern.

Despite our uncertainties, we were both convinced of one thing: real danger lurked in Zubtsov itself. Before leaving, Zahar Kuzmeech had warned us:

"Avoid going into town. Nothing can ever be kept secret in a small place like this. Already everyone knows that Madame Avinov has been exiled from Moscow as an 'enemy of the people.' What with the Party always poking its nose into everyone's business— well, you know; I don't have to tell you! But above all, beware of our local N.K.V.D. chief. A real sadist! He shoots and tortures prisoners himself. He makes his rounds regularly, along with a savage dog trained to go for the throat. You may run into them anywhere."

We dutifully avoided town as much as possible, but hunger sometimes managed to drive us as far as the market. This was a depressing place where ragged figures milled through shabby stalls. For the hungry customer, there was little available besides carrots, half-rotten potatoes, and cabbage. Nadya, the ascetic one, was perfectly content with vegetables, but I always keened at the few scraps of meat that were offered for sale. One day I noticed a small leg of lamb. I was contemplating a juicy, succulent roast, and reaching into my pocket to count my rubles, when I felt a discreet nudge.

"You're the lady from Moscow, aren't you?" whispered a big portly matron at my side. "Well, you don't know what goes on here. Don't buy that lamb; it's really a dog's leg. The butcher killed a dog yesterday, and now he's passing it off as mutton!"

Having saved me from spending my last kopeks on dog-meat, she fell to talking. As we stood there transforming our grievances into pleasant gossip, the crowd around us suddenly gave way before the local N.K.V.D. chief. There was no mistaking his blue uniform, the revolver in his belt, and the brute of a dog at his heels. Quickly I slipped behind my new friend's broad back, and held my breath, while the officer paused to scan every face in the crowd. He passed on without noticing me, but his bestial features stuck in my memory with a strange clarity—it was as if I carried his photograph in my head.

In the meanwhile, Nadya had found some pork in one of the stalls. We met up, compared notes, and trotted home together in high spirits.

That evening, Nadya insisted I eat the lion's share of our little roast, and I finally obliged. After dinner, we went out to sit under the so-called apple tree. Suddenly, a lone airplane appeared out of the west, flying at almost treetop level. We saw swastikas on the wings. As the plane flew over our heads, the pilot leaned out and waved. I sprang to my feet and frantically waved my white handkerchief in return.

"Masha! What are you doing?" Nadya cried. "That's a German plane!"

"Yes, thank God, and may many more of them come soon to wipe out the Bolsheviks!" I kept waving until the plane was well out of sight.

Nadya's eyes were full of shock and reproach. "But that means an invasion of Russia!"

I knew Nika would have had much the same reaction, but I persisted anyway. "I don't care. Any army is a friendly one as long as it gets rid of those foul obscenities!"

Nadya had barely time to frown when Evdokia appeared in the doorway, beckoning. "Quick! Quick! Come and listen to the 'Liar'!" (*Liar* was the then-universal nickname for Moscow's official news broadcast.)

As we arrived in the parlor, Stalin's voice, with its unmistakable

Georgian accent, was announcing that German troops had treacher-
ously invaded the "sacred soil" of Russia. His voice was trembling
with emotion: "Beloved brothers and sisters! Our heroic troops have
already defeated the Fascist dogs, who are in full flight . . ."

"Help us God," gasped Natalia, and crossed herself. "Things
must be pretty bad if he's calling us 'beloved brothers and sisters'!"

Indeed, Stalin had never been known to use such expressions as
"beloved brothers" and "sacred soil." We were convinced that the
situation was desperate and that he had been lying when he spoke
of a German rout.

The very next day, great herds of cattle being driven out of the
west began to pass through our little town—Stalin had ordered the
evacuation of the border regions. Poor unmilked cows, lowing
pitifully, stumbled along in clouds of dust through the oppressive
June heat. Housewives rushed out with pails and pitchers. There
hadn't been such an abundance of milk since before the Revolution,
and the whole town rejoiced for several days. Then came flocks of
sheep, and pigs. The undernourished population around Zubtsov
took their toll, and a delicious smell of roasting meat arose from
every kitchen. Finally the voice of my conscience was drowned
in the rumblings of my stomach. "Nadya," I cried, "let's also grab a
pig!"

"But Masha! That would be stealing!"

"So what? Everything has been stolen from everyone for so
many years, that one hardly knows any more what belongs to
whom!" In the end, however, our two maiden hostesses shared
Nadya's scruples, and so all day long I was obliged to let those
steaks and chops pass by unmolested.

On the morning of the third day after Stalin's announcement,
the eastern skies seemed ablaze. Supplies and stocks of every kind
were being burned in the city of Rzhev, some fifteen miles away.
Even from that distance one could detect on the wind the smell of
burning sugar and flour. People gathered on street corners, muttering in anger.

"Why are they burning food when we're in need of everything?
Why bother, if we are victorious and the Germans are in flight?"

The radio kept feeding us lies until the day when, even as "The
Liar" was crowing over victory, a German unit entered Zubtsov
from the west. A counter-attacking Russian unit moved in from

the east, and a skirmish erupted in the meadow behind our house. Machine guns strafed our walls and smashed a few windows. Nadya and I ran into the garden and down a narrow path to the river bank. Across the path lay the corpse of an old woman, her sightless eyes staring up at the sky. We stepped over her and kept running until a disembodied voice called to us.

"Lie down, fools! Quick! There are Germans on the other bank. *Lie down!*"

We dropped on our faces. The soldier who had shouted at us was hiding in a foxhole, and I could see the tip of his cap. Bullets began to sing over our heads, snapping at overhanging branches. Twigs fell on top of us.

Down by our side of the river, a house had been quickly abandoned. The front door was wide open, and a dog had been left behind, chained to his kennel. The poor animal was howling his head off, and frantically biting at his chain.

"Look at that poor beast," I whispered to Nadya. "He'll be killed, or else starve. . . . I think I'll slide down the bank and set him free."

Nadya seized me by the arm: "Are you mad? You'll get shot!" I tried to free myself of her grip. "Now really, Masha! Death is everywhere, staring us in the face, and you go worrying about a dog! Have you forgotten the dead woman on the path?"

"That's different. That animal's still alive, and suffering."

Her hold on my arm tightened, and we lay very still for a while.

"You know, Masha," said, Nadya, "I wouldn't mind dying here, with the blue sky above and the smell of pines in the air. There'd be no more dangers then, no more striving; nothing but peace and rest then, everlasting peace . . ."

My reaction was instantaneous and vehement: "No! No! I want to live! I want to see Nika again!" I then realized that this was not the safest place we could have chosen for refuge. "Come," I whispered, "let's move on."

We crawled on our bellies until finally we rounded a bend in the path. We were now hidden from the opposite bank, and the firing could not reach us, but we could still hear that wretched dog howling. Over the sound of shooting, that yelping whimper kept on and on. All the world's misery and pain seemed to be expressed in that heartrending cry.

CHAPTER TWENTY-TWO

❧

Shortly after the Russian troops forced back the German unit, there was no food to be had in town. The management of the State Savings Bank had closed its doors and departed with all the savings. "The Liar" was still babbling on: "The conflict is over; conditions are returning to normal . . ." I felt no confidence in such optimistic reports and looked anxiously to Nadya: what if real, full-fledged war were to break out and separate us for good? But Nadya was her most obstinate self that day. Unswayed by my arguments, she boarded a train for Moscow, hoping to bring back money and provisions.

The next morning, I awoke to "The Liar's" cries of alarm: the Germans were on the offensive again! Stalin had ordered instant evacuation! "Back to Moscow," was the order of the day. The broadcast went on to describe German atrocities in graphic detail. Everyone listened aghast to how prisoners were tortured, how women were raped, how old people and children were deliberately crushed beneath heavy armored tanks. But no one felt like leaving.

"Better stick to our homes and trust in God," said Natalia.

The air attack began at noon on a hot, sultry June day. German *Stukas* flew over again and again. The roar of their engines was terrifying as they swooped down for long bombing runs. Naturally, Zubtsov had no antiaircraft defense. Evdokia and Natalia implored me to take refuge in the garden, a plan which seemed the height of folly. I imagined the house and its walls would offer at least some protection. Hurrying indoors, I caught sight of the two old souls, lying on their backs in a ditch near the ungainly skeleton of their beloved apple tree. Each had her eyes tightly closed and wore a small icon over her heart. Bombs were falling all around, and fires were beginning to break out in the afflicted town.

I went straight to my little room and sat down, placing photographs of Nika and Mother before me. Gazing at their beloved
faces, I tried to calm myself. I was trembling from head to foot,
but gradually, an inner serenity began to grow until I was able
to fight my way through to a calm and grateful faith in God. I'm
sure Evdokia and Natalia in their ditch, each clasping her icon,
must have known a similar experience.

By some miracle, our house escaped unscathed except for the
bullet scars of a few days before. At last the *Stukas* disappeared,
leaving havoc behind them—whole streets in flames, and hundreds
of people buried in the rubble. We were told that the Red Army
stood outside Zubtsov, ready for a counter-attack. It became clear
to everyone that our town was to be a battleground, and that the
time had clearly come to run for dear life. Evdokia and Natalia
loaded everything they could into a cart, harnessed their cow to it,
and departed in tears, hoping to reach a village where they had
relatives.

I was left alone. Wandering through the house, I gathered things
of value and hid them under straw in the cellar, hoping that no
marauders, either German or Russian, would find them. For myself, I made up a small bundle of absolute essentials: a toothbrush,
a cake of soap, a towel, a change of underwear, Heredia's
Sonnets, and Flaubert's *Letters*. I intended to walk the five miles to
Darya's village and ask her for shelter; but on leaving the house I
remembered Nadya. It seemed unlikely now that she would return
from Moscow, but if she did, how would she find me?

In my distress, I wandered outside and glanced helplessly at the
devastation. Across the street, on the steps of a small house which
had also escaped destruction, stood the woman who occasionally
sold us fresh eggs.

"Aren't you leaving?" I called over to her. She shook her head.
"But everyone else is!"

"I know. But I can't leave my hens."

I couldn't help smiling. Hers was the kind of attitude, I thought,
that keeps the world moving, and saves people from insanity. I ran
across the street.

"Please, if my friend returns, tell her where I am." I repeated
the name of Darya's village and Darya's full name. The woman
promised she would look out for Nadya. We embraced, blessing

one another with the sign of the cross; and I set off with my bundle slung over my shoulder.

The smoking ruins of Zubtsov were soon far behind. I walked through an empty countryside where wild flowers and fields of wheat rustled under the sun, where a lark in the sky above sang on as gaily as ever. Only when the breeze was right was the peace and quiet broken by muffled gunfire, far, far away.

Darya received me with open arms. "There are refugees everywhere," she cried. "The house is packed. Guests are sleeping on benches, on the floor, in the barn . . . But to you, dear lady, I'll cede my bridal couch!"

She had a strange, pompous way of expressing herself sometimes, which seemed to prove that she had rubbed shoulders outside her class. I deposited my little bundle on her vast wooden bed, wondering whose bride she had been, inasmuch as she seemed to be husbandless. The image of Zahar Kuzmeech flashed through my mind, but I rebuked myself for such indecorous speculations.

Other "guests" from Zubtsov gathered round me, and I was bombarded with questions: What had happened since they left town? What did I think was the best thing to do? Were they to go back, stay here, or retreat still further? These poor souls had been suddenly deprived of everything they owned; but even so, I had to be careful with them. I recognized a couple of Communists in their midst, and an unguarded word might yet have landed me in trouble. So, in my best storytelling style, I began to reel off all sorts of minor incidents that had occurred in and around Zubtsov. Even when I resorted to hearsay, they listened attentively and seemed to derive comfort from hearing the Red Army emerge as the hero. When I was finished, other groups from other houses came to listen, and I found myself again the "Scheherazade of Cell 26." People are intrinsically the same under dire circumstances: whoever captures their imagination can stimulate their courage as well. But on a diet of next to nothing, sheer talk was an exhausting job for me. Two days of it and I was worn out.

I slept well at night, even though Darya's spacious old bed was dangerously rickety. And I felt considerably rested on the morning a German plane flew over and caused several minutes of panic. We saw it coming from afar and ran for shelter. But instead of bombs, a silent shower of leaflets fell over the village. Then the plane was gone, and the thousands of fluttering white shapes settled lightly down over rooftops, fences, and streets.

From all sides men, women, and children came rushing to read the Germans' message. I too picked one up. At a glance I saw it was in Russian—a proclamation addressed to the Russian people. My hopes rose as I started to read.

"We are not at war with you, Russian People, only with your criminal oppressors, the Bolsheviks!" The proclamation went on to make great and solemn promises in the event of a German victory. All land would devolve to the peasants, all political prisoners would be liberated from prisons and concentration camps—I caught my breath. I could see myself scanning every face until my glance struck Nika . . .

A tap on my shoulder brought me back to earth. Darya stood beside me, also with a proclamation in her hand. Her ordinarily shifty eyes for once were fixed upon mine, reflecting my own hopes. I smiled; under the skin we were sisters. She nudged me and pointed to the men and women of the village who had gathered into a crowd. Each was examining a proclamation, while a Communist harangued them all at the top of his voice:

"Comrades! Don't believe a word of it. They'll torture you to death, and rape your women. They'll disembowel your elders and carry your children into slavery . . ."

What a typically Bolshevik approach, I thought, to threaten and bully without once appealing to loyalty and patriotism! Or had Stalin's rule erased all traces of such noble feelings?

"Throw away those filthy leaflets," our speaker shouted in conclusion. "Save yourselves. The Devil himself couldn't have thought of a better trap!"

How fortunate that Nadya was not there at the time! Taking a deep breath, I began speaking in a voice of calm sarcasm:

"Of course, that's one way of looking at it, Comrade Orator. But we all know there's another way, too." I turned and addressed the peasants: "We all know that the Devil is a liar and the father of lies, but I, for one, am still in doubt as to where he really lurks! Now, this proclamation we have here casts doubt on everything our government has told us. We can't say it's a lie just because it's a new viewpoint. I suggest it could be our *government* who's not telling the truth, my friends. Isn't that possible?"

I saw my Bolshevik opponent was yearning for the slightest
encouragement to throw himself upon me, but the peasants remained noncommittal. They glanced sullenly from him to me, their
faces closed. However, not one of them threw away the proclamation. Carefully, they all tucked it into their shirts and slowly drifted
away. Darya nudged me:

"You've scored! They are with you. Oh yes, they're with you
all right."

Next day, as I sat discussing the pros and cons of the German
proclamation with some of our "guests," Darya hurried into the
room. Another "guest" had arrived who was asking for me. Had
my public debate been reported? But when Darya opened the door,
there stood Nadya! The two of us wept with joy, and again
"guests" crowded around, this time to hear the latest news from
Moscow. But Nadya was cautious, as I had been some days before.
Not until we were alone, later that night, did I hear the full story
of her adventures.

Even then, farcical comedy preceded drama. No sooner had
Nadya climbed into Darya's bed beside me, than the whole antique
edifice gave a splintering groan and collapsed. We landed on the
floor startled, but unhurt. Only after our laughter had subsided and
we had settled ourselves amidst the debris, did Nadya begin to
relate her story in hushed whispers.

From the moment of her arrival in Moscow, she had sensed that
something was drastically wrong. There were too many automobiles leaving town, too many queues in front of the food stores.
All day long, a black pall of smoke hung over the Lubyanka headquarters of the N.K.V.D.; the executioners were burning their
incriminating records. When Nadya looked up some friends, they
stared at her in dismay:

"What on earth are you doing? Don't you know the Government is leaving for the Ural? Moscow is to be left undefended. You
will never be able to get back to Zubtsov. For all we know, the
Germans may be there already."

"In that case," answered Nadya, "I'm going back there to help
Masha!" Cramming everything she could into two big suitcases,
she was off to the station again without a backward glance.

Her railroad ticket was issued without hesitation, and the train
even left on time. But at three in the morning, it stopped about

twenty-five miles outside Zubtsov. A conductor hurried through the car, shouting, "Passengers for Zubtsov please get out and walk. The rails have been cut. Those wishing to return to Moscow, keep your seats. This train will go back."

With about a dozen others, Nadya left the train. For the promise of a sizable tip, two men agreed to carry her heavy suitcases. As they moved off into the clear night, the engine blew a mournful whistle behind them and the train backed away. Walking on a road that led away from the tracks, they soon heard what seemed like distant rifle fire. With every step the noise grew louder, and the group bound for Zubtsov began losing travelers one by one. At last, only Nadya and the two men were left. By then the sound of shooting had grown into a thunderous cannonade. Especially loud blasts shook the ground they stood on. The men set down Nadya's suitcases.

"We'd rather not go any further!" She paid them, and they both ran headlong back toward the railroad tracks. Nadya was alone by the roadside until an army truck full of soldiers came rumbling along and swayed to a halt.

"What are you doing there, Citizeness?" demanded a suspicious voice. When Nadya replied she had just come from Moscow, eager hands and arms shot out to haul her and her luggage into the truck. The soldiers clamored for the latest news, until they heard that Moscow was to be left undefended. They sat down again with bowed heads, and kept their heavy silence until the truck reached the Volga, near Zubtsov.

"Well, here we are," said the young officer in command. Nadya climbed down off the truck, and he leaned out to hand her the two suitcases. "You're on your own now, Citizeness. Good luck! Bear us no grudge for leaving you. Well—with God's help, eh?"

The truck bumped and bounced along the rough road following the river bank, and disappeared. But again help was at hand. Through the early morning mist, she saw a ferryman waving to her.

"You're lucky, lady. This is my last crossing. The Germans are expected within the hour!"

When Nadya reached Evdokia and Natalia's house, the good woman across the street was still standing guard over her hens. Nadya quickly learned where I was, but her suitcases had become too much for her to handle any longer and she left them with our former neighbor, after taking out what was most necessary.

"And so, here I am," she said.

Another bright June morning was about to burst in on us, but I was still afraid that Nadya would refuse to see things as I had after the leaflets had been dropped the day before. One by one, I tried various ways of opening the discussion, and cast each aside as unsatisfactory. A long silence fell between us. After several abortive attempts, I finally abandoned the rhetorical preamble.

"Nadya! Honestly now, what are we going to do? The Germans are going to be here any day now. I think we should give ourselves up."

I had expected her horrified shudder: "But that would mean going over to the enemy! We would be cutting ourselves off from Russia, perhaps forever. You know I can't agree to that."

I pressed into her hand the German proclamation: "Read this. Read it and you will see."

She read it through rising tears, and shook her head despondently: "I can't . . ."

"But Nadya, look what they are promising! Frankly I don't believe a word of this talk about atrocities. The Kremlin is merely lying; the Germans are a civilized people, and they wouldn't do anything like that."

Nadya's voice was dry: "Remember what they did in Belgium during the last war?"

"Believe me, in the last war, acts of brutality were committed on all sides. This is different! The Germans are being accused of the most execrable crimes with no proof, mind you, and nothing to go by. I don't believe it. No one can tell me that the people of Schiller and Goethe, of Beethoven, Mozart, and Bach could ever be capable of such inhumanity."

She regarded me coldly: "Oh, have you forgotten what the people of Tchaikovsky and Moussorgsky, of Pushkin, Turgenev, and Tolstoy have been capable of?"

I had to concede the point, but I was irritated that Nadya, who had no real feeling for the arts, should have brought up such an argument. "All right! But I'm sure the Germans would never allow themselves to be led by such utterly godless men as the Russians have."

"*We* are getting better. That young officer yesterday morning, he said 'With *God's* help.' You yourself heard Stalin referring to Russian soil as 'sacred.' "

"Yes! Now that he's quaking in his shoes, he's decided to suck up to us! Of all people, you should see the man is possessed by devils—after what he's done to your father and brothers, to my Nika, to thousands of our countrymen. If Stalin ever comes out of this war as the victor, he'll become even worse. What if he does talk of holiness? That's the way of the Devil, to cringe when in danger, and then attack again later, when the danger is gone. I say *any* power set against Stalin is a blessing to us all, and I really don't understand how we can suddenly be expected to believe everything he tells us about the Germans!"

"It's not that I believe him. It's just . . . well, it's just that he is *with* Russia and the Germans are *against!*"

"But they aren't against us! They say it here, plainly—'We are not at war with the Russian people.' Theirs is merely an attack on Bolshevism, and as such, it's a just attack!" Nadya buried her face in her arms, and began weeping bitter tears. In desperation I shook the proclamation over her head: "These are strong promises, Nadya, like a covenant with the people of Russia! The Germans would never dare break them even if they wanted to. All the land to the peasants! All political prisoners set free! Do you really mind if I get my husband back?"

Nadya sat up, drying her eyes. "No. Please remember, Masha, for me everyone is dead. Everyone is gone." She took my hand. "You are the dearest thing left in my life. I still think you are mistaken, but I'll go with you."

CHAPTER TWENTY-THREE

The next day children rushed through the village streets yelling, "The Germans, the Germans!" From all sides, peasants and refugees came running to me in panic. After my brush with the Communist the day before, I had apparently become a pillar of strength in their eyes, and besides, all the diehard Communists of the village had vanished to a man. Even before the alarm was sounded they had made off stealthily, without a word of warning to anyone.

"Save us," cried the villagers. "What'll happen to us? Will we be massacred?" Now they had singled me out in their desperate search for leadership. I crossed myself.

"Nothing will happen," I said. "If the Germans are coming, then let's go and meet them."

In all seriousness, I did feel like a sort of Moses in skirts as I led a crowd of peasants to a high elevation outside the village. Across the plain below, a dirt road could be seen winding for miles out of the west. One moment it was totally desolate; the next, I distinctly saw activity near the horizon. I prayed that the invaders would keep their promises and live up to what I thought them to be. The breeze carried the still far-off noise of engines, a bit like the sound of cicadas. With my agitation concealed under a fixed smile, I watched what looked like a grayish-green serpent move slowly along the road in our direction: the *Wehrmacht*.

The head of the column was drawing near. I gave the signal to move and led the way down the hill. I could almost feel Nadya recoil, but, never one to turn back, once her mind was made up, she followed close behind me with the rest. The German officer in command of the column called a halt. I approached him.

"*Herr Offizier,*" I said in my best German, "we greet you as liberators. We have read the proclamations dropped by your plane, and know that you have come to fight our Communist oppressors, not us. Therefore, we welcome you and put ourselves in your hands."

Nadya forced herself to mumble a few similar words in German, a concession which must have cost her much. I felt sorry for her, and wondered again whether I had done right in forcing this issue. But the German officer's obvious delight helped reassure me:

"Good Heavens! Can this be true, that two ladies come to welcome us in our own tongue? Are you Germans?"

"No, Russians. But we have often visited Germany. We have admired your literature and your works of art. That is why we have laid our confidence in you."

"And rightly so! I promise we'll do all we can for you." For a moment his probing eyes scanned the faces of the crowd behind me. "But your friends, I see, are not too happy."

I explained to him how for weeks the Moscow radio had fed us tales of German atrocities. A spontaneous ripple of laughter rose from the ranks. The officer joined in the good-natured laughter and dispelled whatever doubts I still harbored about the Germans' honorable intentions.

"Tell the good people that they have nothing to fear. Also, tell them we'll pay for whatever we need."

I turned to the crowd to translate. The peasants looked somewhat relieved. And followed by our excited, chattering mob, the *Wehrmacht* column marched on into the village.

Now that the Communists were gone, there was no one to stop German and Russian from fraternizing. That afternoon and evening, when the German field kitchens had been pitched, there were scenes reminiscent of a "Peace on Earth" allegory with the lion and the lamb resting together. Women sold eggs and milk, and what little else was available. The German quartermaster paid without bargaining. Children gazed spellbound at the unfamiliar German chocolates and candy the soldiers gave them. By nightfall, the soldiers lay around their fires, smoking, while the villagers stood eyeing them curiously. From time to time, individuals exchanged a quite incomprehensible banter in a mixture of Russian and German. But Nadya and I were moved by the pitiable contrast between those clean-shaven, well-dressed, properly fed Germans and our ragged, half-starved Russians. But I also felt an immense personal relief; all miseries seemed at an end. With Stalin defeated, we might all again have cause to hope.

When I look back on that day, I feel that our ignorance was, in a way, our armor. Had we known any real symptoms of Nazi barbarism, we could never have collaborated with the *Wehrmacht*, and would probably have perished in reprisals, as did many other uncooperative Russians. When those first days passed without any brutality or cruelty on the part of the Germans, I strengthened my resolve to help them in every way I could. I did my best to facilitate relations between the invaders and the local population, and was proud to be participating in the great anti-Communist drive.

Next morning we returned to Zubtsov. Our house still stood intact, though Evdokia and Natalia had not yet returned. No sooner did we take possession of it, than two German officers moved in along with their orderlies. We wondered what would happen to us, but they very courteously permitted us to stay. That same evening we were invited to supper. Their frugal army rations seemed to us an epicurean treat: chick-pea soup, canned meat, *ersatz* coffee, and fresh white bread. After the life and company we'd been keeping, it was a pleasure to exchange civilities with two well-bred young men. Our two hosts seemed amazed at our ignorance, and kindly gave us an able résumé of the German view of world affairs.

"Gentlemen, are you members of the Nazi Party?" I asked, rather naïvely.

"We are *all* Nazis," was the prompt reply, "but we are hardly the monsters that Communist propaganda has made us out to be." We leaned forward, listening attentively to their discourse on Hitler's reforms. The New Order, they said, had put the Fatherland on its feet, given people new incentives to work, and revived a German's love of his country and pride in his inheritance. "And we can assure you, we have all been thoroughly briefed, down to the last man. We all know that this is not a war, but rather a Crusade, a Holy Crusade. Very soon now, we will free Russia of her dreadful yoke!"

Now, even Nadya began to put her trust in their words.

German efficiency became immediately evident as work in Zubtsov progressed rapidly. The T.O.D.T.—the engineering units —had moved in with the regular troops and began clearing away the rubble of the air attack. In two days, they had built an excellent bridge across both the Volga and the Vazooza, something Soviet engineers had been trying to do for months. The people of Zubtsov gazed at this feat of engineering, and muttered in awe.

"What chance does the Red Army have against such miracles? They are sure to lose."

A truly glorious autumn shone in the red and gold foliage of the forests that year, but our hearts were heavy with the dread of approaching famine. Fighting had prevented the harvesting of the potato crop, which now lay frost-killed and rotting in the fields. And no one dared touch the rows of cabbage which the Bolsheviks had planted around the town prison.

"They have gone," people would say with a dubious shake of the head, "but who knows when they will be back." Even so, I could not bear to let such a wealth of cabbage go to waste. I went straight to the commanding officer.

"*Herr Oberst*, may we harvest the whole crop?"

"By all means, Frau Marie, harvest all you can."

With these glad tidings, Nadya and I went from house to house, calling on people to come with baskets and knives and help themselves. A good part of the town turned out. Yesterday's fall of light autumn snow gleamed in the sun, while women and children thronged through those cabbage fields. At one point, a squadron of Russian planes flew over, and a few bombs fell. But after the first few minutes, "harvesting" was resumed. Those who had been afraid of the Bolsheviks only the day before were now ready to put up with air raids for the sake of their cabbage.

For several days thereafter, we ate nothing but cabbage unseasoned by salt. Not even in prison (where at least there had been bread rations) had I felt the monotony so keenly. Driven by utter desperation, Nadya and I tottered to the town market in the hopes of finding something besides cabbage. Poor as the market had been before the war, it had now gone completely to seed. Hungry men and women wandered listlessly among the sagging, empty stalls. A barbed-wire fence had been thrown up around the entire market to segregate us Russians from the German troops. Nadya and I had only three rubles between us, and I was carrying all the money.

"Please, Masha, be very careful," Nadya said. "If you find some potatoes, examine each one minutely. If we're lucky, we might be able to get half a dozen. Now you go that way, while I look on the other side."

I glanced with disgust at the piles of "merchandise" heaped on the fresh snow. There were plenty of discarded shoes and rags, but very little food; only a few potatoes and onions here and there, most of them rotten. I had moved only a few steps, when suddenly I saw something that made me catch my breath: atop a cairn of miscellaneous and largely unsalable rubbish lay a splendid eighteenth-century crystal bowl, a real museum piece. My old love of beauty took hold of me, and I turned to the ragged old peasant sitting nearby.

"How much do you want for this glass?" I asked, as carelessly as I could.

"Well . . ." he paused and scratched his beard pensively. "Give me three rubles and you can have it."

I carried off that beautiful bowl in triumph, but when I saw Nadya's face, I didn't know where to look.

"Where are the potatoes?"

"But look," I cried, trying to console her.

"Oh, Masha, that was our last money. What have you done?"

"I bought this exquisite antique for the price of six potatoes!"

"But Masha, we're starving!"

I saw tears rising to her eyes. She turned, and I could see her thin shoulders heaving. I felt dreadfully ashamed, and that same evening, I sold my crystal bowl to a German officer. He was delighted when I accepted his bargain offer of three hundred rubles!

Nadya, however, was too weakened by our cabbage diet to even smile when she saw the money I brought home. The next day I awoke to find her in a dead faint. When I found I was unable to revive her, I naturally ran to the German medical station. The doctor came without a minute's delay, but after looking at Nadya, he shook his head sadly.

"My dear lady, your friend requires no medicine. She is not ill. She is simply dying of malnutrition, and it's not long before you'll be in the same state." He sighed. "God knows, there's little I can give you outside a share of my own ration." Overriding my protests, he insisted on giving us some bread and a sausage. "Wait!" he said. "The chief cook in the canteen is my friend. Let's see what he can do for you." Thanks to that kind doctor, for a while Nadya and I were provided with a daily ration of bread and a container of soup. That extra nourishment undoubtedly saved our lives.

During the first weeks of occupation, regiment after German regiment passed through our town on its way to the front lines; each stopping for a day or two in Zubtsov before moving on. Apparently the only officers permanently stationed there were the two billeted in our house. We grew quite fond of those pleasantly polite young men, but the day eventually came when their unit, too, was ordered into action. On the morning of their departure, one of them came to see me.

"Frau Marie, with all respect, you look half-starved. You are getting thinner every day, so my friend and I decided to present you with a parting gift." He shouted to one of the orderlies: "Fritz! Bring it in!"

I stared dumbfoundedly as Fritz led in a plump, woolly sheep and paraded him up and down the room in front of me.

"What am I to do with him?"

"Why, eat him, of course!"

"But . . . but I don't think I could ever bear to kill him!"

"That too, has been foreseen." He winked at Fritz, who marched away with the sheep as silently and solemnly as he had marched in.

A bit later, I found the carcass on our doorstep. I hated to see the glazed eyes of the poor beast, but hunger was stronger than sentiment. Nadya and I feasted on mutton for a whole week.

Soon after, we both were given jobs as interpreters: Nadya with the civil administration of the town, and I with the Military Police. As was to be expected, Nadya carried out her tasks with meticulous excellence, but remained aloof from her employers. She was never known to smile in the office, and moreover refused to converse on any subject not strictly connected with her duties. As a result, the Germans praised her exemplary work but also looked on her with some suspicion.

In contrast, I was still replete with sanguine illusions and was on the best of terms with most of the Military Police. My chief was portly, middle-aged *Oberleutnant* Heyer. Although overly exacting—"*Befehl ist Befehl,* an order is an order," seemed to be his watchword—he was always cordial. As for his twelve M.P. officers, I found no cause for friction with those efficient and good-natured young men. As with young people everywhere, a joke went a long

way to establish a friendly relationship. I never spared my humor in
their presence. Accordingly, they often sought my advice to settle
disputes with the local populace. After all, they did have a host of
problems to deal with: bombed out families had to be resettled,
houses had to be requisitioned, and despite the sticky point of military security, Russian women had to be hired for housework in
German billets.

The Germans agreed when I suggested they confiscate Communist property first, and leave undisturbed as many innocent
people as possible. But when it came to women, Germans proved
no wiser than anyone else: it was always the girl with the prettiest
face, best clothes, and daintiest figure who got jobs in the officers'
quarters. I knew most of these women were the wives and mistresses
of N.K.V.D. members and other Communist officials, who had
now gone into hiding in the forest. But could I convince twelve
young Germans?

"Don't you realize?" I would say, "the only women in Russia
with such good clothes are the girlfriends of Bolshevik bigwigs?"

But my answer was always an incredulous smile: "Ach, Frau
Marie, such lovely girls with such candid blue eyes!"

At last, I became exasperated. "You can't see what's happening
right under your noses! When they're off duty, your chamber-
maids go into the woods to 'gather mushrooms,' and that's where
their men are hiding! Why do you think the Russian planes are
bombing only the most significant targets?" Gradually, reluctantly,
all "lovely girls with candid blue eyes" were weeded out from the
barracks, and the accuracy of Russian bombing attacks promptly
declined.

We knew, however, that Communists were still hiding in the
woods nearby. One day Heyer sent me with some papers to the
Kommandatur. I entered the central office where secret maps and
plans hung on the walls and officers telephoned vital orders in harsh
whispers. In one corner, mending boots, sat a Russian with a long,
dirty beard and glasses. He looked humble enough, but I swallowed
hard. Under his disguise, I instantly recognized the features of the
former chief of the Zubtsov N.K.V.D. I realized that he probably
understood German and was merrily listening to plans for future
attacks, troop transfers, and God knows what else! Fortunately,
he was bending low over his work and did not see me. I gave him

no time to look up; turning on my heel, I rushed to the adjutant's office. When I appeared before him, panting and shaking with anxiety, the adjutant rose to his feet with an amused smile.

"Why, Frau Marie, you look all flustered!"

"I am! Do you know who you have in the main office there, mending boots?"

The adjutant's smile became almost patronizing: "Yes, I know. Our boots were falling apart, and then this old man turned up. He's a godsend who's doing an excellent job."

"He must be doing a fine job indeed! He's neither an old man nor a shoemaker. He's the former chief of the Zubtsov N.K.V.D." I didn't have to say another word. The adjutant turned pale and bolted out of his office. That same day, the *ersatz* shoemaker was apprehended and shot.

Although I was directly responsible, I honestly felt I had done my duty for a noble cause. I kept repeating to myself, "To a dog a dog's death" and "That degenerate animal deserved to be destroyed"; but still something in my conscience refused to be rationalized away. Only a few weeks later did a chance come for me to restore my mental balance.

Our maiden landladies, Evdokia and Natalia, had returned to Zubtsov from visiting their relatives. As I came home from work one evening, Natalia came to meet me in tears.

"Oh dreadful, dreadful," she moaned. "You know that kind old neighbor of ours, Ivan Stepanovich? The Germans have arrested him! To be sure, he's a Communist, but we all know what kind of Communist he is! He's always helping people, and trying to save people's lives. He even believes in God! He has an icon in his room hidden behind Lenin's picture!" She wrung her hands: "His poor old wife is frantic. She's in the kitchen waiting for you. The Germans trust you, you're her only hope. Please! Dear Madame Avinov, please intercede for him. They'll shoot him for sure if you don't!"

The arrested man's wife threw herself at my feet, weeping. I knew her husband was indeed loved and respected despite his Communist affiliations. *So,* I thought to myself, *here's where I try to save a Bolshevik's life for a change!*

Knowing that the Germans made short shrift of captured

Bolsheviks, I went at once to my chief. But when the *Oberleutnant* heard my story, he threw up his hands.

"There's nothing I can do. He was arrested by the Gestapo. They are rounding up all the Communists in town. It's the *Sonderführer* who is in charge."

"Very well then, take me to him."

At this the *Oberleutnant* grew very red in the face, and his jowls trembled with something close to revulsion. "Certainly not," he cried. "I've told you time and again never to have anything to do with the Gestapo or the S.S.! They are . . ." Heyer stopped himself abruptly, then scowled into a corner of the room. But I was determined to try and save this old man, and I told him so.

"Frau Marie," he muttered helplessly, "that . . . that . . . the *Sonderführer* I mean . . . he might suspect *you* of being a Bolshevik!"

"I don't think he will, but I'll take the chance. Remember the incident with the N.K.V.D. chief? By now I'm sure the *Sonderführer* knows as well as you do how I act when it comes to *real* Bolsheviks."

After some further hesitation, due to his aversion to the *Sonderführer* rather than worry over my safety, my chief took me to Gestapo headquarters. I felt my skin tighten as I followed him into the office, where the *Sonderführer* sat, enormous and malevolent, behind his diminutive desk. I wondered where he had found such a dainty piece of furniture, but needless to say, I never found out. Having introduced me, Heyer turned sharply on his heel and hurried out of the room.

Silently I prayed I would find the right words and the accent that convinces; again, it was as though someone else began to speak through me, in calm and measured tones. I began by citing the old man's character and reputation: "I'm convinced that his release will make an excellent impression on the local population. 'The Germans are stern,' they will say, 'but they are also just and discriminating.' Of course, *Herr Sonderführer*, you know as well as I do that many people were forced to join the Party, in order to save themselves and those they love. Do you know what we call such 'Communists' in Russia? We call them 'Radishes': red outside, white inside!"

The *Sonderführer* leaned back in his chair and a smile slowly spread across his beefy face. But he said nothing. With a curt nod he signified that our "audience" was over. I went home, wondering. At least I had cause for prayer and hope: a smile such as the one he left me with was usually a prelude to a thaw.

As I sat working at my desk the next morning, Heyer marched into the office. He was beaming. "My dear Frau Marie, your old neighbor owes you a big candle! The *Sonderführer* was impressed, not only by what you said but also by your personality. He has released your man."

In my immense relief, I jumped to my feet and gave Heyer two resounding kisses, one on each cheek. For a few seconds, he stared at me in surprise, and the young officers around us roared with laughter and clapped their hands. I blushed thoroughly at my lack of self-control. *Masha, you impetuous thing*, I though to myself in a tone that might have come straight from my mother's lips, *when will you learn to behave?*

CHAPTER TWENTY-FOUR

᠅

The winter of 1941 set in early, with frightful snowstorms and bitter cold. Roads were buried under drifts several feet high, and trucks and tanks could no longer move along them. Peasants from the nearby villages were recruited to clear away some of the snow and plant stakes to mark the roadsides. But even though the Germans were paying for this work with rations of food and tobacco, this forced labor fell as a heavy burden upon the rural population. The same townspeople who during the previous summer had marveled at the "miraculous" German bridge across the Volga and Vazooza, now winked smugly at each other. "It's 'Father Frost' again, fighting the Germans today just as he fought the French in 1812!" They were rather proud; after all, there was no denying that for cold weather, Russia took first place over Germany! Yet the peasants' pride was soured by secret fears that winter's icy triumph might land them with the Bolsheviks around their necks once more.

After seeing how, every morning, the German soldiers plunged into holes hacked in the icebound Volga and then ran naked along the shore, some Zubtsovites went so far as to cast doubts on Father Frost's virility. Of course with a sufficient supply of calories, any human body can withstand extremely low temperatures. The German troops had rations adequate to maintain their caloric intake, but to the half-starved Russians, their braving of the cold seemed an almost superhuman feat. One often heard murmurs in the street. "What can anyone do against these devils, when even ice water doesn't faze them?"

As it turned out, the peasants greatly overestimated the Germans' resistance to the devastating powers of a Russian winter. The number of frostbites in their ranks soon became appalling. For all its efficiency, the German High Command had failed to provide its troops with *valenki*—the native Russian footwear indispensable in low temperatures. In subzero weather, German sentries stood for hours on end with only straw wrapped round their leather boots. Men with frozen feet and advancing gangrene had to be hospitalized and even sent back to Germany. I understood this lack of foresight was laid to a German general named Beck, who was promptly sacked by Hitler himself.

But there was no one to blame for what the Russian people suffered from "Father Frost," together with hunger and typhus. Every morning on my way to the office I saw women and children with swollen, greenish-yellow faces, often emaciated and skeletal. I was virtually sickened by my inability to do anything for them.

After some tentative overtures, though, I did contrive to get permission for them to go to the fields and dig up whatever undecayed scraps of potatoes they could find. To my chagrin, this enterprise ended in disaster. Some of the women decided to use this opportunity for limited travel to get in touch with Communists still hiding in the woods. But in the midst of their clandestine rendezvous, they were apprehended by the Germans and gunned down on the spot. I was shocked at their fate and frightened that there would be fast retribution for my unwitting mischief. But all I got from the Commanding General was a frown and a light reprimand: "No more of this, Frau Marie!" he said, shaking his finger at me. "You know your Russians better than we do. Now in the future, use your brains and not your susceptible woman's heart!"

I owed his clemency to the intervention of two German officers stationed in Zubtsov, Heinrich von Lange and Joachim von Wehrs. They were decent, upright young men who would have been a credit to any nation. Often they had gone out of their way to help Nadya and me in our search for food; for although we received a fairly adequate salary as interpreters, there were hardly any supplies to be bought in town. The German canteen that had supplied us with our daily ration of soup and bread had long since moved on into the great Russian beyond, and accordingly, we went hungry for much of the time.

One day, however, there was a windfall. I was sitting at home when an orphan boy I had befriended came running in with good news. A horse had just been killed by a Russian bomb, he said, and the carcass was lying in a nearby field. In no time I collected a sledge, some empty sacks, a hatchet, and a large kitchen knife, and went off after my young guide. We hadn't gone far when he stopped and pointed to where, straight ahead on the dazzling white snow, lay the dead horse—a splendid Belgian Percheron.

I had never butchered a horse before, but hunger is the best of teachers. I hacked and cut and sliced and chopped until I had filled my sacks with meat and given my young friend a good share to take home with him. Then I sent him to fetch Klavdia, a peasant woman whom I knew to be starving, along with her six children in their unheated cottage. Her whole family came at a run and went straight to work. Joyful grins creased their hollow cheeks with tiny little wrinkles. Soon nothing remained of the horse but an impression in the snow. Even the bones were take away to be boiled down into soup.

Horsemeat was no novelty to me, for I had eaten it on a silver platter in the early stages of Bolshevik rule. But when I tried to induce von Lange and von Wehrs to taste it, they flatly refused.

"Look," I said, "in the old days, I had one of the best chefs in Moscow, and he once told me that the juicy steaks served in some of the best restaurants were nothing but horsemeat!" Wehrs, the more squeamish and articulate of the two, gave a grimace of disgust, and they both turned up their noses at the idea.

Nadya and I devised a plot: if the customers in the old Moscow restaurants could be fooled by a bit of good cooking, why couldn't our German friends as well? We invited them to supper. Our story was, that by a stroke of luck, a peasant had sold us some good fresh meat, and that Nadya, who was an excellent cook, was making a delicious sausage. How those two ate that evening was a joy to behold! "I haven't tasted anything so excellent in months," cried Wehrs. "I haven't eaten such good fresh meat in weeks," smiled Lange. Before leaving, they thanked us profusely, pressing and shaking our hands over and over again.

It took us several days to pluck up courage enough to tell them what they had relished that evening. Lange seldom laughed, but when he heard our confession he burst into sudden peels of merriment which were caught up by Wehrs. In the end they were both doubled up with laughter. But as a French writer once said, *"On ne peut pas faire le bien impunément,* One cannot do good without getting punished."* In no time at all, word of the excellence of Russian horsemeat spread among the Germans. Even horses dead of exhaustion or killed by fire were so eagerly sought that it became difficult for us to replenish our larder. Sometimes Lange would present me ceremoniously with a chunk of freshly sliced horsemeat: "To our pioneer in such delicacies, my tribute." His smile then lit up his dark eyes and dispelled the sadness which always seemed to lie in their depths.

Besides Lange and Wehrs, I had made friends with two army chaplains: a Protestant parson named Heyken, and Father Lawrence, a Catholic priest. Nadya merely tolerated Lange and Wehrs, but genuinely warmed to these two. Father Lawrence was serious and conventional, a bit pensive and withdrawn, and occasionally given to pious platitudes. But Heyken was one of the warmest, most outgoing men I have ever come across. He seemed to breathe love and compassion, and gave of himself freely. In giving moral support to Nadya and me, he became our pillar of strength. When we felt low in spirit, he spent whole evenings with us in long but lively talks.

He knew the difficulty we had in procuring even the most elementary necessities of life: one day, upon returning from the front where a Russian supply train had been wrecked, he brought us tea, sugar, and soap—commodities of priceless value. While Nadya busied herself brewing the tea he had brought, Heyken and I settled in a corner for one of our intimate chats.

"Something has been puzzling me," he said. "Aren't there any intellectuals in this town? If so, where are they? Everyone I've seen looks like a peasant."

"They're about all we have left," I replied, "or very close to it: just small shopkeepers—the former ones, I mean—and working men. The 'anti-Communist' intellectuals have long since been either liquidated or sent to concentration camps. The few who did escape went into hiding, and if you saw one today, you might easily mistake him for a peasant."

I told Heyken of the fears that still dominated the town: neighbors might turn out to be informers; Germans might take it into their heads to stand you against the wall; the N.K.V.D. still had ears, and might actually return. "Why, only the other day, a school teacher told me he was afraid to read Pushkin's poetry to his pupils! He said the Bolsheviks might come back and accuse him of being a counter-revolutionary."

We sat in silence for a while, sipping the tea Nadya had brewed. Heyken was turning over in his mind what I had said. "You see," I continued, "there are practically no educated people left. Consequently, there's no real competition for jobs. If need be, almost anyone can take anyone else's place."

Pastor Heyken almost grinned: "Ah no, Frau Marie, there you are wrong. No one could replace you! You'd be indispensable to us under any circumstances. And by that, I don't mean just as an interpreter or a go-between, but as a boost to our morale. We are all of us homesick, naturally, and an evening spent with you is a haven for us poor wretches. Didn't you notice the other day, when we were discussing music and you sang some German *Lieder*, how moved Lange was?"

I may have blushed; I had a secret weakness for that tall, reticent Lange. He had taken a fancy to me too—that much I had sensed—but there was never the slightest flirtation between us. Whenever we met, always in company, he would naturally drift over to me and talk at length about his little son Hansi, aged five or six, whom he idolized. (His wife had died three years before.) He would tell me his plans for little Hansi's education and future; of little Hansi's health, good looks, and robust little body. Childless and alone myself, I never found it hard to give Lange my undivided attention. He was perhaps the only man who ever reminded me strongly of Nika.

One night late in November, Nadya and I were sitting at home huddled over a small stove while a blizzard raged outside. Suddenly the door flew open and Lange came in, accompanied by Wehrs and the two chaplains. All were wearing full battle dress. "Pardon us for intruding at such an hour," Lange said. He fell silent, not knowing how, or perhaps unable to go on. The always voluble Wehrs continued for him: "We've come to say goodbye. A Russian attack has been rumored for tonight. Give a thought and a prayer for us—even a victory will be no picnic in this storm!"

Wehrs and the chaplains trooped out of the room after clasping our hands. I involuntarily drew back a few steps, and Lange came up close to me and looked me in the eye. "Give me your blessing, Maria," he whispered. "If I die, I want to carry your blessing with me, since I dare not hope for anything else." It was the one and only time he'd ever addressed me by my first name.

I made the sign of the cross from his forehead to his chest, and from shoulder to shoulder. He kissed my hand. "Put your kettle on tomorrow morning, ladies," he said aloud for Nadya's benefit, but looking only at me. "Put your kettle on and make some tea. If I'm not back at noon, raise a cup in my memory."

He came back. They all did—drenched in melting snow, bloodstained and exhausted. While Nadya prepared tea, Lange, who was deathly pale, slumped into a chair and covered his face with his hands. I glanced to his companions in alarm. Wehrs drew me aside.

"His boy . . ." he stammered, "you'll understand when I tell you." And then he continued on into the whole ghastly story.

At daybreak, their unit had been posted on the outskirts of a village. A meadow lay between them and the forest from which the Russian attack was expected to issue. It was snowing hard when abruptly, out of the forest appeared a long line of small figures, walking slowly toward the Germans. As the line drew nearer, they discerned with horror that it consisted of about fifty little boys, none older than six or seven. The Russians were counting on the children to hobble the Germans' fire until the Russians themselves had a chance to assemble on the forest border and prepare their attack. Naturally, every second counted. It was Lange, in charge of the machine guns, who had to give the order to fire. In seconds, the whole line of little boys was mowed down.

"They lay in the snow like little puppet soldiers," said Wehrs. "After that, we never fought harder in our lives. We took no prisoners, not even those who surrendered and begged for mercy. We shot them all!" He pounded his clenched fist hard on the table as he uttered oaths against "these Russians . . . this war . . . and everyone of us." He sank into a chair, leaned across the table, and buried his face in his arm. His shoulders were trembling.

"You are overwrought, Captain Wehrs," said Father Lawrence. "You are not making sense. Go and rest."

At this, Lange rose to his feet and faced the priest: "Maybe he's not making sense, Father. But did we, or did we not, commit an unforgivable crime?"

Father Lawrence began speaking familiar rhetoric about a soldier's duty, and God's mercy; but I didn't let him finish. "But—but it's the *Bolsheviks*!" I exclaimed in an emotion-choked voice. "The Bolsheviks! *They* sent out the children—*they* alone are guilty!"

Lange looked at me with a smile of something like pity at the corners of his lips.

"No, they're not the only ones to blame." He fell silent for an instant, and then spoke as if he hadn't time to say all he wanted.

"I might have told my men to shoot in the air, and all those frightened little boys would have run like a pack of rabbits; or else we might have taken them prisoner right off, and then shot their abominable elders when they appeared." He stopped as abruptly as he had begun: "Oh what's the use? A crime is a crime, and you can't talk yourself out of it."

I think at that moment I admired him more than ever: strong enough to commit the atrocity that discipline demanded, yet also man enough to acknowledge the guilt that was his.

Lange left the room, and behind me Pastor Heyken was muttering ". . . Abominable crimes. May God indeed have mercy on the human race . . ."

CHAPTER TWENTY-FIVE

❧§❧

My faith in the German "Crusade against Communism" soon received the first of several rude jolts. One day in the late fall of 1941, a long column of Russian prisoners of war was driven through Zubtsov. They staggered by, bedraggled, filthy, and vermin-ridden. Not only we Russians, but even the German garrison stood aghast at the sight of great dark fevered eyes set above skin stretched drum-tight across the cheekbones.

The column halted many times as though its members were about to expire. To a few of the prisoners I managed to give what I could —a piece of bread, a lump of sugar, or a cigarette—and at the same time questioned them anxiously. Their stories were always the same: "We believed the German promises, and we surrendered in order to fight for them. Now look at us. . . . Oh, they'll pay for this," they added in barely audible whispers.

This ghastly procession dragged itself past for several hours. At one point Wehrs came, tight-lipped and glum, and stood beside me.

"Why haven't they been fed and armed?" I asked. "Where are they being driven to now?"

Wehrs, not caring to meet my eyes, looked straight ahead with his chin high. "They are being taken to Germany," he said abruptly. "There is field and factory work to be done. Germany is where they are needed." I had never heard him speak in that tone before.

"But don't you see," I cried, "that they'll never get there? They're starving! It's an outrage! They believed your propaganda and you treat them this way! Don't you realize they *gave themselves up* to fight the Bolsheviks?"

"I do." He shrugged, perhaps in annoyance at having to discuss the distasteful matter. "We didn't expect four million of them, though."

I gasped, "Four *million?*"

"Or, thereabouts." Wehrs drew himself to his full height and threw out his chest. "Anyway, war is war," he exclaimed curtly. Turning on his heel, he walked briskly away.

That night, still thinking of the forced march, I was unable to fall asleep for hours. As usual, Nadya was not about to change her opinion on the strength of only a single piece of evidence. "It's probably one of those dreadful things that happen once in a blue moon," she kept repeating. "It sounds like the action of some particular sadist, and hardly the general rule. They couldn't be treating *all* their Russian prisoners that way!" Typically, Nadya had cast aside her usual pessimistic view of the Germans in order to comfort me; also typically, I let myself be persuaded that what we had seen was merely an isolated instance of cruelty, which would be swiftly punished. For the next two days, I felt optimistic and willed myself to feel better. But on the third evening another blow fell that crippled my resolve.

Lange had brought a friend of his to see us, an officer just back from Germany. During our conversation, this man suddenly brought up the subject of Russian prisoners of war.

"I tell you, Lange" he said, "one has to see them to believe it. A couple of weeks ago when I was on duty, a whole batch of them were brought to our compound. Those miserable creatures just crept by me. All trace of the soldier in them was gone. One actually collapsed, and in the instant he was down, before I could do anything about it, the others were on him like starving beasts. They smashed his skull open and started devouring his . . ."

"Stop!" Lange cried; "these ladies are Russian!"

Noticing how shattered Nadya and I were by the man's story, he soon took his disconcerted friend away. Like Wehrs this man had shown that peculiar, instinctive refusal to admit that German treatment had driven those poor Russians to such extremes. This time Nadya did not argue for my benefit. In her silence she stared at the floor. Immobilized myself, I could only remember the decimated prisoners' ghostly whispers: "They will pay for this, oh they will pay . . ."

Word of such despicable treatment had been grist to Stalin's mill, and retribution was not slow in coming. Leaflets, vividly describing the plight of Russians under Nazi rule, had been dropped over

Russian lines for all troops to read—"Comrades! Your Father Stalin warned you! Now you may read how right he was! Now that you know the truth, fight like lions to save Holy Mother Russia!" Fairly soon after, malcontents hid in forests instead of defecting to the enemy. With the resources of a true underground resistance, they formed themselves into guerilla bands which soon became a menace to the *Wehrmacht*. Moscow wisely kept the guerillas supplied with ample food and ammunition that was airlifted and parachuted into forest clearings. Fortified by clandestine supplies, Russian resentment soon became widespread and virulent, and it was not long before I witnessed a tragic example of it, right in Zubtsov.

Shortly before Christmas shaggy little peasant horses had begun to arrive, drawing sledges laden with parcels for the German garrison. At distribution time, each soldier would reach for his gift with a trembling hand and a misty eye, displaying the homesickness that he normally kept so well concealed. At such moments, I felt pity for those young Germans. Like our own Russian citizens during World War I, they had simply been thrust forward to conquer and subdue, to satisfy some abstract principle of "National Honor." But to most Russians, these same Germans were only hated oppressors who deserved a reward of the kind that does not come in Christmas packages.

One morning I found my boss—now *Hauptmann* (Captain) Heyer—restlessly pacing up and down in his office. "Frau Marie," he exclaimed, "a most tiresome thing has happened! A great many Christmas parcels were stolen from the sledges during last night's snowstorm. We found the empty sacks on the road." He mopped his thick neck and forehead. "It's the work of an organized gang, that much I know. I haven't yet discovered how they're operating, although we suspect a very disreputable woman of being the ringleader. In any case, we'll soon find out. The whole town's being searched."

On entering his office the next morning, I found six little boys lined up facing the wall. Heyer himself was sitting at his desk, talking with the comparatively new M.P. officer, Herman—the only man in the outfit I could not abide. This man's washy-blue eyes and secretive mouth had given me chills the very first time I saw him, and my antipathy was thoroughly reciprocated. Whenever we were thrown together, he would watch me stealthily as though expecting to catch me at some clandestine project.

I must have shown my feelings. "Why do you dislike Herman so?" Heyer once asked me. "He's completely loyal and reliable. One can trust him with the meanest jobs. After all, someone has to do the dirty work."

"But that's precisely why I find him repellent. I feel he's a cruel man, a sadist. He reminds me of that N.K.V.D. chief you arrested and shot!" Neither Heyer nor I said any more at the time, but later I thought I detected a certain coolness in his attitude toward Herman.

But now they were together, almost touching each other's foreheads in secret consultation. My anxieties for the six children were heightened by Herman's last words, the only ones I was able to catch: ". . . let me handle this my way. Give them to me, sir. In ten minutes you'll have the whole truth."

Seeing me, Heyer hesitated. "No," he said after a while. "First let Frau Marie talk to them." He ignored the contemptuous sweep of Herman's hand: "That'll be all, Herman. I'll call you when I need you."

Herman stood up and clicked his heels with a deferential "as-you-wish-sir" smile. But on his way out he threw me a look of deep loathing.

"Now, Frau Marie," said Heyer, rubbing his hands together, "let's get down to business. Will you please tell these six boys to give you the names of all their accomplices? Tell them we found the Christmas parcels in the woman's cellar, along with quite a lot of other stolen goods. Tell them that this woman they're protecting is a procuress, who's looking out for herself only. She's sold what they stole for her at exorbitant prices, and given them nothing. She's a filthy speculator, that's what she is. Be sure to tell them that!" He put as much venom into "speculator" as any Bolshevik official; the term, of course, was calculated to impress these Soviet-bred children with the magnitude of the woman's guilt.

"This one seems to be the leader," Heyer continued. "Start with him." He turned the boy around, and I saw a charming little face with wavy golden hair. A pair of candid blue eyes looked straight up into the slightly bulbous ones of the German. "*Ein schöner Bub*, eh—?" Heyer chucked the boy under the chin, but those steady blue eyes never wavered. "He's twelve or thirteen, wouldn't you say, Frau Marie? It looks as if butter wouldn't melt in his mouth, but I think you will find him a tough little nut to crack."

I cleared my throat and spoke up in Russian. Instanly, the boy's eyes left Heyer's and fixed themselves on me in a most disconcerting way. I felt self-conscious and spoke a bit too fast and too loud. I reminded him that he and his friends were risking execution. Death was the usual punishment for their offense, I said, but if he would give us the names of the others, the Captain might persuade the General to pardon them. The boy said nothing. When I told him that the woman was a procuress and a speculator, he never changed his expression. Perhaps he already knew. I talked myself hoarse trying to break through that impenetrable little mask. All I got was an occasional sullen toss of the head or a silent, unflinching *nyet*. Finally, I turned to Heyer, defeated.

"Nothing doing, *Herr Hauptmann*."

"Well then, *Befehl ist Befehl!*"

"But they're only children," I cried. "Think of the temptation for a boy to try playing highwayman. Think of the dreadful conditions these boys have been living under, starving most of the time! Why, under similar circumstances, any boy anywhere, here or in Germany—even your own son, *Herr Hauptmann*, might turn to crime in order to get something to eat!"

Heyer's heavy gray eyes came to rest on mine. At last, he signaled to the boy to turn back to the wall. Slowly he rose to his feet and left the room. I remained seated, sipping water for my dry throat, and wondering what lay in store for these children. I felt a glow of perverse pride in the courage of those tough little Russian boys.

Not one of them moved. It was almost as if they had ceased to breathe altogether. After an oppressive half hour, Heyer returned looking visibly relieved. This being their first offense, the general had decided to spare all six.

"But warn them," he said, "if they're ever caught stealing again, they will be hanged."

All six were released that day. Herman, it seems, had been ordered to lie in wait for them outside Heyer's door and to give each one a lashing. He couldn't have shown any of them the slightest mercy, for at one point, the piercing shrieks of those normally taciturn children could be heard all the way from the stone-walled basement. I clamped my hands to my ears and sprinted to the nearest washroom where I threw up.

But if Herman thought that his brutality could crush those six boys, he had another guess coming. Apparently no amout of punishment would have deterred them from further acts of patriotic sabotage—for that's how I think they viewed their activities. Profit and gain held an undeniable place among their motives, but it could not have been *that* compelling. Ten days later, the Germans caught all six of them red-handed, along with two new offenders. All eight were hanged that same night.

It was painful to see how mistaken had been my image of a noble German "Crusade of Liberation." In instinctive self-defense, my mind returned to the more deeply rooted concept I had always carried of the German people as a whole. I began to dwell on the memory of Dr. Krueger, that gentle old German teacher of my youth. My friendship with Pastor Heyken deepened especially. With men like him in sight, I still could keep telling myself that Germany hadn't completely lost her head. The Nazis at least still used chaplains to solace their soldiers. Communist troops, on the other hand, were given plenty of sheep dogs, but never a shepherd. Though Hitler did seem brutal at times, I felt sure that his Austro-German background would stand proof against his stooping to anti-religious propaganda. But before long this illusion, too, had to go the way of the rest.

Again, an officer just back from Germany was the courier of shocking news. Pastor Heyken had brought a tense, high-strung young man to our place for tea, and before Heyken could stop him, he began explaining Hitler's forthcoming decree to abolish Christianity. In all of our discussions, Heyken had never touched on religious affairs in Nazi Germany, nor had he ever reflected upon politics or the personality of the *Führer*. His guest's revelation, therefore, came as a surprise that illuminated the conflicts which must have been wracking Heyken's conscience.

Dumbfounded, I listened to this officer's story, whose abrupt sentences were accentuated by nervous jerks of the chin. The *Führer* had ordered total abolition of Christianity and a return to the fold of the old Germanic gods—Thor, Wotan, Helga, and the rest. All churches, Catholic and Protestant, were to be closed. All crosses were to be removed from soldiers' graves. In their places, nothing would remain but markers bearing a swastika and the name of the deceased.

"Yes, Pastor Heyken," the young man said bitterly, "that's how things are with us. And I'm sure it'll come as no surprise when I tell you that the S.S. and *Einsatz Truppen* are already fervently embracing the *Führer's* beautiful new dream. I'm told that they get married in forests by jumping over burning bushes, and afterward sing odes to Wotan!"

Heyken blanched. "I can't believe it!" he stammered. "This is madness!"

"Of course it is." The officer leaned forward, lowering his voice. "Don't worry, *Herr Pastor*, it's not going to be easy for Hitler to do this. I have it from reliable sources that the High Command is furious. They have already brought it home to the *Führer* that if his crazy measure is put through, the morale of the troops will plummet along with his own popularity."

In his distress, Heyken shot me a pleading glance. At once I understood that this conversation was not meant for my ears, and I retired discreetly into the next room. I heard nothing more for a week, when suddenly everything the young officer had predicted took shape in almost satirical fashion.

A train carrying an S.S. unit from France was wrecked by Russian bombs outside Zubtsov. The train crew and personnel had to be temporarily quartered in town. From the wreck, the S.S. officers had salvaged a carload of *pâté de foie gras*, roast chicken, smoked ham, and French wines, cognacs, and liqueurs—in short, delicacies which I had almost forgotten existed. Since many of the tins had been ruptured, the food had to be consumed as quickly as possible. The S.S. officers requisitioned a large room in the *Kommandatur* for an improvised feast, to which they invited all the officers and two chaplains of the German garrison. How or why I don't know. but invitations were also extended to Nadya and myself. Despite the splendid fare, we looked with some distaste on the idea of attending the S.S. party. But Heyken insisted it was better to go. A refusal on our part, he said, would probably be misinterpreted and followed with possibly dire results, not only for us, but for any German who had befriended us. This of course settled the matter. Even Nadya felt she could not jeopardize the chaplains' safety. I required even less persuasion; I've always adored roast chicken.

We were installed at a long table literally creaking under the piled weight of such food as we had not seen in years. Wines and spirits were being poured lavishly. Nadya and I were, incongruously, the only women present. On my right sat Pastor Heyken, and on my left, a young S.S. officer whom I tried to ignore. Instead, I made a close survey of our other hosts. All of them were young, all extremely good-looking in a clean-cut, milk-and-honey sort of way; and all wore the black S.S. uniform that seemed very dapper in spite of its skull and crossbones insignia. But I realized that each of those clean-shaven young faces had been chosen for cold-blooded cruelty and blind obedience. They reminded me of the kind of fallen angels our Russian artist Vrublev used to paint. It was men such as this who would jump over burning bushes and sing hymns to Wotan. They would not take pledges to any Krimhildes and Brunhildes, but rather to their *Führer* and perhaps later, to one another. As if to awaken memories of the robust pre-Christian days, the S.S. had insisted on a total absence of cutlery, so that we had to tear chickens apart with our bare hands, dig fingers into the *pâté de foie gras*, carve ham with communal pen-knives.

The flow of wines quickly loosened tongues and turned the conversation into a bedlam of coarse jokes, shouts, and laughter. Some S.S. officers stared insolently at our two chaplains and in loud voices began to eulogize the new religion's "uplifting beauty."

"It's time we got rid of the Christian faith," one of them roared; "it can only undermine the inborn strength and virility of the German male!" In response, strong youthful voices rose in a song of praise to the Nibelungen gods. The faces of our chaplains were a study, yet none of us dared say a word, not even when those *Nibelungenlieder* gave way to ballads with ribald reference to Jesus Christ.

The young S.S. officer beside me suddenly seized my hand under the table and leaned close to my ear. His face was pale and taut.

"They are mad, *Gnädige Frau*, mad!" His whisper was so low that only I could hear him. I suppose his comrades figured he was starting a flirtation, and so paid him no attention.

"I'm of the same outfit as they are and underwent the same training, but—oh God! Only four days ago death was all around us. For twelve hours those Russian shells never stopped falling! Only the thought of Christ the Redeemer and the prayers my mother taught me kept me sane. Ach, they are mad! *Mad!*"

Deeply moved, I pressed his hand. "God bless you," I whispered back. "God help and protect you." His words helped me to endure the rest of that "banquet."

For me at least, it didn't last too long. When the bawdy songs again broke out, Father Lawrence got up and mumbled something about "Boys will be boys, but ladies shouldn't be present when they are." The four of us—the two chaplains, Nadya and I—bowed to our hosts and thanked them as nicely as we could. We retreated from the room to loud cries of *"Heil Hitler!"* and *"Wotan über Alles!"* I can only say that I had not been so much horrified by this quasi-Wagnerian travesty of religion as disgusted by its utter vulgarity.

When we got home, I let go an indignant tirade against the Germans for not living up to my expectations. Nadya, my sole audience, did not say "I told you so," but simply, "You are right, they were abominable. But we have to thank God for one thing— even among *them* we have found Father Lawrence and Pastor Heyken. Two such friends as these we can never forget."

Father Lawrence was her special favorite. His reserve, his quiet sense, and even his pedantic streak all struck responsive notes from her. Personally I found him a bit of a bore at times, but he was beyond doubt a good, brave man, and faithfully dedicated to his calling.

To let my emotional energy escape, I couldn't refrain from teasing Nadya a little. "Yes," I smiled, "they *are* the clergy, and seeing as they're men of God, you naturally forgive their being German. *Well!* I think our lay friends are all right, too . . . that wonderful Lange, for instance."

"Oh, *him!*" Nadya returned with an equally disdainful sniff. "He's just another of those 'Masha worshipers,' that's all!" We both ended up laughing.

But the S.S. banquet had a sequel which gave us a few uncomfortable hours. Information had reached the Gestapo that there had been discussions of religion—a thing strictly forbidden in the *Wehrmacht*—as well as derogatory voices at the party. An investigation instantly went into full swing, and we were regaled with

threats of severe punishments for the guilty. There was the shadow
of the Gestapo here, the shadow of the N.K.V.D. there; the whole
situation depressed me beyond words. I felt incensed that my
"cultured" Germans should submit to such a degrading yoke. But
fortunately, the whispers of my young S.S. neighbor had gone
undetected, and a sufficient number of his colleagues had testified
that the two chaplains and the two Russian ladies hadn't uttered a
word. Father Lawrence seemed to have delivered a parting reproof,
but if he had, it was admittedly ambiguous. The matter was dropped
the same day, and everyone heaved a sigh of relief. Even my grudge
against the Gestapo faded into the background.

With the coming of the spring of 1942, an upsurge of renewed
hopes hung buoyant in the air. Grain and potato seed had been
brought from Germany in large quantities, and the Russian population began to smile again at the German soldiers. Work had begun
in the fields and in kitchen gardens. Women helped with the plowing, for hardly any horses had survived the winter. Even the rumors
of a possible Russian offensive and an intensification of air raids
on Zubtsov did not dampen our spirits. Going to work, I often had
to take cover wherever I happened to be, and listen to the drone
of aircraft overhead and the whine of falling shells. Strange as it
may seem, this precarious living had an exhilarating effect on me.
I felt as though I were standing on top of a plateau, surveying life
with detachment, and preparing myself for another world.

CHAPTER TWENTY-SIX

❧

Summer came and went. Potatoes and grain were harvested and stored for the hard months ahead. It was September now, and already the chilly breezes of winter could be felt on the night air. The intermittent air raids had become less frequent of late. Neither Nadya nor I, nor the German garrison of Zubtsov, nor even the German High Command itself had any apparent inkling of what was creeping up on us. When the blow did fall, it took us entirely by surprise.

One night, a loud pounding on the door tore us out of our sleep. Hysterical shrieks of "The town's on fire!" and "The Bolsheviks are here!" sent shivers down my spine. Nadya and I scrambled blindly into whatever clothes came first to hand, and then stuffed whatever we could into our knapsacks.

"Here, take this," cried Nadya, throwing a sweater onto my bed. "You'll need it. I have no more room."

"Neither have I."

I was squeezing Heredia's *Sonnets* and Flaubert's *Letters,* into my bulging canvas bag. For a moment Nadya froze.

"Are you out of your mind?" she raged. "Here we are running for our lives on this cold night, and you're packing those stupid *books!* Oh!"

She was almost sobbing with rage. In order to appease her, I threw the sweater over my shoulder, tied its arms around my neck, and with a "There! Now let's go," swept out of the room with my two books still tucked safely in my knapsack.

The moment we emerged from the house we realized that the screams about a Russian invasion had been a bit premature. Thunderous boomings from "Katyusha," the famous Russian cannon, sounded quite close, but there was still time enough to escape. We

234

begged Evdokia and Natalia to come with us, but they only threw
up their hands in despair. "How can we leave the cow?"

We begged Groosha, their great-niece, who was living with them
at the time, to persuade them, but she only shook her head sadly.
So alone, we ran to join the retreating Germans.

When we reached the *Kommendatur,* the roof was on fire.
Radios, maps, and files were being thrown out of windows and
hurriedly piled into trucks. Several wounded lay groaning on the
ground. The town was being abandoned. We joined a long convoy
already snaking its way out of town toward the westward forest
from which it had originally come. "The Russians are still ten miles
away," someone said.

"Our artillery will hold them for awhile. But it's shameful to be
taken unaware! Our Intelligence was caught napping! *Schande,
Schande!, Ach ja, ein grosse Skandal!*"

It didn't take us long to reach a plateau in the forest, from which
we could see the burning town we had left behind. The sun had
risen. The forest was full of wild flowers. As we looked back, I
thought of Evdokia and Natalia with a heavy heart.

Our unit came to a halt on the plateau, set up its artillery, and
lit its kitchen fires. They intended to hold the plateau, they said,
until the rear guard caught up with them. Nadya and I were all
set to wait too, but Lange, who seemed to be in command, ordered
us on.

"That truck there is packed with the wounded. There's no room
left in it for you, but it will be creeping over these roads at a snail's
pace. You can easily keep up with it on foot." He looked very
grave, sensing perhaps as I did that this might be our last farewell.
Noticing our hesitation, he added: "The young corporal at the
wheel knows that you will be following him. I told him not to let
you fall too far behind. Now please go."

We had no choice. All that day we walked behind the creeping
truck, which emitted moans, groans, and even screams of pain
whenever a wheel jolted over a bump in the road. Every hour or so,
the truck slowed almost to a standstill, and the Corporal, craning
his neck from behind the wheel, would shout, "Are you there?"
When we responded, he would drive on.

I still had my sweater tied over my shoulders, but otherwise,
neither of us wore anything more than summer clothes and sandals.

Soon it began to rain. We walked on, shivering as our wet dresses clung to our bodies. When at last a halt was called for the night, we had to settle down in wet grass under dripping trees, and on empty stomachs to boot. Nadya's fortitude was truly amazing. When I fell to weeping from cold and hunger, Nadya looked at me rather grimly.

"Just think of what our Russians would have done to us and you will feel better."

I realized then how *she* must have felt, she who had never wanted to welcome the Germans in the first place. Ashamed of my tears and guilty for having dragged her into this sorry plight, I embraced her, begging forgiveness. We spent an hour in prayer before falling into a restless sleep.

Before sunrise we were on the move again, but without the warming benefit of tea or coffee. Our feet were dragging when at noon we reached a large village. The truck ahead of us came to a stop, and the Corporal jumped down from his seat.

"There's a big unit of the *Wehrmacht* here," he said. "I will report to the C.O." In less than ten minutes he was back with another soldier who conducted us to a barn.

"Your billets, ladies, with the compliments of the Commanding Officer. *Heil Hitler!*"

This Nazi expletive seemed to punctuate all German thought and action, like the inverted exclamation mark at the beginning of a Spanish sentence. It usually put Nadya's nerves on edge, but on this occasion she hardly noticed it. With sighs of relief and gratitude we both sank into the hay. For a while we lay there with closed eyes, and allowed our fatigue to slowly ooze away. But before long, hunger began to assert itself again. Unbearably delectable cooking smells were reaching us from the barn across the road that housed the army canteen. After a quarter of an hour I could stand it no longer.

"Say what you like, Nadya, I'm going over there and beg."

Nadya said nothing, but she nodded her assent. I believe she was actually praying for my expedition to meet with some measure of success.

I came out of the barn. Outside the canteen, a group of German soldiers stared at me in blank amazement. Then they began to shout, whistle, laugh, and clap their hands. Still laughing and whistling, they surrounded me with cries of "Welcome, Beloved Adele,"

"How are you?" "Welcome, welcome!" "You look tired, *liebchen*, but no wonder—it's a long, long way from Berlin!"

It was my turn to stare at them. A sergeant joined the group, also laughing and shouting until he saw my look of consternation.

"You don't mind a joke," he asked, "do you, *Gnädige Frau*? You see, it's your likeness—simply amazing! You are the spitting image of Adele. You might pass for her anywhere!" Seeing that I still didn't understand, he went on. "Our famous movie star, Adele Sanrock, looks just like you. So please, lady, join in the fun. Pretend you are Adele and see how generous my boys can be."

I went along with the make-believe, and complained how hungry I was after my long flight from Berlin. Soon the Sergeant had called his men back to duty, and I was staggering back to our barn under a wobbly load of food-stuffs: cans of hot soup and *ersatz* coffee, loaves of bread, slices of salami, sausages, chocolate bars, cigarettes, margarine—in fact, everything that the soldiers had been able to lay hands on.

Nadya almost wept at the sight of it all. We ate to our hearts' content and hid for the morrow what remained. I felt a bit drowsy after such a meal and stretched myself out in the hay, but Nadya was simply rejuvenated and went out for a brisk walk. In no time at all she was back, her big eyes bright with excitement.

"Masha! Masha, guess who's here? Heyken! Our dear Pastor Heyken!"

I sprang to my feet, with all trace of drowsiness gone. Heyken stepped into the barn a few minutes later.

"Just fancy finding you two!" he laughed. "I was sent here to tend to the wounded and bury the dead, and look what I find—you two, alive and unhurt!" He had been sure that we had been left behind in Zubtsov, and on catching sight of Nadya in the village, he had hardly believed his eyes. But when we asked him where we were to go from here, his face clouded.

"This unit is moving in the morning to Vyazma." (Vyazma was the largest city in that part of Russia.) Heyken shook his head: "The real trouble is, we are forbidden to take any refugees with us." But he brightened suddenly: "I will see the Commanding Officer, though. As official interpreters, you should be in a class apart, and the rule should obviously not be applied. I think he'll understand."

Heyken was as good as his word. Scarcely an hour later he was with us again with a smile of encouragement. We walked with him to a crossroads outside the village where he paused.

"Here," he said, "the main road branches off to Vyazma. Be sure to be back at this same spot before dawn tomorrow. There won't be anyone around, but don't worry. When you see an army truck coming down that road, get ready. When it stops and the driver raises his hand, jump in!"

Inexpressibly grateful, we returned to the barn and had just settled ourselves in the hay when a tall young *Oberleutnant* hurried in.

"I am looking for the Russian lady who worked for the Zubtsov *Feldpolizei* . . ." I stood up. He saluted courteously: "My friend Pastor Heyken said you would not refuse to help us." I nodded readily. "Thank you. You see, a Russian four-motor bomber was shot down a couple of hours ago. The pilot bailed out. He landed all right, but his stomach has been ripped open by machine-gun fire. Still, we hope to get some information out of him, and in this you can be of help. Pastor Heyken said you would know how to talk to a Russian boy."

"Boy?" I drew back in astonishment. "I thought you said he had piloted a four-motor bomber?"

"Yes. But you will see . . ."

A few minutes later, as I entered behind the *Oberleutnant* into a small shack converted into a field hospital, I had to marvel again at German efficiency. The walls were covered with clean white sheets, and the floor was laid with spotless linoleum. A doctor in a white smock was bending over the operation table where a wounded man was moaning horribly. I saw at a glance that he was very young, with a typical blond Russian peasant's face. At the moment though, his face was convulsed with agony and bathed in a cold sweat. From the terrible wound in his stomach, blood dripped slowly onto the floor.

"Can he answer questions?" asked the *Oberleutnant*.

"No," replied the doctor in a harsh, disagreeable voice. "But I can give him a shot to pep him up. He will then be able to talk, if he wants to. These Communists are stubborn animals."

I glanced at the doctor. "Couldn't you give him a shot of morphine? He is in terrible pain."

"No. Our supply is short, and I'm not going to waste it on this Russian dog!"

My blood boiled, but there was nothing I could do other than turn pleadingly to the *Oberleutnant*, who seemed to be a kind man. I was not mistaken.

"Doctor," he said curtly, "give this pilot a shot of morphine. That's an order!"

"*Jawohl*," growled the doctor. After a moment of what seemed like spiteful hesitation, he obeyed.

When the morphine had taken effect, I bent over the lad. He opened his eyes, and I saw animosity and contempt in them.

"*Golubchik*," I said as gently as I could, "you see, there are kind people here too. Your pain has been eased. Now try to answer me . . ." I began to translate the German officer's questions: "How old are you?"

"Eighteen."

"Where is your base and how many bombers are there?"

He shook his head from side to side in silence.

"How long were you in training before piloting a four-motor bomber?"

"Two weeks."

"No!" exclaimed the *Oberleutnant*. "Impossible! *Gnädige Frau*, you must have misunderstood him. Repeat the question."

The shade of a proud smile touched the boy's swollen lips. "Two. Weeks," he repeated, very distinctly.

"How many times have you jumped before this morning?"

"Twice."

"Incredible!" the *Oberleutnant* exclaimed again. "Ask him what he and his comrades think of the war. Who will win—we or the Red Army?"

The boy managed to steady his barely audible voice:

"It's not for us to think. Our duty is to fight and die, if necessary, for our beloved Communist Fatherland and our great Stalin."

"Great Heavens!" said the *Oberleutnant* with some awe. "I hope 'the great Stalin' has not many such soldiers!"

"Well, at any rate, this one is through," interjected the doctor. "He is dying."

I bent over the peasant boy. His eyes were closed and his shrunken face twitched with pain.

"*Golubchik*," I said softly, "you are a Communist. You probably don't believe in God. But very soon now you will be in His presence, and it is He who will give you peace forever and ever. If your mother were here, she would bless and kiss you. I will do it for her . . ."

I made the sign of the cross over him. When I leaned forward and kissed his forehead, two large tears broke through his eyelashes and rolled slowly down his pale cheeks.

I must have swayed as I turned away from the dead boy, unable to restrain the tears that choked me. The *Oberleutnant* was right there, offering me his arm. And thus, ceremoniously arm in arm, we left.

Outside in the village street, Nadya stood waiting for me. But before handing me over to her, the *Oberleutnant* looked significantly at me:

"Believe me, *Gnädige Frau*, I understand. I too know the pain that comes from a 'split personality.' Many of us suffer from it. There is our allegiance to our oath, to our *Führer*, and then comes something like this doctor—to those of us who have remained Christians, the clash is heartrending. But one thing every one of us has to remember . . ." Here he repeated almost word for word what my friend Lange had said before: "If a single link in our iron chain—the *Wehrmacht*—breaks, it is Germany that will perish."

He saluted, clicked his heels, and was gone. Very gently, Nadya took me by the hand. I let her lead me back to the barn.

"When everything is comfortable and easy, God's blessings are often lost on us," she said. "When we come face to face with horror, it shakes us up, but it also sharpens our perceptions. Isn't that so, Masha dear? And now you must take advantage of the soft aromatic hay, and try to rest."

But there was no rest for me yet. The impact of that sadistic German doctor was still fresh upon me. Moreover, when we reached our barn we found three refugees from Zubtsov resting in the hay. These three women had been former neighbors of ours. Their clothes were now torn and caked with mud, and they looked ready to expire. Nadya and I hurried to the corner where we had hidden our food supplies. We gave them to the unfortunate women, who gobbled them up and then sank back wearily onto the hay. But a few minutes later, when their energy began to return, they sat up again to tell us the gruesome details of what we had avoided in Zubtsov.

At the first alarm, they said, they had hidden in a ditch. "By some miracle the Russians never saw us. But we saw them—Oh God, for our sins we saw them! They dragged poor old Evdokia out of the house and shot her. Then they did the same with Natalia. As for pretty little Groosha, they tore her clothes off, called her a German whore, and then easily a dozen of them raped her, one after the other. Finally they slashed her throat. At last darkness came, and we managed to crawl away undetected."

Darkness was now descending again, and the women got ready to leave. "There's a village not far away where we have a family."

Nadya and I were alone in the night, having to keep vigil so as to be up at the appointed hour for our predawn rendezvous with the truck. From where we lay, we could see a few stars through a broken rafter. Dead silence reigned in the village. Not even a dog barked. Heyken had warned us not even to strike a match, since the slightest flicker of light would be a signal to the Russian Air Force, which, he said, was bound to stage a bombing raid. Sure enough, after a while we heard the ominous drone of engines above us, and saw dark-winged shapes cross our little patch of sky and blot out the stars. Birds of death, I thought, come one by one to avenge a brave young hero. But even though the planes passed over several times, they dropped no bombs. The German camouflage had been effective.

Even to me, who knew nothing of military science, it was clear during those long wakeful hours that the German offensive had failed. We were retreating now, away from Russia and even further away from Nika.

Before sunrise, Nadya and I were at the crossroads, wondering whether that truck would appear in time. The sky was paling, and larks were already trilling over the fields. We could hear the rumbling of Russian artillery to the east. As the sun came up, we saw with horror a dense, rose-colored cloud of dust advancing slowly over the plain in our direction: Russian infantry!

"Here it comes," Nadya whispered, clutching my hand.

Oddly enough, at this crucial moment, one thing kept reverberating through my brain—the howl of that poor dog who had been left chained to its kennel in Zubtsov. *We are all chained dogs,* I thought, *howling in our helplessness.*

"Look!"

Nadya's voice was shrill with excitement, and the sharp nudge of her elbow gave me a start.

Seemingly out of nowhere, a German army truck had appeared from a side road. The driver slowed down and raised his hand. We virtually threw ourselves into the back. The hard floor actually felt good against our knees. Then the truck turned into the Vyazma road, shifted gears, and gathered speed.

CHAPTER TWENTY-SEVEN

❧❦❧

Before the war, Vyazma had been a thriving city of considerable size. Now after many heavy air raids, half of it stood in ruins. What was left of its population was in a state of near-starvation. Large numbers of the *Wehrmacht* had concentrated in Vyazma, and the former City Hall had been taken over as an officers' quarters. From the pains those officers had taken to make their rooms neat and livable—even the walls and ceilings were freshly painted—it was clear that they had been expecting a long sojourn.

Fortunately, Pastor Heyken had accompanied the detachment that brought us to Vyazma, and was therefore able to put in a good word for us with the Commanding General. The General received us with kindness, but his appearance made it rather difficult to take him seriously. He was a little butterball of a man whose silly round face sported a turned-up mustache like the former Kaiser's. Even more incongruously, he bore the lofty name of Adlerhorst, meaning *Eagle's Nest!*

His fighting days were long past, but like most German generals in command of occupied cities away from the front, he had been recalled from civilian life. Now, in the three rooms he occupied, he had surrounded himself with specifically civilian luxuries—carpets, mirrors, paintings, sculptures—in short, the best of everything that could be found in the ruined town. This in itself was a marked contrast to the frugal habits of German regulars. In other ways, though, General Adlerhorst was both modest and chaste (or perhaps just old). The other officers of his numerous entourage all had Russian women to tidy their rooms, do their laundry, and minister to their other nightly comforts; but the general was satisfied with the services of one old orderly, who I believe had been his lifelong servant.

During that first interview, the orderly served us *ersatz* coffee with cookies. "Max made them himself," the General boasted. When we told him how good they were, he grew enthusiastic and instantly offered us jobs. I became interpreter to the town *Kommandant*, while Nadya entered the office of the civilian government in the same capacity.

I soon got to know the whole of the *Kommandant's* staff, from the fatherly *Kommandant* himself (who gave me much good advice) to the youngest of his officers. But my special friend was the simplehearted *Hauptfeldwebel* (Master Sergeant) Engelhart, who was nicknamed "Mother of the Company," or sometimes in affectionate derision, "*Unsere Gute Frau Mutti.*"

Engelhart first endeared himself to me through the compassion he showed to the Russians who were fleeing into Vyazma from nearby rural districts reoccupied by the Red Army. They appeared like miserable shadows, pushing carts filled with their pathetic belongings or driving skeletal horses, with an occasional goat or sheep bleating behind them on a long tether. According to standing regulations, Engelhart was not supposed either to house or to feed them, but his ingrained goodness outweighed his discipline in this case. He let refugees sleep in an empty church, and regularly supplied Nadya and me with cabbage, potatoes, and even bones and tripe from the regimental butcher, so that we could make soup for the poor souls. I never asked him how he could manage it, and he never told me, even though he had ample opportunity to do so whenever he invited me to his room for a drink or a smoke. But then, on such occasions he was homesick, and talked of nothing but his wife Martha, his children, and his beloved Hamburg.

Even though translating orders for the *Kommandant* took up little time, my work was far from easy. The problem lay in the two jobs I held besides my routine office work. I had to supervise the women who cut wood and fed the stoves—at least four dozen of them—at the officers' quarters. It was also my job to manage a crew of about fifty young men, recruited to clear debris and repave the shell-pocked streets. These workmen were paid with the same rations of bread, soup, and tobacco that German soldiers received—a boon to those long deprived of the barest necessities. Yet many of them would try to slip away as soon as the rations had been handed out, hoping to get as much as they could for as little

as possible. Over and over I pointed out that they were being paid
to work for their *own* town. But having been reared under Communism, their sense of obligation had been replaced by mere fear
of punishment, and my feeble threats had little effect.

In the end, I asked the Lieutenant who oversaw all these working
gangs to have the ringleaders arrested and kept on bread and water
for a few days. At first the Lieutenant balked, protesting that he
had no authority to ask the Military Police to arrest Russians, but
he capitulated when I threatened to go to the *Kommandant* and
resign. Three of the worst offenders were picked up, deprived of
their rations, and held in prison for three days. When released,
they went down on their knees before me and promised to behave.
I pretended to think it over for a while, but of course in the end I
took them back. And I didn't regret it: now that my authority
seemed fully supported by the German Command, I had no more
trouble.

During the fall of 1942 it rained incessantly. Vyazma's shelled
streets became an endless, impassable quagmire for cars and motorcycles. Everyone went about with wet feet. The German officers,
who possessed only thin, shiny boots, suffered severe colds. Many
were confined to bed with grippe and even pneumonia. Watertight
footwear was plainly the answer, but where was one to get it in this
devastated city? I gave the matter much thought and finally had a
brainstorm.

"Engelhart," I said to our "*Gute Frau Mutti*," "your companions
are in very bad health. Something has to be done. How about getting galoshes for everyone?"

"Galoshes?" He stared at me, dumbfounded. "In this Godfor-
saken hole? You're joking!"

"Not at all. There's a dump of discarded rubber tires in the forest,
and any number of unemployed shoemakers in town."

"Discarded tires? Perish the thought! A special commission will
be coming to take them away to be reprocessed."

"But my dear Englehart, this is Russia, not your orderly Germany. Doomsday will be over before your commission gets here;
and meanwhile, winter is just around the corner. All that good
material will rot in the snow. Be realistic, my friend!"

But Engelhart remained adamant. "*Nein, nein, nein! Befehl ist
Befehl!*"

I then knew that only a personal order from the General would do the trick, but to get through to him, one had to go through channels. Etiquette and protocol had to be rigidly observed.

I applied to his adjutant for an appointment. I was asked some questions, which I answered evasively, and submitted patiently to a long wait. Finally, after a few significant squints by the adjutant at his wristwatch, I was finally ushered into the "Presence."

As always, at the sight of Adlerhorst enthroned behind his immense desk and surrounded by carpets, mirrors, and statuary, I had trouble keeping a straight face. But as always, too, he was disarmingly courteous.

"What can I do for you, my dear Frau Marie?"

"For once, General, I have come to ask permission to do something for you and for your staff." I explained about the rain, the mud, and the colds, adding: "I think I can provide galoshes for all of you. They may be clumsy, but they should also be solid and waterproof."

Altogether, the general's reaction was similar to Engelhart's: "Galoshes? In this accursed place? You're joking!"

I tried to answer with the utmost dignity: "Indeed not, General! All I need is a written order from you permitting me to use whatever old rubber I can find, and to pay shoemakers for their work."

"But of course, of course! Take all the old rubber you can, pay as much as you like. You are a miracle of ingenuity, Frau Marie! I can't thank you enough."

He wrote out the order, stamped it, and signed it with an elaborate flourish. Then he called Max in and told him to measure the feet of all the officers and N.C.O.s on his staff. I departed in triumph.

At the time, we had with us in Vyazma a detachment of eighteen Don Cossacks attached to the *Wehrmacht*. Loathing the Bolsheviks for having deprived them of their land, their horses, and their cherished traditions, they had defected to the Germans. In this instance, the Nazis had done the proper thing to everyone's satisfaction. The Germans profited by the services of these born scouts and first-class shots, and the Cossacks earned adequate supplies of food and clothing in addition to all the decorations available to foreigners serving in the *Wehrmacht*. Whenever I had time, I spent an evening with the Cossacks to listen to their songs and tales about life before the Revolution. They were more entertaining than the best of novels.

I now approached my particular Cossack friend—a brave, simple fellow named Andrey. "You know that big pile of old tires in the forest? Well, the next time you go for firewood, please take some empty sacks with you. Pick out the best tires you can find and bring them to the woodshed. But don't go until after dark, so that no one sees you—those are the general's orders. You'll get vodka and sausages for your trouble."

Andrey would have obliged me even without the promise of a reward. It didn't take me long to round up competent shoemakers who were delighted to get a well-paid job. In a few days the galoshes were made, and I was able to give every man a pair that fitted him. The General was so pleased with his that for a moment I was afraid he might kiss me. But instead he gave me something far more pleasant—a carton of cigarettes.

My friend Engelhart was one of the last to receive his pair. "My good sergeant," I said, "here is a little present for you. Now your dear Martha no longer needs to worry about your going around with wet feet!"

When he saw the galoshes, he was outraged. "I forbade . . ." he cried, but I interrupted him.

"Could I have disobeyed the General? Have you forgotten, *Befehl ist Befehl?*" I handed him the order. He read it through once, and then a second time. His face changed from purple to an even, rosy tint.

"I must say . . . I must say . . ." he stammered. Then suddenly, he flung out his arms as though to embrace me: "Frau Marie, you are the best woman in the world!"

"Second-best, Sergeant. After Martha!"

"Yes, of course, second-best!" We both laughed.

Again winter set in early, with heavy snows and bitter cold. One evening the General summoned me to his office. His round face bore a sheepish expression: "Frau Marie, I have a favor to ask." He looked to the right, then to the left, and for a moment I thought that he was about to hide under his desk. But finally he mastered his embarrassment.

"Before the war, in Berlin, I saw a beautiful Russian ballet. The chief male dancer—ach, I will never forget him—he was wearing such a beautiful, marvelous costume of white fur! It was all white, you understand—the cap, the gloves, the coat, the trousers, and even the white felt boots. I was told it was a copy of the hunting suit worn by Russian Boyars!" Shyly, almost coyly, he looked at me out of the corner of his eyes: "Frau Marie, I want to have such a costume."

"Well," I mumbled, steadying my voice as best I could, "I suppose, *if* I can find a first-class tailor, and *if* you are prepared to pay a fancy price for rabbit fur . . ."

"Ach, spend anything you like! But please, have the felt boots made with *very* high heels."

"But won't high heels be dangerous with all the snow and ice on the ground?"

"Ah, there's no danger at all! My feet and ankles are solid. It's my height I'm worried about. There's a . . . shortage there, so to speak. Well, you understand yourself, for a Commander in Chief it is a . . . a bit awkward!" I agreed in the most commiserating tone I could muster. "Ach, and one more thing, Frau Marie! Please have everything ready by Saturday, because Sunday morning I plan to go to church. Here is a requisition. The paymaster will give you whatever you need."

At home I told Nadya about the general's strange fancy. She only shook her head, tapped her forehead, and waved me away. The shoemaker laughed when he heard my order—"*Valenki* with high heels? Is he daft?"—and the tailor almost split his sides: "Is he nuts or something? Boyars! Rabbit fur! All white! What a get-up!"

"Well," I said, "He *is* paying. All you have to do is make it."

The suit was ready by Saturday afternoon. At nine on Sunday morning I held my breath. The local grapevine had been buzzing, and a crowd of curious citizens had gathered outside City Hall. As bad luck would have it, there had been rain the day before, followed by a hard freeze. The front steps had been scraped and sanded, but the yard itself was still sheer ice where the general's long limousine stood waiting. A guard of honor lined the stairway on both sides. When at last the big door flew open, the crowd gasped at the incredible sight.

At the top of the stairs, very pleased with itself, stood a small, round, excessively fat figure entirely wrapped in white fur. A small red face peered out of a circle of fluff. The pointed mustache looked like a cat's whiskers. Slowly the squat apparition began to descend the stairs. All went well until he reached the yard—there, no sooner had the General put a toe on the ice, than both his feet flew up into the air. He went skittering over the ice with his white-gloved hands frantically clutching at thin air. By the time he managed to roll over onto his stomach and come to a stop, his civilian audience had melted away, doubtless fearing possible reprisals for having witnessed the fall of an Eagle. But the well-trained German soldiers didn't move a muscle. Members of Adlerhorst's staff came rushing down the stairs to help him up.

It suffices to say, that for my pains I received two cartons of cigarettes. The General himself held no brief against me—not for long at any rate. When he summoned me into his presence again later that day to vent his spleen, I forestalled him by buttering his vanity.

"Ah, General, it could have happened to anyone! No Boyar could have withstood that ice! And really, what a splendid costume!"

At this, he perked up, all smiles and dimples:

"Yes, wasn't it? *Colossal!* And so typically Russian, too!"

CHAPTER TWENTY-EIGHT

◆§◆

In spring of 1943, the siege of Stalingrad collapsed; General Paulus and his army, some 200,000 strong, surrendered to the Russians. With every bit of such news, my gloom settled deeper: What hope was there now for the liberation of Soviet prisons and concentration camps, and moreover, of Nika? In my misery I had no one to turn to. Though Nadya felt sorry for me, I knew that at heart she couldn't help but rejoice over Russian victories. Sergeant Engelhart tried to comfort me: "Chances of war, Frau Marie, just chances of war. We're down today, up tomorrow! We still have our *Führer* and our *Wehrmacht*. That's all that matters!" I was grateful, but I could see that he, too, was shaken.

Then one day he turned to me in agitation; "Have you heard? General Adlerhorst has been sent packing! His replacement, General Mittelmeyer, arrived last night. He's a high officer in the *Leibstandarte des Führers*, and is said to be a frightful disciplinarian!"

"Well," I replied wearily, "a little discipline around here would do no harm."

"Ach, but who can tell how a new broom will sweep! The first thing he did this morning was to clear everything out of Adlerhorst's three rooms—all the armchairs, carpets, pictures, and statuary. He said, 'Sergeant! Out with this junk! All I need is a bed, a table, and a few chairs.' "

"Ah, a real soldier for a change."

"*Ja*, but listen to this! I'm to get rid of all the women working for the officers, at once! From now on their orderlies are to look after them."

"High time, if you ask me, my good Engelhart!"

"I suppose so, but who's going to wash the floors? Who's going to clean the rooms? The place will become a pigsty in no time at

250

all! The General said to me—and mark these words, Frau Marie—
'Sergeant!' he said, 'no more women! This is the *Wehrmacht*, not
the Swedish baths!' "

I knew what Engelhart meant: while the remark about the
Swedish baths could only apply to Russian "Dulcineas" in the
officers' quarters, there was a clear implication that all women
would be discharged. What would this severe new General do with
Nadya and myself?

I was soon to find out.

Three days hadn't gone by when General Mittelmeyer's adjutant
sought me out in the woodshed where I was supervising my female
wood-chopping and wood-stocking brigade. He introduced himself, and clicked his heels with great formality.

"The General wishes to see you, *Gnädige Frau*. Kindly step this
way."

An old green military coat that was falling to my heels and huge
clumsy galoshes tied on with strings were not exactly the garments
I would have chosen in which to meet the man who was to decide
our fate. But I had no choice. I hurried along behind the adjutant,
putting on the best face I could.

My guide came to a stop in front of the door I knew well, from
behind which I had often heard General Adlerhorst squeak: "Come
in!" Now, in answer to the adjutant's knock, came a strong rich
baritone, *"Herein!"* Stepping aside and bowing slightly, the adjutant opened the door and motioned me in. I squared my shoulders and held my head high, as a tall, elderly, handsome man rose
courteously from his desk to greet me.

"Thank you for coming, *Gnädige Frau*."

"I am very honored to meet you, *Excellenz*."

He pointed me to a chair opposite him and resumed his seat. "I
have been watching you these two days working with the women
in the yard. You don't waste time."

Again I squared my shoulders, "I work, General, not only because
it's my job but also in hopes of being of some use to the 'Cause.' "

Thin aristocratic eyebrows rose in mild surprise:

"The 'Cause'?"

"Yes, the Crusade." I saw that he still hadn't understood: "I mean
the Crusade against the Bolsheviks who have enslaved my country."

"Oh, I see . . ." He leaned back in his chair with an amused smile hovering around the edges of his mouth. A moment later, he picked up a pencil and tapped it gently, pensively on the desk. "Well now, tell me about yourself, about your friend . . . Fräulein Shipov, is it not? All right. Tell me how you escaped from the Communist Paradise."

I could not have asked for more. I told him of the manner in which Nadya and I had surrendered to the *Wehrmacht*, and then plunged with gusto into a recital of our life before the Revolution. I mentioned our estates and my family's big house in Moscow, laying light but deft stress on my Grandfather Scherbatov and his princely Rurik descent (Germans love names and titles). As briefly as I could, I then told him about Nika's arrests, his final disappearance, and my own imprisonments and exile.

He listened attentively. Now and then he asked a question, from which I soon gathered that we were what the Russians call "berries from the same field": our nurseries, as one says, had been the same, and our backgrounds similar. He asked me if we had been well-treated by the *Wehrmacht*? When I told him that to me, personally, the *Wehrmacht* was like a throng of Lohengrins riding tanks and motorcycles instead of swans, he threw back his head and laughed:

"Well, well! That's all to the good. But don't forget, there are also monsters in Wagner's operas."

I nodded knowingly: "Oh, yes, I was warned to beware of . . ." But here I stumbled and fell silent. I had suddenly remembered that this man belonged to the *Leibstandarte des Führers*, which I understood to be an S.S. unit.

He looked at me closely: "Yes? Go on, *Gnädige Frau*, to beware of whom?"

I had to answer. "The Gestapo, *Excellenz*. And the S.S., and *Einsatz Truppen*."

"Quite right! Remember, besides the 'Crusade,' there are political and international problems that have to be met with harsh measures."

His manner softened, and he smiled. He pulled a paper from his pocket, and to my amazement I recognized it as a poem I had written, a kind of Ode to the *Wehrmacht* (I still believe it was one of the best things I had ever done). General Mittelmeyer held it up: "One of your 'Lohengrins' gave it to me. He was deeply moved by it." He gave me a long probing glance: "Do you really believe these eulogies?"

"Do you think I would have written them if I did not?"

"*Nein*." He seemed to weigh the matter with half-amusement, letting his "*Nein*" sink into a skeptical pause: "Nein," he repeated with deliberation. "Now that I have seen and spoken to you, I don't. And I might as well confess I, too, was moved by your poem. Very much so." A sad little sigh escaped him: "Ah, long may you live in your fool's paradise!" Taken aback, I was about to ask what he meant when his own clarification staggered me even more: "When you get to Berlin you may be somewhat disillusioned."

"Berlin, General? But I don't understand!"

"That's where I am sending you and Fräulein Shipov in a day or two. This is no place for ladies. The Russians are preparing a massive offensive. You ought not to be here at all. I will put a call through. A room and job will be awaiting you and your friend in Berlin. Also, you will be able to replenish your wardrobe. High time, too, I should say, what?"

We both laughed. I thanked him profusely; but he, very deliberately, shook his finger at me, as if trying to impress every word upon my mind. "Remember, dear lady, no matter where you go, be it Russia, Germany, France, or anywhere else—you will always find both angels and devils."

He took my hand as I began to thank him again. "I am delighted to have been able to be of service to you." A slight hesitation, a deeper look, and then: "May I ask you a favor? Please remember me sometimes in your prayers. Life is difficult, and death is often near."

I was so impressed with General Mittelmeyer that I sought to find out all I could about him. It puzzled me how such a gentleman, in every sense of the word, happened to be so high up in Hitler's immediate entourage. That evening Sergeant Engelhart dropped in to see us and tell us what he knew. General Mittelmeyer, it seems, was Austrian. He had commanded an Austrian unit during the First World War, and Adolf Hitler had been among his men. It is well-known that the then-Corporal Hitler got himself into some scrape and was threatened with a court-martial. As Engelhart explained with emphasis and enthusiasm: "It was Captain Mittelmeyer who intervened in Hitler's favor. The *Führer*, of course, never forgets a good turn. That is how General Mittelmeyer is where he is today!"

CHAPTER TWENTY-NINE

❧❦❧

Nadya and I left for Berlin in July of 1943, a month or so before Vyazma fell to the Red Army. Russian civilians were never permitted to ride in German Army trains, but General Mittelmeyer's express order made our case an exception. Russian planes had already bombed the Vyazma station, and our train was entirely blacked out; all blinds were down, all lights out. In the compartment assigned to us, it was so dark that upon entering, I could barely distinguish the figure of the officer who had sprung to his feet at our approach and clicked his heels with a loud "*Heil Hitler!*"

"Our two esteemed ladies, I presume?" His tone was deferential. He clicked his heels once again. "Excuse me, *Mesdames*. It won't take me long—I must call my comrade who has been assigned to help me entertain you and see that you are in no way disturbed. General's orders!"

This new attention on the part of General Mittelmeyer was not to Nadya's liking. I could sense it in her stiff silence. For her, this would be an unnecessary "fraternization," which she wanted no part of. Once the officer was out of earshot, I was not surprised when she whispered to me in Russian, "Be entertained by these Krauts, if you like [she used the Russian derogatory *nyemchura*]. I'm going to sleep!" With that she climbed into her bunk, turned to the wall, and at least pretended to fall fast asleep. I settled down in a corner, near the blacked-out window.

Presently our officer returned with another officer who, after the usual "*Heil Hitler*" and heel-clicking, introduced himself as an *Oberleutnant*. Upon learning that Nadya had already retired, one of the officers—I could hardly tell which in the darkness—settled down opposite me and soon fell asleep. The other seated himself beside me, and I felt him nestle up to me in the dark.

I could not see his face, nor could he see mine. But I was very slender in those days—scrawny, I should say—and he doubtless thought that I was a much younger woman. A passionate whisper suddenly broke upon my ear.

"What luck for me, *Gnädige Frau!* I think Russian women are divine, the most enchanting in the world! They are clever, courageous and—ah, so beautiful! Roses in bloom, I call them. It has always been my dream to get to know a Russian woman real well. And now—ach, and by our general's orders, too—if you would only condescend . . . What bliss! Two days and two whole nights together!"

Good Heavens, I thought, *what a beginning!*

For a while his voice carried on this romantic rigamarole about Russian women. Then, before I knew it, his arm was around my waist and his hand creeping up in bold exploration. I moved away as far as the wall on my other side would let me:

"You are very kind, *Herr Oberleutnant*, and very flattering. I hope I won't be a disappointment to you tomorrow. But tonight I'm dead tired. I simply must have some sleep."

He was on his feet in an instant, clicking his heels: "Ach, how thoughtless of me! How inconsiderate! Forgive me! Of course, of *course*, you must rest."

He helped me climb into my bunk and covered me carefully, almost tenderly, with a *Wehrmacht* blanket. "*Gute Nacht, Gnädige Frau,*" he said in a loud and faultlessly correct voice. Then he added in a hot, passionate whisper: "My lovely Russian rose! Until tomorrow then, pretty one!" *Ah, my ardent cavalier!* I thought to myself, *as the French say "at night all cats are gray." Tomorrow you will see!*

As the first rays of the sun filtered through the chinks in the black-out curtain, I turned over and looked down at my *Oberleutnant*. He was awake too. His was about the youngest face I had ever seen on a grown man, with barely perceptible beginnings of a blond mustache above soft red lips. He looked up at me with a smile of happy anticipation, all prepared to cover the fingertips of a casually proffered girl's hand with passionate kisses. But instead of a blooming young girl, he saw the wan, lined countenance of a middle-aged woman whose graying wisps of hair protruded from the handkerchief around her head. His back

stiffened, his smile froze, and his face fell in disappointment and—
I'll admit—disgust. I had to dive under my blanket to hide my
laughter, but the young man's ego was wounded nevertheless. For
the rest of the trip, he never spoke to me again except in cold
and very formal short sentences. General's orders!

All that day we traveled through dreary Polish fields dotted
with burned-out villages. My youthful wooer of the night before
continued to sulk, so his comrade—about the same age but with
more manly features—took on the work of entertaining us. I tried
to make up for Nadya's sparse replies by chatting pleasantly with
him in German, in the Russian he had been studying, and in the
French on which he prided himself but spoke with an atrocious
German accent. Altogether, we were a well-matched foursome—
one couple monosyllabic, the other polyglot.

Next morning we reached the German border. The train came
to a stop before a large white gate adorned with greenery, bunting,
and a huge sign reading: "Welcome to the Fatherland!" Everyone
on the train was given a food parcel containing sausage, cheese,
butter, bread, and a small bottle of Schnapps—compliments of the
Führer. Nadya and I were escorted to a row of charming white
cottages run by an organization known as *Kraft durch Freude*
(Strength through Joy), where we were received by a buxom,
pink-cheeked maid in a starched apron. After enjoying a hot bath,
we were served an excellent meal. The night was spent in soft beds
with clean white sheets. Even Nadya heaved something between a
sigh and a little groan of delight as she sank back onto her clean
white pillow.

We reached Berlin the next day. The protecting influence of
General Mittelmeyer was still with us; we were assigned to a room
in a hospice for people attached to the *Wehrmacht*. A handsome
building, the hospice had once been a Roman Catholic convent, and
a few nuns were still there to look after us. As they hurried down
the long corridors, their sad, pale faces expressed no feeling beyond
a mute resignation to the will of God. They added a mournful
touch to a place which otherwise breathed comfort and efficiency.
The floors were spotless, the rooms well aired, the beds soft and
clean, and the meals well served, though utterly tasteless. Yet it
was in this meticulous hospice that what General Mittelmeyer had
called my "fool's paradise" came to an end.

Living there were three young Russians, former prisoners of war. We met them at breakfast and instantly fell to talking. Nadya became her old self again, at once outgoing and shy. We exchanged news of the front for word about conditions in Germany. It was soon apparent that our stories were heartening by comparison. I was stunned. I listened as they told us how Jews had been gassed by the thousands, of the beastly treatment of "Osts" (imported Russian slave-laborers), of the cruel indignities inflicted upon anti-Nazi Germans. I learned the awful plight of Russian POWs, who either died of starvation in camps or were subjected to inhuman tortures as the subjects of "medical research."

"They throw them into freezing baths," exclaimed one of the young men, "and then into boiling water. They want to see how much the human body can stand!"

"We know this for a fact," said the second. "Some of our best friends perished that way!"

"Yes," the third added. "The only reason we three were spared and treated decently was because we spoke such good German. They said it made us human."

In momentary bitterness, my thoughts flew back to my friends at the front. In his simplicity Sergeant Engelhart might plead ignorance, but how could such men as Lange and Wehrs still endure hardships and dangers, knowing what they knew? How could any decent man die for such an abominable regime, for a demented *Führer?* Then something Lange had once said returned to me: "If a single link in our iron chain—the *Wehrmacht*—breaks, it is Germany that will perish." Lange's love for his country was on a par with Nika's love for Russia, and resulted in the same tragic weight upon the heart. Now that I understood their moral torments, my affection for Lange and others like him remained unaltered and perhaps even enhanced. Many years later, when I was already settled in the United States, I was to receive a letter from Pastor Heyken in which he wrote, "Wherever you go, whenever you can, dear friend, put in a good word for us." This I shall always do. In the final analysis, as General Mittelmeyer said, "Be it Russia, Germany, France, or anywhere else—you will always find both angels and devils."

To me, Berlin was full of surprises, staggering revelations, and unexpected comparisons. I was struck by the long, wide, almost deserted streets. There was no traffic, no young people to be seen anywhere—only the old and the very young, with sad, drawn faces. This was a far cry from the rich city seething with life and energy that I had visited often before the First World War. All parks, gardens, and squares were planted with food crops—potatoes, cabbage, turnips, and even oats. The atmosphere was altogether gloomy and charged with discontent. Although *Heil Hitlers* were heard everywhere, the Berliners' irrepressible humor was still in evidence. Cynicism took the form of whispered anecdotes. I had seen the same thing in Communist Moscow, where the "have-you-heard-this-one?" became a means of giving voice to political opinions one dared not express openly.

In the midst of a conversation, a Berliner would pause and ask, "Have you heard this one? The *Führer* buys a carpet and the store manager asks him, '*Mein Führer*, shall I send it to the *Reichskanzlei*, or do you wish to chew it here?" Or, "Have you heard this one? Hitler, Göring and Goebbels are circling in a plane over Berlin. Hitler says, 'What shall we drop as a gift to please our dear Berliners?' Goebbels suggests cigars; Göring prefers sausages. So Hitler asks the pilot: 'You, as one of our dear Berliners, what do you think they would like best?' '*Mein Führer*,' the pilot says, 'What better gift could you drop than your own beloved self? The people would be overjoyed to see you on your way down.'"

On my first day in Berlin I went into a bookshop and asked for Mussolini's biography. The salesgirl stared at me and sighed, "Are you still reading that trash?"

"What do you mean, trash? Isn't Mussolini the *Führer's* faithful ally?"

"So what? They're two eggs in one basket. *Heil Hitler!*"

In the beginning I used to gasp at such irreverences, particularly when I thought of the front, where words of this sort would have soon had the speaker court-martialed. But here, the tittering Berliner, whispering behind his hand, had only his inherent Prussian sense of obedience to chastise him.

General Mittelmeyer's influence proved invaluable. We were issued new clothes, new underwear, overcoats, and shoes. After having heard all we had about the Nazis, to be forced to accept even these much-needed gifts with a smiling *Heil Hitler* was a bitter pill to swallow. On the other hand, our work in a government translation office gave us no qualms. We merely had to translate propaganda leaflets, so asinine that they could only harm the Nazi cause. I recall a sample: "Russian peasants clad in national dress, crowned with flowers, and carrying icons, bread, and salt, danced in the fields to welcome their German liberators." Nadya and I could only chortle up our sleeves while translating such abysmal nonsense.

Our office hours were long—from nine in the morning to seven at night. After that we had to walk to the hospice through a total black-out, although we were provided, as was everyone else, with phosphorescent lapel buttons to save us from bumping into one another. We felt fairly secure.

Our Chief Herr Hohensee was a member of the S.S., but for some reason or other, he did not seem to bear any military rank. He must have known General Mittelmeyer, for during the six months we worked under him he showed us nothing but courtesy and consideration.

In the fall of 1943 came the devastating British and American air raids. As soon as we heard sirens, we had to rush to the shelter assigned to us, no matter where we might be at the time. All were warned that persons injured through failure to take proper shelter would receive no medical care. Our designated refuge—a curious place—was in the basement of the hospice. Armchairs, with the names of their owners embroidered on antimacassars, were lined along the walls. During an alert, elderly Germans would take their places in there and sit, mute and impassive through the long night, with their hands folded across their stomachs. We Russians (the three former prisoners of war, Nadya, and myself) would gather together in a corner, where before long we would be engrossed in long and sometimes heated discussions. As the bombs fell, we talked over all kinds of subjects—philosophy, religion, Tolstoy, Dostoevsky, the pros and cons of democracy as against absolutism. Ours were good, endless, *bona fide* Russian talks. I could hear a German stir now and then in his chair, and mutter, "*Diese verrückte Russen*, Those crazy Russians!"

As in Zubtsov the year before, life in the constant shadow of death had a stimulating effect on me. Night after night, the bombers came over in waves. The noise was terrific, but by some lucky chance our hospice was never hit. One morning, after an all clear, one of the POWs and I came up from the shelter to find every house in the street on fire. Many had already crumbled into smouldering ruin. My friend, who had been unable to smoke all night, lit a cigarette. Instantly a policeman pounced upon him: "*Polizeilich verbotten hier zu rauchen*, Smoking here is strictly forbidden!"

"But," the Russian protested, "the whole street's on fire! What difference could one cigarette possibly make?"

"That's none of your concern. Put out your cigarette—*Befehl ist Befehl!*"

Soon alarming rumors began to travel all over town: the eastern front had collapsed, Russian armies were invading German soil and converging on Berlin. Nadya and I knew all too well what would happen to us if the Red Army invaded Berlin. Nor was the strain made any lighter by our three Russian friends, who kept bemoaning our horrible fate in advance.

It was Nadya who ended the tension by forcing me to act. We had worked in the translation bureau for six months, and a leave had been promised us at the end of that period. "Masha," said Nadya, "we have no choice. We must go to Paris!"

"But that's impossible!"

"Your sister can put us up."

"That's not the point. It's just impossible! No permits are issued for France."

Nadya drew her mouth into a tight line that made her look more obstinate than ever. Her eyes were deep and luminous, full of light and strength. "Nothing is impossible. Think of your mother, and of her great faith. And have you forgotten all Saint Seraphim has done for you? I, for one, not only believe in miracles, I count on them!"

There was nothing else to be done but to go and see our chief. "Herr Hohensee," I said, "my friend and I would like to spend our leave in Paris. Would you please advise me how to go about getting a travel permit?"

"No private individuals are issued travel permits for France."

"I know, I know, but this is most important. You have always been so kind and helpful. Please do what you can."

He cut me short: "I can't do anything. Only the Gestapo can issue such a permit!"

"Oh no!" I all but groaned. "Not the Gestapo!"

There was a twinkle of amused speculation in his eyes: "Come to think of it, why not? I have watched you now for six months, Frau Marie. I do believe you could twist even the Gestapo round your little finger."

"Oh," I cried in desperation, "this is no time to make fun of me!"

"But I'm not making fun." His eyes looked mischievous, and a gambler's cool smile curled his lips. "What's more, I'd like to see you get away with it!"

I began to protest, but he picked up the telephone and silenced me with a wave of his hand. A moment later, he was clicking his heels to an invisible superior, talking rapidly and urgently at the same time. At last he put down the receiver and sat back in his chair:

"There! *Hauptmann* von Braun will see you. And hurry! He says he is free now."

I knew I was facing danger, but as in all such critical moments of my life, my poised and confident "Over-self" took control.

The Gestapo had its headquarters in a grandly beautiful mansion. I was ushered into a most imposing room with marble walls, parquet floors, and fine furniture. I was received by a perfectly tailored officer seated behind his desk: *Hauptmann* von Braun. He seemed true to type: broad-shouldered and handsome, he was obviously addicted to the cult of his body, but his eyes were cold and piercing, and his mouth thin and cruel. Our conversation began in strict accordance with Nazi protocol:

"*Heil Hitler!* Why did you ask for an appointment?"

"*Heil Hitler!* To request a permit for me and my friend to go to Paris."

"What?" There was ominous silence, during which I could almost see his fury rising: "Do you have the nerve to disturb me with such a preposterous request? Only members of the *Wehrmacht* and the High Command are allowed to go to France. Now get out of my office!"

His rude dismissal was another of the unexpected comparisons I found between Nazi and Communist officials. But as on previous occasions when facing the rising ire of a Bolshevik, I began to talk *at* my adversary. The trick was to weave a quick mesh of words in a tone at once propitiating and insistent:

"*Herr Hauptmann*, you have granted me this interview, but you have not heard what I have to say. Please let me speak before you shout me down." I gave him no time to either protest or interrupt: "General Mittelmeyer of the *Leibstandarte des Führers*, as I took leave of him in Vyazma, said to me . . ." I paused for just an instant to see what effect the general's name might have. I could almost hear the mental click of heels as the *Hauptmann* pricked up his ears and looked at me closely. I went on as if I had noticed nothing: ". . . he said, *Gnädige Frau*, please do me a favor. When you get to Berlin you may have occasion to meet some of the higher authorities. The higher the better, because any high-ranking man you will be dealing with will be intelligent and courteous. I ask you merely to be as frank with him as you have been with me, and if you are, I'm sure any reasonable request of yours will be granted.'" Again I paused and looked straight into the *Hauptmann's* steel-gray eyes. They actually gave way, and I summoned the sweetest smile I could: "You know, *Herr Hauptmann*, I have found General Mittelmeyer's advice invaluable. Never once has a request of mine been refused. I can't believe that you will be the first to prove the General wrong!"

I really can offer no explanation as to why this hard-bitten Gestapo officer should have suddenly capitulated, unless he thought he was being threatened through someone close to the *Führer*. He looked at me for a few seconds in silence, then bent his sleek head over the papers on his desk.

"Well," he said, "apparently I have no choice in the matter." He stamped and signed the two forms then and there. This time he stood up, handed them to me, and clicked his heels:

"*Heil Hitler, Gnädige Frau!*"

"*Heil Hitler, und danke schöhn, Herr Hauptmann!*"

Nadya had been entirely right.

Nadya and I left Berlin for Paris in the spring of 1944, when it was forbidden to take *Reichsmarks* out of Germany. Before leaving, we had to convert all our earnings into the special currency used in German-occupied countries. We were warned that all travelers would be searched at the border. If any smuggled *Reichsmarks* were discovered, a concentration camp was waiting for the offender and any of his associates.

We had just exchanged all our money when an aunt of mine in Rome sent me an unexpected present—a splendid fur coat. A German woman saw it and offered me what seemed a very large sum at the time. I sold her the coat on the spot. Seeing as there was no time to change this windfall into occupation currency, I sewed the *Reichsmarks* into the bodice of my dress. This was of course an insanely dangerous thing to do, but I was so elated over my miracle with *Hauptmann* von Braun, over the prospect of seeing my sister Sonya and our Swiss governess Alice, that for a few hours I gave the matter no thought.

The Paris train's first-class carriage was packed with generals, colonels, a sprinkling of junior officers, and a few important civilians. Everyone's curiosity was aroused as to how two Russian ladies came to be aboard, and Nadya and I became the focus of attention. At once two young officers sprang up and gave us their seats. I settled down in mine, still without a thought to the forthcoming inspection at the frontier. Only when the train pulled out of the sation did I remember those *Reichsmarks* around my waist and bosom. Fervently I wished I had left them behind or could now find some way to get rid of them. Nadya was, of course, completely innocent, and I tried not to dwell on what would happen to her were they discovered.

As we approached the frontier, the Commandant of the train entered our carriage and saluted.

"Ladies and gentlemen," he announced in a loud, casual voice, "a Customs Officer will be here shortly to search everyone for *Reichsmarks*. This is a mere formality, of course . . ." Soon after that appeared a pretty girl (probably French or Belgian, judging from her accent), wearing an officer's uniform.

"Ladies first," she smiled and came over to me.

I must have looked very odd, for she looked at me with concern: "Are you unwell, *Madame*?"

I could barely mutter a few disjointed words: "Yes . . . I'm sorry. Two years at the front, six months of Berlin . . . Too much, too much . . ."

"I understand," she said with sympathy, but her eyes seemed

questioning as her hands traveled over my shoulders, breast, and
waist. For a second she seemed to hesitate. Then she turned to the
train Commandant with a bright smile.

"This lady has nothing, but she's ill and overwrought. She may
sit while I go through her luggage."

I leaned back in my seat and shut my eyes. I believe I actually
lost consciousness for a few seconds. In all my danger-ridden years,
this must have been my narrowest escape.

As our train neared Paris, Nadya and I began to discuss in French
the problems we would face there. We had been told that it was
difficult to get a porter at the Gare du Nord, but even if we
found one, we had no French currency to pay him with. "How can
we get a taxi, or even the *Métro*?" A distinguished, well-dressed old
man overheard this, rose from his seat, and came over to us:

"Excuse me, ladies, I am a Belgian and I speak French. Permit me
to be of assistance to you." He held out a hundred franc note!
Overwhelmed, we thanked him, and demanded that he give us his
name and address so that we could return the loan. He wouldn't
hear of it: "It's a trifle, *Mesdames*, I assure you, a mere trifle. It
makes me happy to be of help." A couple of hours later, the train
pulled into the Gare du Nord.

It was getting late. Hundreds of people milled around us in the
blackout. Somewhere outside the station, sirens were screeching an
air raid alert. With little hope of getting an answer, I stood on
the crowded platform shouting, "*Porteur! Porteur!*" To my surprise, a porter materialized out of the surrounding gloom to get us
a taxi and pile our suitcases inside. Twenty minutes later, I was
knocking on a door I'd often doubted I would ever reach.

"*Qui est là?*" A tremulous but very familiar voice came to me
through the locked door.

"It's me," I answered in Russian. "Masha!"

The door flew open and I embraced my dear old Alice. Over her
shoulder I could see my darling sister Sonya smiling.

CHAPTER THIRTY

❧❦❧

Miracle by near miracle, we had made our escape, leaving behind us a crumbling Hitler and a triumphant Stalin, birds of a feather who had plucked each other. But for all that lay behind us, we had not yet reached safety. The Germans still held France and might easily have looked on us as a pair of deserters from government jobs. We had to go into hiding upon the expiration of our official leave. We found refuge through my nephew, Igor Demidov, the son of my sister Katya, who had died in Paris in 1931. A friend of Igor's owned a lovely villa on the outskirts of the forest of Fontainebleau, where together with our charming French hostess, we lay low until the invasion of Normandy.

The war was barely over when the volatile Parisians, with an amazing shortage of memory and gratitude, began shouting, "Americans, go home! We could have won the war without you." Just about that time, letters from the Avinovs began arriving, inviting Nadya and me to join them in America. They promised to attend to all the formalities necessary to get immigration visas for us. It frightened me to think of leaving my hopes for Nika on this side of the Atlantic's vast expanse, yet at the same time a secret inner voice kept whispering for me to go west. It didn't seem to make sense at all. I knew Nika could not be anywhere on the American continent, or he surely would have contacted Ellie and Andrey. But Nadya was also in favor of emigrating to America, and the fact that the invitation came from Nika's own brother and sister seemed like a good omen to me. I wrote our acceptance, and Andrey wrote back to say that he had already begun to pull strings.

As months went by, Nadya and I grew puzzled, then impatient, and finally anxious. We knew that all the necessary papers should have long since been dispatched from Washington. I called at the American Embassy every week to see if they had arrived. The charming, efficient, and gracious ladies working in the outer offices told me that such delays were almost routine. Invariably the consul who was handling our case would call me into his office, offer me a chair beside his desk, and put me through a long and tedious interrogation that would end in a polite but discouraging, "Sorry, nothing yet. Come back next week."

Most of the time we conversed through a Russian interpreter. My English had grown pretty rusty after many years of disuse and, moreover, the consul had a strong American accent, which I could hardly understand. During our many interviews, the Russian interpreter stood behind the consul's chair, leaning forward deferentially to translate his employer's questions and my replies. This slowed our conversation enough that I had time to study the consul. He was immensely tall, and equally heavy. His face was round, his eyes slightly bulbous, and a smug smile lay half-concealed in the folds of his cigar-smoking mouth. Needless to say, I kept my observations strictly to myself, but after a dozen or so fruitless interviews I was beginning to develop a strong dislike for him. On one occasion, my quick temper finally got the better of me.

On that particular day, he had grilled me for over half an hour, as usual. "And now, Madam," he said, "I must ask you for some money."

"Why? I thought all expenses had been paid in advance?"

"Correct, but there is this unforeseen expense. I must send a wire to the Moscow police and verify what you have told me about yourself and your friend."

Giving the interpreter no time to translate, I burst forth in volcanic English. What I neglected in grammar, I compensated for in strength of feeling.

"Have you no notion, Mister Consul, what the Russian Revolution is? Have you not perhaps read books about it?"

In my rage, I switched to Russian again, and the interpreter hurriedly began translating (for the umpteenth time) how Nika and I had been hounded for years by the Communists.

"And now," I cried, "I'm living in danger right here in Paris. Just the other day, I was warned that I'm on the Soviet Embassy's blacklist. They might have me murdered or kidnapped any day, just as they've kidnapped and murdered other more prominent White Russians." I pointed an accusing finger at the consul, as if to accuse him of responsibility for any possible misfortune.

He merely raised his eyebrows in slow surprise: "Oh, is it as bad as all that? All right then, calm yourself. I won't send the wire."

I muttered a "thank you," and swallowed a few angry tears.

"But I must have your birth certificate."

"I haven't got one!" I shook my head dolefully. "As you know from my papers, I was born in Germany."

He eyed me suspiciously. "Why in Germany?"

"Because it so happens that my pregnant mother was there at the time!" I broke into English again, too quickly for the interpreter to catch up: "At Freiburg, in Bresgau. As perhaps you don't know, that city was heavily bombed during the war. As perhaps you can't understand, all archives were destroyed!"

The consul shut his eyes. "You will have to do something about it," he drawled.

Surely, I thought, this could not be just a case of hidebound ignorance. There must be something else behind his hesitations— perhaps our two years' work with the *Wehrmacht*! I had heard how shabbily Americans and Britons were treating Russians who had collaborated with the German army. In their eyes, such persons were out-and-out traitors.

But whether or not my speculation was true, I lost no more time arguing. Characteristically, I wrote to the mayor of Freiburg to explain my predicament in detail. I begged him to help a woman in distress. Believe it or not, five days later, the morning mail brought me my birth certificate, together with a polite note from the mayor: "As luck would have it, *Gnädige Frau*, our archives for your particular birth year were safely stored in a cellar."

The consul had no excuses left. Nadya and I were issued visas and given permits to board a plane for New York. I was brimming over with happy relief, and I wanted to share the feeling.

"You know, Nadya," I said, "we ought to express our appreciation to all those nice American girls at the Embassy. They were so thoughtful and kind to me. Let's get them an immense bouquet of flowers!"

Nadya agreed.

At six the next morning, we were in Paris' famous Marché aux Fleurs. In the early morning dew sparkled a paradise of blossoms: roses, lilies, carnations, pinks, sweet peas, and dozens more. We bought a whole armful and carried it to the Embassy. The young ladies thanked us over and over again. "Ordinarily we get nothing but grumbles and complaints." I was warmed at their delight, but secretly hoping that our lavish gift and their profuse gratitude would somehow convey to the consul how little help he had afforded me.

The moment of departure had come, and I had never been near a plane before. Like a thrilled, fascinated child I took in every detail: the long, luxurious cabin of the airliner, our soft comfortable seats, the subdued reading lights in the walls and ceiling, and the two smart young hostesses in uniform dispensing magazines, foot stools, and pillows. But as the plane's wheels rose from the ground, my mind played a curious trick on me. For a moment I lost all awareness of my surroundings.

Again, I found myself on the hard boards of a Soviet prison train. So vivid was the memory that again I felt the torturing thirst, again heard my own anguished cry for water that had threatened to land me in a freezing cell. I could not hear the vibrations of the mighty airborne engines. In their place, two beautiful voices rose, singing to win a cup of water for me. Hot tears filled my eyes. But the illusion passed. Instead of a cellmate whispering, "Have a drink, my poor dear," a trim American Airline hostess was leaning over me anxiously.

"Are you all right, Madam? Would you care for some orange juice?"

I swallowed the delicious, ice-cold drink at a gulp. She fixed a soft pillow under my head. I felt terribly sleepy. The plane flew on and on, but into what new night or dawn I could not yet care.

We landed in America in May of 1947.

EPILOGUE

The Message

~ஃ~

After a week or so, my brother-in-law Andrey, Ellie, and I had had ample time to talk our way backward and forward through our long years of separation. "Tomorrow," said Andrey, "I will go to Washington. Perhaps there's still some way of prying poor Nika out of that infernal paradise!" He then mentioned the name of someone high up in the Administration whom he intended to see: "If there's the slightest chance, he'll unearth it for us. He knows the conditions over there better than anyone else. He has studied Russia for years, and has been over there on highly important missions. Altogether, he's an expert."

A few days later, Andrey was back with us on Long Island. He was crestfallen: "Just imagine, the man knew all about Nika —he remembered the position he had held in the Provisional Government, his role in preparing the way for the Constituent Assembly, and even his reputation as an economist! 'We'd be glad to do anything we can to get him out,' he hold me. 'We might try to exchange him for some Bolshevik spy or even offer money, but believe me, Professor—the moment we broach the subject to the Kremlin, your brother will be no more. They'll think we want him because he worked for us. And we'll be told he died years ago of pneumonia or something, in some hospital somewhere!' "

Knowing Stalin's Russia as well as I did, I had to admit the truth of Andrey's words. But I refused to give up—I turned to the International Red Cross, hoping that they could trace Nika's whereabouts and send him food packages. When I learned they could do nothing, I began interviewing Soviet defectors whenever I had the chance. Some were former inmates of concentration camps, but none had heard of Nika.

As long as dangers, sufferings, and privation had been my lot,

271

as long as I had had to struggle for life, there hadn't been time
for me to lose heart. But now, returning to a life of comfort and
ease, I began to sink into periodic spells of despondency. My futile
and perverse anger flared against the circumstances that had led
me so far away from Nika, but no voice now came, as it once had,
to whisper that I should go west. Sometimes I tried to evoke it, but
only succeeded in wishful thinking. Whenever the real thing had
occurred, I had always experienced a momentary elation, but now
my mind only played tricks and tried to recreate only the elation.
It took the strictest self-honesty to admit that nothing had stirred,
that no voice had murmured, that the innermost had lain fallow
and empty.

That emptiness lasted for many years. Andrey died in 1949
without ever hearing of his beloved older brother. The fifties came
to replace the forties. Nadya had grown old and weak. We fixed
her up in a nice Russian Rest Home in California where she was
to die a few years later, very peacefully, with a prayer on her lips.
I had already moved in with Ellie, when one day the telephone rang.
On the other end was a man's voice, speaking English with a strong
Russian accent. "You—Madam Avinov?" he asked abruptly.

"Yes . . ."

"Wife of Nikolay Nikolayevich Avinov?"

My heart began to race wildly. The man was speaking Russian
now.

"Marya Yuryevna? Oh! I must see you. I have a message for you
from your husband."

I sank heavily into a chair. "Yes," I muttered incoherently.
"When? Now? At once! As soon as possible!"

I don't think he even heard me. Instead of answering, he gave me
his name: Leonid. It seemed to ring a faint, very distant bell that
died away unrecognized. He began to explain himself, voluble
unrestrained now that he could speak our native tongue.

He himself had been arrested during Stalin's Great Purge—the
so-called "Yezhov Purge"—and had been condemned to many
years of hard labor as an incorrigible "enemy of the people."
Through the stupidity or overzealousness of his concentration camp
commandant, he was repatriated to Germany because, like me, he
happened to have been born there. He had arrived but recently
from West Germany, through the graces of some welfare organiza-

tion, and had heard of me through another Soviet refugee whom I had recently interviewed.

Again he told me his name, apparently disappointed that I didn't react to it. But when he let drop some remark, I realized with a flash that this was the young man whom, years ago, Nika had provided with a ready-made Master's thesis. I remembered my indignant reproaches at the time, and smiled to realize that Nika had done the right thing after all. Leonid, then a young man, had never forgotten his generosity. A budding economist himself, he had been filled with admiration and boundless gratitude, and had kept in touch with Nika whenever he could throughout the years.

Soon Leonid was sitting opposite me in Ellie's large, comfortable living room. But search as I might, I could not find the face of Nika's round-cheeked and rather naïve young protégé among the symptoms of this prematurely aged fifty-year-old: he now had thin white hair, bags under tired, watery eyes, a heavily scooped underlip, and cheeks grown puffy from many years of semi-starvation.

"Yes," he said, "I remember November 1937! It was a terrible month."

"That's when they took Nika!"

"Yes . . . One hundred thousand of us were rounded up at that time. I was taken to the Lubyanka, thrown into a crowded cell, and grilled for nights on end . . . But, ahem! I daresay you know all about that sort of thing."

"Yes, but go on. Where did you find *him*? And what condition was he in?"

My visitor leaned forward, and in his unexpectedly bright smile I saw a reflection of the Leonid I could remember.

"You see, our cell was so crowded we could hardly find room to sit down. We all groaned when the guards opened the door and pushed in this new group. The new arrivals were all university professors, scientists, journalists, or literary men, intellectuals. They'd been bruised, beaten, and torn, though I did not notice all this right away. When I first caught sight of your husband, he was helping an old professor who was in a state of hysteria. The poor man could no longer stand on his own. Your husband must have been badly mussed up himself, yet somehow he looked as if he'd just stepped out of his room, freshly groomed. I don't know

what it was that gave him his unruffled, unself-conscious air. When
I called his name, he turned around and his whole face lit up.
'Leonid, my poor friend, are you in this too!' He was about to say
more, but at that moment the stricken professor was deprived of
Avinov's strong arms, and sank sobbing to the floor." He sighed.

I sat motionless. "What was his message," I managed to murmur
at last. "Was it . . . was it a death message?"

Leonid inclined his head. "All of the new arrivals were shot
that same night." But just before the fatal call had come, it seemed
that Nika had managed to give Leonid what amounted to his last
words on earth. I shut my eyes, closing myself in to keep out the
shock and absorb the message:

" 'If you ever get out of here alive, promise me one thing: Find
my wife, Marya Yuryevna—my Masha. Tell her I love her, and
that my thoughts are with her. Tell her that for me, death comes as
a release and a blessing. And tell her to believe this, and to treasure
it in her heart.'

"Believe me, Marya Yuryevna," added Leonid in a low voice,
"the final bullet was a blessing in disguise. With his unusual
physique, Avinov might have survived years of torture."

My face must have gone very white, for he glanced at me
anxiously. But how was I to explain the complexity of my emotions?—the deathblow to my last hope of ever seeing my beloved
again; the distress at my seeming selfishness in holding him in a
concentration camp all these years, as if willing him to live on in
agony; and the quiet joy of having him, through that final message,
back with me and never again to be taken away. But oh! What a
long and arduous road a woman has to travel before she can accept
as a blessing the brutal murder of the man she has loved above all
else in life!

Considering all I have been through, friends have asked me how
I can appear so calm and serene. They say when I'm settled comfortably in a corner of Ellie's living room, one would think I had
always sat in the lap of luxury, with only summer breezes to ruffle
my composure. If so, this must be a reflection not of my past but
of my present state of mind. I can sum it all up in the curtain line
of Sophocles' *Oedipus at Colonus*, where the blind and anguished

king has finally reached the end of his wanderings and is absorbed
into holy splendor by forgiving gods:

> Now cease,
> And lift no more your wailing cry,
> For in the events
> Which now have been fulfilled
> There lives divine authority.